£18.95

Corporate
Communications
Handbook

Who's versatile enough to get more people to sport Jockey underwear, think Digital and buy everything from Taiwan?

Shandwick is the largest PR group in the UK. But that is only half of the story. We are also the most versatile. Because, with a skill base of nearly 400 people, we have a remarkably wide mix of resources and expertise.

Every single aspect of our client's business can demand a specialist PR solution. So our diversity and collective strength means the sum of our parts really is greater than the whole. The right resources and the specialist skills are here in Shandwick, in the UK or worldwide. It also means that there is virtually no PR need or problem that we have not seen before.

We structure our business around our clients and have won numerous awards in recognition of our skills. We've also won the appreciation of almost one third of the top 50 companies in the Times 500. They already rely on us for everything from a snapshot view to an authoritative understanding of the big picture.

If you would like to find out how Shandwick teamwork can help your business, call Colin Trusler on 0171 355 1908 or write to Shandwick UK, 18 Dering Street, London, W1R 9AF.

Shandwick

Corporate Communications Handbook

CONSULTANT EDITORS

Timothy R V Foster and Adam Jolly

KOGAN
PAGE

Published in 1997

Kogan Page Ltd
120 Pentonville Road
London N1 9JN
kpinfo@kogan-page.co.uk

© Kogan Page 1997

British Library Cataloguing in Publication Data
A CIP record for this book is available from the British Library
ISBN 0 7494 2233 5

Typeset by Northern Phototypesetting Co Ltd, Bolton
Printed and bound in Great Britain by Biddles Ltd, Guildford and King's Lynn

Contents

Part 8 – Opinion Communications

Part 9 – Crisis Communications

THE BNFL CORPORATE COMMUNICATIONS UNIT

The BNFL Corporate Communications Unit hosts a group of researchers working in The Management School at the University of Salford. The Unit was established in early 1995 with financial support from British Nuclear Fuels plc. The group is conducting original research in order to gain insights, through rigorous academic analysis, into how the emerging field of Corporate Communications Management can be taught, practiced, developed and evaluated. As well as conducting research in the field, staff teach courses in corporate communications and marketing communications for The Management School's MBA and MSc programmes, and a part-time MSc in Corporate Communications Management.

WHY CORPORATE COMMUNICATIONS MANAGEMENT?

There are clear indications that Corporate Communication is evolving as a specific field of management which has long-term and 'whole enterprise' perspectives on the problems of communication between the key influential groups of a business enterprise, and is distinct from, and includes the strategic management of, corporate communications which are the events and mediums by which communications takes place and which can be subject to strategic management.

AIMS OF THE UNIT

The BNFL Cororate Communications Unit aims to enhance the standing of The Management School, the Research Institute for Design, Manufacture & Marketing, and the University of Salford by achieving recognition as a centre of excellence in academic research in the emerging academic discipline of Corporate Communication (the management system of communications within management, organisation, and marketing).

The Unit conducts original research and publishes findings in the field of Corporate Communications in academic journals and conferences, management journals, books and a Management School Occasional Paper Series. Events are also organised to stimulate debate and disseminate findings amongst practitioners (seminars, lectures, professional executive programmes, conference presentations. Consulting projects facilitate insights and decision-making. Members of the Unit contribute to the teaching programmes of the University's Management School and IT Institute.

The Unit aims to meet the needs and interests of the primary sponsor and other collaborating organisations, which include understanding the development of the trust in relationships with stakeholders, and the teaching of communications management principles and techniques to staff.

THE UNIT'S CURRENT RESEARCH PRIORITIES ARE:

- To develop a theoretical framework for the practical development of the Cororate Communication field, which will provide and promote a more coherent way of thinking about communication problems by focusing on organisation as a whole;

- To demonstrate how Corporate Communication can harmonise all forms of managerial, organisational, and marketing communication - by integrating corporate strategy with organisational development, human resource management, public relations, and marketing - this requires convergent thinking;

- To illustrate how organisations need to be responsive to a diverse range of stakeholders, in which influence and distribution of power changes over time.

RESEARCH APPROACH

To achieve its broad aims, the Unit is studying, synthesising and disseminating, through a planned programme of publications and teaching, a clear coherent theoretical framework. We aim to surface implicit theories of managerial, organisational and marketing communication at the intrapersonal, interpersonal, group/organisation, and technological levels. These pragmatic theories will be translated by analysing cases of corporate communication practice and by drawing widely from a multi-disciplinary theoretical perspective to achieve an all-inclusive view. Specifically, we wish to understand why and how many organisations are moving away from a reliance on directive mass communication methods.

Our work is partly theoretical and partly application and this naturally places us in a position to undertake research and development work for a range of organisations who have unresolved issues of communications management. We seek opportunities to co-operate on suitable projects in this field.

PROJECTS

Current projects cover internal marketing, the integration of communication functions and development of the Public Relations function, the application of chaos and complexity theory to communication events, the diagnosis of emotional labour in service encounters, the managerial and communication issues of virtual teamworking, the ideology of employee communications, the sociology of Corporate Communication in new forms of organisation, the development of computer-mediated 'business breakfast' business skills programmes using broadband technologies, the business case for operating an Internat site, and examination of the impact on competitive advantage of broadband technology capabilities.

Foreword

Sir Colin Marshall, *President,*
Confederation of British Industry, and
Chairman, British Airways

The UK is on course for steady growth over the next two years and it is no wonder that our performance is much admired by other countries.

The CBI is committed to playing its part in making sure that industry has the means to create jobs, build wealth and achieve competitive success for Britain.

One of the key areas involved in making this happen is that of corporate communications. It is to help ensure that this important subject receives the attention and commitment it requires that the CBI has produced this handbook.

Assembled to present the cutting-edge thinking of the leaders in corporate communications, it covers the gamut of the subject, from research to strategy, from crisis management to updates on the media. It even makes more than a passing mention of the Internet!

I would like to take this opportunity to thank all the contributors for sharing their valued knowledge and ideas.

List of Contributors

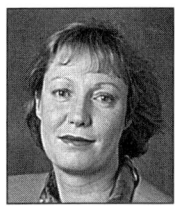 **Annette Allen** is director of Words into Action. Words into Action use a proven, international research method – successfully transforming some of the world's top brands – to show clients the link between customer commitment, employee motivation and financial performance. They help directors create a clear and compelling vision focused on lifetime customer relationships, with appropriate action plans; integrate internal and external communication strategies; and ensure involvement at all levels.

 **Caroline Bainbridge** is a consultant specialising in research for communications. She works with several leading public relations agencies and is research adviser to a leading trade organisation, operating as Caroline Bainbridge Communications Planning.

 **Claire Beale** is associate editor of *Campaign*. Prior to this she was media editor for the *Campaign* and *Marketing* magazines and account director at MediaTel.

 **Ed Bickham** is managing director of public affairs and corporate policy at Hill Knowlton (UK). He was special adviser at the Foreign Office (1991/93) and Home Office (1985/88) and was director of corporate affairs at British Satellite Broadcasting (1988–90).

Richard Birtchnell is a director of 2Cs Communications Ltd, which offers corporate communications services including video, film, event management and multimedia. In 1990, following a career in marketing at well–known retail companies such as the Burton Group, he became chairman of the conference production company Forum Communications Ltd, which was merged into 2Cs in 1996.

Clive Bonney is director of The Solutions Organisation, and principal of Sales Management Partners. He is accredited by the Training and Enterprise Council to help organisations achieve the national standard of Investors in People. He is author of *The Business Writing Pocketbook* and *The Salesperson's Pocketbook* (Management Pocketbooks).

Colin Browne joined the BBC in April 1994 as director of corporate affairs. He is responsible for the communication of the corporation's policies, aims and achievements. He is a member of the BBC Executive Committee. Prior to this he was director of BT Vision, responsible for the company's developing interests in cable TV and satellite TV programming. He oversaw six cable TV franchises and was a founding director of MTV Europe, chairman of the Children's Channel and a director of the Home Video Channel.

Lord Chadlington is founder and chairman of Shandwick International Plc, now the largest independent public relations group in the world. He is also chairman of the Royal Opera House, Covent Garden and a director of the Halifax Building Society. He writes extensively on business and marketing matters and has been widely recognised within the PR industry in the UK and overseas.

John Clare is a former Daily Mail and ITN journalist. He is now managing director of Lion's Den Communications Management, experts in issues and crisis management and all aspects of media training and broadcast strategy.

Peter Cochrane joined BT Laboratories in 1973 and has worked on a wide range of technologies and systems. He is a visiting professor to UCL, Essex and Kent Universities and a member of the New York Academy of Sciences. He has published and lectured widely on technology and the implications of IT. He led the team that received the Queen's Award for Innovation & Export in 1990; the Martlesham Medal for contributions to fibre optic technology in 1994; the IEE Electronics Division Premium in 1986; Computing and Control Premium in 1994; the IERE Benefactors Prize in 1994; the James Clerk Maxwell Memorial Medal in 1995; IBTE Best Paper Prize and received honorary doctorates from Essex, and Stafford Universities in 1996.

Nicholas Comfort has been a political and media consultant with Politics International since July 1996. Prior to this he was a national newspaper lobby consultant for 18 years, principally with the *Daily Telegraph*, and worked in Washington and in Europe. He is a regular broadcaster and author of Brewer's political dictionary.

Alan Coon is president of Coon–Riffone Communications, a Los Angeles based marketing communications and public relations firm specialising in technology and interactive media. He writes extensively on interactive media and marketing and speaks on the topic at industry conferences.

Alan Cooper spent his formative years in advertising at Leo Burnett and Gold Greenlees Trott during the 1980s. In 1989, after a year running his own business, he moved back into the sharp end of advertising when he joined Simons Palmer soon after it had set up. He is currently planning director at Simons Palmer and is chairman of the Account Planning Group – the advertising planners' industry body.

Barry Cox joined Granada Television in 1970, where he was a reporter and later producer/director on *World in Action* for nearly five years. In 1974 he moved to LWT and became head of current affairs three years later. He created and produced *Saturday Night People*, and devised *The 6 O'Clock Show*. In 1981 he took over the post of controller of features and current affairs, and in September 1987 was appointed director of corporate affairs. In April 1995 he took up the post of director of the ITV Association where he is responsible for strategic policy issues.

Steve Cox has had several roles during his time at the RAB. He was instrumental in setting up the Media Planning Services helpdesk and now runs the RAB's training programme for advertisers and advertising agencies. His media career began in 1984 selling airtime for Anglia TV. Two years later he moved to the media business where he negotiated TV airtime rates on behalf of clients such as IPC magazines and Nestlé. In 1989 he accepted a job at GGT and began planning and buying across all media. After four valuable years working with advertisers such as Cadbury, Holsten, and the Post Office he was finally tempted away when the RAB began operating in 1992.

Stuart Crainer is a freelance business and management writer. He is the author of numerous books, including *The Real Power of Brands* (FT/Pitman 1995) and *Key Management Ideas* (Capstone 1995) and is editor of *The Financial Times Handbook of Management* (FT/Pitman 1995). His latest books are *The Ultimate Business Library* (Capstone 1996) and a biography, *Tom Peters, From Corporate Man to Corporate Skunk* (Capstone 1997).

Steve Cuthbert is the director general of the Chartered Institute of Marketing. He is a member of the CBI's Council and Education and Training Affairs Committee, a former member of the President's Committee and an ex–chairman of the CBI's Southern Region. His background is in applied technology, finance and industrial marketing. He is also on the advisory board of the International Corporate Identity Group and the Management Board of the European Marketing Confederation.

David Davis is senior vice president of International Medialink Worldwide Incorporated. He moved into broadcasting in 1992 after a long distinguished career in print journalism and public relations. He joined Medialink's first overseas office in London to develop the company's operations worldwide which currently spans 18 countries. He was previously with *The Times* and vice chairman of Edelman Public Relations Worldwide.

Charles Dawson is managing director of Neomedion Ltd, a European media market consultancy which provides strategic intelligence, research and documentation for media and advertising-related enterprises in Europe and beyond.

Peter Dear is deputy chief executive of PPA, the association of magazine publishers in the UK – a post he has now held for seven years. Among his particular responsibilities are advertising and marketing, and the business magazines sector. He represents the magazine industry on several UK media and advertising committees, and is director of National Readership Surveys Ltd and the Advertising Standards Board of Finance. He is chairman of the International Federation of the Periodical Press (FIPP) Business Magazines Group and is a member of the Executive Committee and chairman of the Market Committee of FAEP, the association of European magazine publishing associations.

Colette Dorward is managing director of Smythe Dorward Lambert. She has consultancy experience in a wide range of industries and has worked with leading organisations such as Bass Plc, Britvic Soft Drinks, Royal Sun Alliance, Tesco Stores and WH Smith.

John Duhig is a consultant at GPC Market Access Europe, the leading public affairs consultancy in Brussels. He advises clients in GPC MAE's expanding Non–Governmental Practice (NGO) area and on R&D and various EU funding opportunities. He is particularly involved in the environment and energy sectors.

Jackie Elliot joined Manning, Selvage & Lee as joint managing director in 1990 from The Rowland Company. She became managing director and chief executive in 1994. She worked for some years in advertising, journalism and public relations before moving to Hong Kong. In 1981 she joined Hill & Knowlton in Hong Kong as senior consultant, specialising in corporate and financial communications. She returned to London in 1984 as a director of Hill & Knowlton in the City, moving to Rowland in 1986 and becoming Rowland's managing director in 1989.

Chris Forrest is planning director at Duckworth, Finn, Grubb, Waters. Prior to this he worked for Ogilvy & Mather as an account planner, the Strategic Research Group and the Qualitative Research Centre.

Timothy R V Foster is the author of 20 books, including *101 Ways to Succeed as an Independent Consultant*, *101 Ways to Generate Great Ideas*, *101 Ways to Get More Business*, *101 Ways to Get Great Publicity*, *101 Ways to Better Business Writing*, *101 Ways to Boost Customer Satisfaction* and *101 Great Mission Statements*, for a total of 707 Ways! All are published by Kogan Page. He was previously advertising and sales promotion director for Merrill Lynch, Pierce, Fenner & Smith in New York and creative director for Burson-Marsteller in New York and London.

Cheryl Freeman is marketing director for Andersen Consulting, covering the UK, Ireland, Scandinavia and South Africa. She started her career at Unilever, left to take an MBA and then spent a number of years in management consultancy, specialising in marketing strategy.

Ray Gallager is director of public affairs at British Sky Broadcasting (BSkyB), the world's largest and most successful pay-TV direct-to-home operator. In this position he is responsible for government and regulatory issues, both at the UK and European levels, affecting BSkyB's multi–channel operation. From 1983 to 1988 he was an independent consultant on broadcasting and new media. Before this he served as a new media specialist for the American Newspaper Publishers Association in Washington DC and a communications consultant to the US Government.

Alfred Glossbrenner is president of FireCrystal Communications, and the author or co-author of over 40 books, including *Making More Money on the Internet* (McGraw-Hill, 1996), *The Little Web Book* (Peachpit Press, 1996), *Online Resources for Business* (Wiley, 1995) and *Finding a Job on the Internet* (McGraw-Hill, 1995). He is also a long-time columnist for several major computer magazines.

Mike Hayes is a classically trained marketer and worked in the FMCG industry for several years. In the mid 1980s he was responsible for the launch and marketing of the Trivial Pursuit board game. Between 1989 and 1994 he was the marketing director for Nintendo. He joined the Cable Communications Association in 1995 and united the industry to produce the first ever national cable marketing campaign. He is now an independent consultant working in the interactive, media and communications markets.

Roger Hayes is director general of the British Nuclear Industry Forum, the trade association of the British nuclear industry. He was previously vice president of public and government affairs at Ford of Europe Inc, director of corporate communications at Thorn EMI and manager of corporate communications at PA Management and Technology Consultants.

Peter Hehir is president of ICO – the worldwide organisation representing all registered public relations consultancies. He is chairman of Countrywide Porter Novelli, the UK's third largest public relations consultancy, voted 'Consultancy of the Year' three times. He is also joint chairman of Porter Novelli International, the world's fourth largest public relations group, with 1,800 staff in 92 offices spanning 39 countries.

Peter Hill is head of corporate communications at Lloyd's of London. A former president of the UK Chapter of the International Association of Business Communicators (IABC), he is presently director of IABC's Europe/Africa region and a member of IABC's executive board.

Neville Hobson, ABC, is a senior consultant at William M Mercer Limited, specialising in communication technologies. He has helped many organisations integrate technology tools into their strategic communication processes. An accredited member of the International Association of Business Communicators (IABC), he is a past-chairman of IABC's international technology committee.

Janet Hull has worked for the advertising agencies Ted Bates, Abbott Mead Vickers, Geers Gross and Young & Rubicam and the PR company Burson-Marsteller. She was head of account management and assistant managing director at Young & Rubicam, and creative director at Burson-Marsteller. In 1994 she was appointed to the new post of consultant director of advertising effectivness at the Institure of Practitioners in Advertising (IPA) on a 3 day week consultancy. In June 1995 she also became a consultant to The Marketing Council. She is a long-term member of the Women's Advertising Club, a main committee member of Women of the Year Luncheon, a recent fellow of the Royal Society of Arts and an elected member of The Reform.

Pamela A Jameson managed the investor relations programme for three New York Stock Exchange listed companies and was a securities analyst for ten years. She now advises corporations on investor relations strategy, operating as Jameson Investor Relations Inc. She is a chartered financial analyst and on the board of directors of the National Investor Relations Institute.

Jeremy Keohane is the client director of UXL Ltd. A company founded to offer tangible business benefits to businesses using internet technologies. He combines strong IT knowledge with in-depth marketing and communications experience. This has enabled UXL to become the market leader in providing innovative and functional Internet/Intranet solutions. Their client list includes several prestigious blue chip organisations as well as many of the top 100 listed companies.

Alex Letts is chairman of the SMI Group. After graduating from Oxford, he joined Young & Rubicam where for five years he worked on multinational consumer brands. In 1990 he incorporated SMI Group as a dedicated new technology full–service agency for the European markets. SMI Group has already become the largest business–to–business agency in the UK and in the past 12 months has been one of the fastest growing agencies in Europe as well as a leader in the new interactive marketing sector.

Simon Lewis is president of the Institute of Public Relations, the professional body representing more than 5,000 practitioners in the industry. He is director of corporate affairs at British Gas Energy, the gas supply business to be created from the demerger of British Gas plc. Previously he was director of corporate affairs at NatWest Group and has worked in politics and consultancy.

Daphne Luchtenberg is European marketing manager for Shandwick International Plc where she is responsible for directing the group's marketing activities for UK, Europe and the Worldwide Affiliate Network. Previously, she worked as new business manager for the pioneering communications management consultancy, Smythe Dorward Lambert in London. She has published numerous articles on international public relations management.

Kate Lynch joined Leo Burnett as a media researcher in 1988. She took over as head of research in October 1993, and was promoted to the board in 1995. She ran the UK and European media research facilities until February 1997 when she left to join the worldwide headquarters in Chicago as director of media research for North America.

Michael Lyons is a group leader in business modelling at KT Laboratories. He leads a team developing computer-based simulation techniques to support strategic decision making. The team's work includes research into regulatory issues, industry structure and future service demand, as well as the development of new modelling techniques based on complex systems and evolutionary approaches. The group is also using scenarios development as a means of understanding the assumptions underlying the quantitative models. He is a member of the Royal Society of Chemistry and has 20 years experience in telecommunications research.

Iain McLeod is managing director of Easy i Ltd – a leading multi–media company specialising in developing business information programmes – and has extensive experience in marketing, media and communications. Before establishing Easy i, he held senior management positions at the BBC, Rank and Pearson.

Mohammed T Mirza graduated from the University of Huddersfield in Business Studies and followed on to take a Masters in Marketing. He is currently researching into corporate communications and integrated communications. He also undertakes some consultation work in the area of communications.

Mike Monkman is an independent media research consultant, whose list of clients includes most of the major media companies in the UK. He has been the technical consultant to the Institute of Practitioners in Advertising on television research for the last eight years. He is also the co–editor of the *MRG Guide to Media Research*.

Dugal Nisbet–Smith was publishing adviser to HH The Aga Khan, based in Paris but working mainly in Kenya, Pakistan and the Far East until 1983 when he joined the Newspaper Society as director designate and took over as director in 1984. He was a member of the Executive Committee of The International Federation of Newspaper Publishers (FIEJ), a member of the CBI Director General's Group, and a council member of the Commonwealth Press Union, the Advertising Association and the Audit Bureau of Circulations.

Gerard J O'Neill is a member of McCann-Erickson's 'McCann Strategy Group' – a think tank comprising external advisors to McCann management and clients. He is currently director of the Henley Centre's Ireland office. He is also a non-executive director of London-based Relationship Marketing International.

Shaun Orpen joined Microsoft in February 1988 as spreadsheet products manager, developing Microsoft's role within the spreadsheet market. Throughout his time at Microsoft he has undertaken a number of roles, including groups application marketing manager, which gave him responsibility for all Microsoft Windows applications and channel marketing. Subsequently, he moved on to develop Microsoft's strategic marketing, before becoming director of marketing services in July 1995.

Ray Palin is a director of the Energy from Waste Association which represents the major Energy from Waste developers and operators in the UK. Prior to joining EWA in March 1994, Mr Palin served for over 15 years as a consultant with the international PR firm Burson–Marsteller, specialising in corporate and environmental communications and community involvement.

Nick Phillips became director general of the Institute of Practitioners in Advertising (IPA) in 1989 and represents them on a number of industry bodies, including the Council and Executive Committee of the Advertising Association and the Advertising Liaison Group of the ITC. His previous career in marketing and advertising included two spells at Granada Television where he was sales director and then director of strategy. He was marketing services director of Beechams Products from 1978–84 and head of research at the Central Office of Information 1973–78.

David Pollock was seconded to the merchant bank Robert Fleming in 1983, and made a more permanent transition to the City in 1986 when he joined the Stock Exchange as head of the Industry Policy Unit. He left the Stock Exchange in early 1991 to join the Newspaper Publishers Association as designer designate, a post he held until the 1st January 1992 when he succeeded John LePage as director.

Arthur Pryor is a consultant with the Public Policy Unit. He previously held a number of senior positions at the Department of Trade and Industry where he worked extensively on EU issues. From 1993 to 1996 he was head of DTI's Competition Policy Division. He now advises on competition and regulation.

Bill Quirke has consulted internationally over the last fifteen years on internal communication and the management of change, in both the public and private sectors. He is one of the leading authorities on linking internal communication to delivering on business strategy. He was a board director of Burson-Marsteller and is now managing director of Synopsis Communication Consulting, which develops internal communication strategies designed to sustain change.

Michael Robertson is responsible for media relations for the ABB Group. He spent 16 years with British Brown Boveri in London, heading a sales and contracts department for the company's activities in the field of electrical power transmission and distribution. In 1985 he transferred to the parent company Brown Boveri in Switzerland as global marketing manager for two business areas and took up his present position in the group's Zurich headquarters in 1993.

David I Robottom is director of development at the Direct Marketing Association. This is a new role focusing on the development of the industry across all sectors. Prior to the DMA , he held a series of senior management positions at GUS and was a direct marketing manager with Midland Bank Group. His career started at General Foods where he was classically trained as a FMCG brand marketer, one of his positions being associate product manager for Maxwell House. He is a founder member of the IDM, a member of the Marketing Society and the Institute of Directors.

Johnnie Seidler is an account director at Sampson Tyrell Enterprises where he has worked with companies from most of the service industries and particularly organisations facing major industry change. Prior to joining Sampson Tyrell Enterprises five years ago, he spent ten years in investment banking at Lazard Brothers and National Westminster Bank.

Mike Seymour is managing director of issues and crisis management at Burson-Marsteller. He works with UK and international companies. He has wide experience of preparedness planning and simulation training for multinationals operating in USA, Europe and Asia Pacific.

Amy Smith is marketing director of McCann-Erickson Advertising. She began her career in marketing as client services director at AUB in Sydney, Australia. She then moved on to develop international business for Telstra Corporation (Telecom Australia) which involved forming strategic alliances with other carriers and managing agency relationships. In 1994, she moved to London to join Simons Palmer Clemmow Johnson as business development director. In the following two and a half years she worked on Sony Playstation, Hoverspeed, COI, Department of Health, Fuji and British Gas Goldfield.

Tim Sutton is chief executive of Charles Barker plc, one of the UK's largest public relations consultancies, and a member of the management buyout team which acquired the company from its previous owners in July 1992. He is currently an advisor to the worldwide oil industry on communications issues arising from the decommissioning of offshore installations. For the last eight years, he has been personally responsible for the whole of British Midland's corporate and public affairs programmes in Europe, reporting to the chairman. This campaign earned the IPR's Sword of Excellence in 1994 as the best PR campaign in the UK. He has been involved in advising a number of companies at senior level on major restructuring and branding strategies and is also a recognised authority on crisis management and employee communications.

Kevin Thomson has pioneered internal marketing and communication for more than a decade. He is chairman of the Marketing and Communication Agency (MCA), the first internal marketing and communication consultancy. He is a leading authority on applying external marketing concepts internally and has developed strategies and processes that have proven highly effective in blue chip organisations.

Dr Roger Till recently joined the Electronic Commerce Association as chief executive. Prior to this he worked for three years at PFA, the consultancy specialising in electronic commerce. He worked for many years at BP, initially in software development in BP Exploration and then in the BP head office IT and Telecomms Strategy Team, where he became their worldwide EDI co–ordinator.

Julian Treasure established TPD Publishing Ltd in 1988, following an extensive career in magazine publishing, latterly as marketing director of IDG Communications. TPD is now the UK's largest independent contract publisher and has offices throughout the world, employs over 140 people and works with some of the world's most successful companies, including Microsoft and Toyota. Julian is now the chairman of the TPD group of companies.

Dr Richard Varey is active in research and teaching in corporate communications, marketing communications, service marketing and related areas at the University of Salford. He has previously lectured in marketing management and business quality, and has completed over 80 consulting projects, mostly in the SME sector.

Gloria Walker, ABC, holds BS and MA degrees in journalism and public relations from two American universities. Throughout her career she has gained experience in the US and Europe in corporate and internal communications, public relations and public affairs. She is an accredited member of the International Association of Business Communicators and is currently president of the UK Chapter.

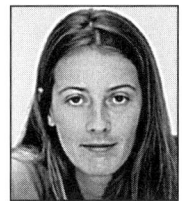

Rachel Walker is deputy planning director at Duckworth Finn Grubb Waters. Prior to this she was an account planner at both BMP DDB Needham (1989) and Duckworth Finn Grubb Waters (1992).

Alan Watson, CBE, is chairman of Burson–Marsteller Europe and a director of Burson–Marsteller worldwide. He is also chairman of Corporate Television Networks Ltd, Burson–Marsteller's joint venture with ITN, providing business services throughout Europe. He advises many major UK and international companies on their communication strategies. His career spans public relations, broadcasting, politics and academia.

Dr Tom Watson is managing director of Hallmark Public Relations Ltd. He gained his PhD in 1995 for a research programme on public relations evaluation. He has written extensively on evaluation and is currently writing a book on the subject.

Jeremy Weinberg is public relations manager at the Institute of Public Relations. He has worked in both print and radio journalism and, as public relations consultant, he has held both in–house and consultancy positions. Prior to joining the institute, he worked for Edelman Public Relations where he specialised in business–to–business and consumer accounts including Commercial Union and the National Dairy Council.

Dr Jon White is a consultant in management and organisation development, and public affairs. As a visiting faculty member at City University Business School and the London School of Economics and Political Science, he also teaches corporate communications. He has written a number of books and articles on the management of communication within and by organisations.

Bob Wootton is director of media services at The Incorporated Society of British Advertisers, which represents the interests of British member advertisers, many of which are the UK arms of multinational companies.

Information Society Initiative, Easy i Ltd and UXL Ltd.; case histories in various aspects of communications are provided by ABB, Andersen Consulting, Lloyds of London, Microsoft and One 2 One; academia is represented by the BNFL Corporate Communications Unit of The Management School at the University of Salford.

The media are reviewed in detail, with the latest from the BBC, British Sky Broadcasting, the Independent Television Association, the Newspaper Publishers Association, the Newspaper Society, the Periodical Publishers Association, TPD Publishing and the Radio Advertising Bureau.

Issues management is discussed from the point of view of Lucas Industries, the British Nuclear Industry Forum and the Energy from Waste Association, while dealing with government is addressed by experts at GPC Market Access, Politics International and the Public Policy Unit.

Public relations, called opinion communications in this book, is represented by useful *Rashomon*-like thinking from the Public Relations Consultants Association and leading agencies Burson-Marsteller, Charles Barker, Countrywide Porter Novelli, Hallmark Marketing Services, Hill & Knowlton, Manning, Selvage & Lee and Shandwick International, plus Medialink Worldwide, the Institute of Public Relations (reviewing their Sword of Excellence Awards) and some wisdom about crisis on the Internet from the US newsletter, *Interactive PR News*.

Communications management is the subject of stories from the International Association of Business Communicators, the Chartered Institute of Marketing, the International Consultants Organisation, the Marketing & Communication Agency and Smythe Dorward Lambert, while corporate identity is discussed by Sampson Tyrrell Enterprises.

Global communications are covered by the International PR Association, Shandwick International and the SMI Group.

Top authors Stuart Crainer, Alfred Glossbrenner and Bill Quirke have written using their specialised expertise, as have independent consultants Annette Allen, Caroline Bainbridge, Clive Bonny, John Clare, Charles Dawson, Neville Hobson, Pamela Jameson, Mike Monkman and Dr Jon White.

To everybody who contributed and who helped with useful suggestions for contributors, a warm and heartfelt thank you. I particularly want to acknowledge and thank Bruce Abrahams of the Origination consultancy for his advice in helping me strategise the content of this book.

Introduction

Timothy R V Foster

The idea of assembling this handbook by taking editorial contributions from people at the cutting edge of their businesses has produced what I believe will stand as a useful source of information, strategic thinking, interpretation and analysis about the state of the art in corporate communications today.

Two words keep cropping up in these pages: Internet and stakeholders. Everything you need to know about the Internet is here. Meanwhile, stakeholders are defined as the key array of audiences a corporation must address, from employees, customers and suppliers, to shareholders, the Government, and the specialised media.

We have the voice of experience right here for you. The heads of the leading professional organisations and relevant key business interests speak within these covers. If it's advertising that interests you, we have words of much wisdom from the Institute of Practitioners in Advertising (IPA), including a review of the winners of the IPA Advertising Effectiveness Awards. We also hear from the Incorporated Society of British Advertisers, the Account Planning Group, the Advertising Standards Authority, the Media Research Group, The Slogo Register, and from ad agencies Duckworth Finn Grubb Waters, from Leo Burnett, McCann-Erickson, from Simons Palmer Denton Clemmow Johnson, and a neat look at the Broadcasting Act, courtsey of *Campaign* magazine's Claire Beale. More specialised interests are covered by input from the British Direct Marketing Association, the Cable Communications Association and the Electronic Commerce Association.

Tomorrow's business practices are forecast by BT Laboratories, the DTI's

Part 1

Corporate Communications

1
Strategic Overview: Where We Are Headed

Simon Lewis
President, the Institute of Public Relations, and Director of Corporate Affairs, British Gas Energy

The corporate communications business is in better shape than ever before. The production of this handbook is testament to the growing importance of the discipline within the business community; the demand for public relations services both through consultancy and in-house is continuing apace. As the pressures on business to perform in highly competitive markets increase, there is a growing appreciation that corporate communications can make a difference.

Some people ask, what is the difference between public relations and corporate communications? To me, they are synonyms for a discipline which is about effective communication, for or on behalf of an organisation. The RSA Tomorrow's Company Inquiry recognised the crucial importance of effective communication in its analysis of the UK's relatively poor competitive performance. In setting out the 'inclusive approach' to managing a business, the Inquiry emphasised the need for a company to define clearly its purpose and values, and to communicate them consistently to its stakeholders. As corporate communicators we have a key role to play in this process.

But in order to play this role there are some key issues which need to be addressed to ensure the most effective use of the discipline.

Where should the function sit in the organisation?

To be most effective, corporate communications must be a strategic, rather than tactical discipline. It belongs in its own right, and not as part of another function or specialism, but with close working relationships with other key strategic functions.

Should the function be centralised or devolved?

In any organisation, the relationship between the head office and individual businesses needs to be actively managed. The key issue is not whether the discipline is devolved, but the establishment of clear guidelines for managing that relationship. Corporate communications belongs at the centre of any organisation.

What should the reporting line be?

Given the strategic significance of corporate communications, the discipline should report directly to the Chief Executive. This provides access and information, two of the most important ingredients for success in corporate communications.

What should be the relationship with strategy?

The relationship should be as close as possible. In too many organisations, the process of communicating strategy, both internally and externally, is seen as separate from day-to-day communications activity. The communication of strategy should be a continuous and planned process.

If these questions provide a framework for organisational success, what will we require as corporate communicators to develop the discipline? The key, in my view, is to identify those trends which will shape the world in which we operate. What are these trends?

Demand for greater transparency

The combination of better-informed customers, greater public scrutiny of corporate decisions and actions, and more active shareholders has led to a demand for greater transparency from government, corporations and other institutions. The expectation is that organisations should be prepared to explain and justify their actions across a range of issues. To give an example, it is now common practice in the UK for publicly quoted companies to provide full details on the remuneration of their main board directors and also, increasingly, to provide descriptions of environmental and community policies. We have also seen in recent years how companies' failures to explain their actions can have damaging business consequences. As communicators, therefore, we must understand these pressures to be more accountable and anticipate what other areas of corporate life are likely to be subject to public scrutiny in the future.

The ethical agenda

The issue of ethics has moved from the periphery to the mainstream of the business agenda. Companies are much more aware of the importance of balancing the interests of all stakeholders (including customers, staff, suppliers, shareholders and the community) in decision making. This entails a willingness to explain the principles of business as much as the business strategy itself. More companies are committed to explaining their ethical stance and publishing Codes of Conduct. For corporate communications practitioners, the ability to understand how the ethical debate has moved from academia to the boardroom is vital.

The rise of pressure-group politics

Political parties in Europe have been losing popularity over the course of a generation. Fewer people are prepared to join political parties and new political alliances are emerging. The phenomenon of the single-issue pressure group is having a major impact on the way in which business and political life is organised. People want to support specific causes outside the broader political process. There are now a number of pressure groups in the UK, including the RSPCA, the RSPB and the National Trust, which have more members than any of the major political parties. Their organisations are well organised, highly professional and expert in understanding the new media. Pressure groups are not a threat to the democratic process unless they are unaccountable and unrepresentative, but to understand their role in our modern society is a crucial part of the competency of a communications professional.

The regulatory framework

We live in a world of regulation. As privatisation rolls out across the world and new markets open, the need for regulation is apparent. What is less clear is which is the most effective model of regulation in different industries and whether self or statutory regulation provides the blueprint for the future. Although we operate in regulated industries as practitioners, our own industry is largely unregulated and, therefore, at risk from practices and traditions which threaten to undermine the reputation of what we have built. We must try, therefore, to put our own house in order as we seek to understand the changing regulatory framework.

What do these trends mean for corporate communicators?

We need to be as forward looking as possible as it is no longer enough simply to respond to today's problems and issues. As a strategic discipline we have the opportunity to help shape the influences which are likely to impact most on the business environment of the future. The challenge is to prove that, as corporate communicators, we are best placed to lead that process.

2

Meeting Today's Audience Expectations

The Six Dimensions: The Inside and Outside Story*

Kevin Thomson
Vice President, Professional Development, International Association of Business Communicators, and Chairman, The Marketing and Communication Agency

Once upon a time life was easy for those who dealt with corporate communications. The external part was handled by either by a PR 'expert' whose job was to handle media relations, or by the marketing 'experts' whose job was to handle customers. So far so good; two external dimensions to the corporate communication jigsaw piece. The third internal dimension was even easier; someone handled employee communications. Generally an 'editor' was appointed who produced a variety of media which cascaded down the organisation in a one-way 'tell' mode. This internal responsi-

*This article is based on work being conducted into the roles and goals of the new communicators in organisations for the International Association of Business Communicators (IABC). The results will be presented by Kevin Thomson at the IABC international conference in Los Angeles in June 1997. It follows a major study by The Marketing and Communication Agency (MCA) and the Corporate Communications Unit of Salford University, entitled the 'Time Warp Survey'.

bility was usually held somewhere down the chain of command, often in Human Resources. Every now and again an outside video or conference company produced something 'motivational' like a roadshow.

Oh that life were as simple today! We now live in a world where everything has changed. Who is today's target audience for corporate communication? Everyone. We have sophisticated customers who demand greater levels of service and quality from every contact with an organisation. This leads to firms like British Airways and NatWest (not just those in the entertainment industry like Disney) developing strategies for a 'total customer experience'. Who gives this customer the experience? Everyone. Who needs to be targeted to get buy-in to wanting to give the customers this experience? Everyone. The concept of 'Brand Ambassadors', where not just the product but also your people are your brand, is being discussed by marketeers at events like the Chartered Institute of Marketing International Conference and in the marketing press.

Today's customer communication strategy goes way beyond even the concept of 'relationship marketing' with its idea of customers for life. The communication strategy looks to making the product or service a part of someone's life. Brand strategies go beyond 'share of voice' in the media to 'share of mind' in the customer's head. In the case of an airline flight with British Airways and its rivals like Virgin, the 'experience' extends from the point of even thinking about a trip to returning and telling people about it. Did the chauffeur add to the 'experience' – and how about the ground staff and cabin crew? Every 'moment of truth' along the way is not just a link in a very complex chain delivery of the product and service, it is a part of a critical link in the chain of communication. Get this wrong and the 'experience' goes wrong. So who is the target audience? Everyone! This goes way beyond customer-service type programmes.

The level of communication needed is phenomenal, to ensure everyone is 'on board' and communicated with fully so they know what they are doing, why, when, how, with whom and where. This is made even more complex when, in many organisations, the downsizing, right sizing, reorganising (and fears of capsizing!) lead to complex problems of communication logistics. We used to have 'employees'. Some organisations now have more people contracted out than those who work for the organisation. Who communicates with them? Who are they committed to? How do you capture their hearts and minds?

So, external customer communication forms one dimension of external communication that ranges from mass marketing to lifetime relationships centred on a total experience. The same principles of external marketing are now being applied in the internal dimension of communication.

Internal communications

Internally we now know that treating people as 'internal customers' is the way forward. We know that by using marketing strategies that match their needs in a two-way flow between the organisation and themselves, we can get far greater degrees of buy-in to corporate messages. A powerful study conducted by The Marketing and Communication Agency (MCA) and Salford University Corporate Communications Unit with leaders in UK businesses came up with two conclusions. First, 'employee communications', in its old 'top-down' form has failed British industry. With an appalling rating of effectiveness of 5.6 out of 10, the old models of team briefing and company magazines are seen not to work. Sadly the new tools of technology, like e-mail and even intranets, are having little more effect other than adding to the overload of information. The second major finding is that 'internal marketing' is rapidly being recognised as the way forward – although many were not quite sure what it was!

But internal marketing does not stop at the two dimensions of top down and bottom up. Empowerment has meant that almost everyone, from individuals to teams to departments and divisions, must target themselves to each other – or be outsourced, or plain old got rid of. The newest dimension of side-to-side communication is the result of the quality revolution, business process re-engineering, outsourcing, strategic alliances and all those other radical changes of the last decade or so. As the three academics Professor William Halal and Drs Ali Geranmeyeh and John Pourdehnad say in their book, *Internal Markets*:

> 'Internal Markets carries today's evolution of management through to its logical conclusion by providing a broader conceptual foundation based on the principles of free enterprise; complete internal-market economies that bring all the advantages of free markets INSIDE large organisations, just like external economies.'

In other words, side-to-side communication is as much a part of corporate communication, because to those individuals, teams, and departments, it *is* their corporate communication. The old functional silos are being replaced by businesses that must communicate and market themselves, or go out of business.

Three-dimensional communications

This gives us three dimensions of communication with internal customers – top down, bottom up and side-to-side. There are also three dimensions externally. The first must be with customers, from simple advertising to lifetime relationship-building. The second dimension is to people who may be customers, but who also wear any number of other hats under the recently elevated status of 'stakeholders'. Corporate communication through the PR department has long dealt with all manner of interested parties from unions, politicians, pressure groups, city institutions, small shareholders, the local community etc. What's new? What is new is that this responsibility cannot be held by the PR department alone.

The role of the individual

Everyone in an organisation, if they are living its values and delivering its message, is a corporate communicator. Everyone can voice an opinion from a seat in the pub to their friends, or to the nation in their armchairs, or as they are interviewed on TV outside the factory gate. Getting the people in and around organisations on your side is no longer a 'nice to have'. The threat to your business if these stakeholders are 'against' you can be considerable. From strikes about pay, driven by the unions, to pickets of middle-class shareholders complaining of the pay of the 'fat cats', as they protest both outside and inside the AGM – they all damage businesses. The 1996 Royal Mail strikes, for example, led to politicians discussing a loss of their monopoly status. The 'fat cat' rumpus around the Greenbury report is doing big business leaders no good at all. Managing this element of the corporate communication mix now means getting the buy-in of a variety of often very vociferous stakeholders.

The supplier

And so to the last dimension of corporate communication. Long considered the responsibility of the sales and purchasing department, are the suppliers. If they are a part of your customer supplier chain, then they are as much a target audience as everyone else. The Procter and Gamble (P&G) and WalMart experience in the US points to a paradigm shift. No longer do a few people communicate on an adversarial purchaser and supplier basis, everyone in both organisations works together. Indeed P&G do not get paid when WalMart accepts the goods. They get paid when the customer purchases the goods. Buy-in, from everyone in both organisations to delivering their part of the chain, is a feature of the success of supplier communication.

Six Dimensions of Corporate Communication: three outside and three inside. Many new target audiences, for new types of messages about change, as well as the 'old' messages, like visions, missions, business goals, best practice, innovation, re-structuring, partnerships, alliances etc. Two- and three-way communication is no longer a 'nice to have'. Integration of communication is now a critical business strategy not a distant dream. Listening, research, targeting, launching, sustaining, promoting to everyone, not just customers is the order of the day.

What is the bottom line to all this change? Everyone is a customer of everyone else; everyone is a supplier. Everyone has stakeholders who have an impact on what they are trying to achieve, from the global corporation to the individual on the shop floor. Corporate communication is now breaking out of the time warp of PR, marketing and internal communication, into a new dimension – in fact six new dimensions.

3

Management of Reputation

Tim Sutton
Chief Executive, Charles Barker plc

As you would expect, as public relations advisors, we spend a good deal of our time with the boards of major and indeed less major companies, helping them to say what they mean.

The changing face of PR

A less obvious and more difficult part of the job is also to help companies to mean what they say. As you will appreciate, it isn't always the same thing. As recently as 20 years ago, the role of the public relations advisor was quite different from what it is today. Basically the job was twofold: to keep a hostile world at bay in the event of bad news; or to turn on a well-crafted eulogy press release in the case of good news.

Things have changed and companies quite rightly expect considerably more these days from their corporate-communications-relations advisor than that. It's no longer about lobbing over information to the enemy. Nor is it about building fortification walls against a siege of unwelcome requests or brickbats.

If we are looking for a better definition of what corporate communications is really about, we could do a lot worse, as so often in life, than turn to Shakespeare, who gives us one of the best clues to the value of goodwill. It is Othello who laments:

'Reputation, reputation, reputation, I have lost my reputation! I have lost the
immortal part of myself and what remains is bestial.'

Poetic it may be, but it provides a wonderful insight into the fact that
reputation (be it personal or corporate), however hard it may be to pin
down and define, is something of wonderful and tangible value. And
when we lose reputation, either gradually or suddenly, Othello tells us that
there are some very dire consequences.

The power of reputation

Corporate communications is best understood as the management of reputation. If we think of the idea of someone's personal reputation, the
process by which we reach a view of that is far more complex than making
a simple judgement of what that person tells us.

Turn the words 'public relations' round and, of course, you get relations
(with) public(s). Publics in plural because every company, by virtue of
existing, has to have relationships with a number of different audiences.
Typically, these include: investors, customers, suppliers, employees, politicians, opinion formers and so on. For many companies, the list can get
more complex, including regulators, trade associations, business competitors, dealers or other intermediaries, business providers and so on.

In this sense public relations is different to any other form of marketing
activity. We can choose whether to advertise, or whether to have direct
mail or whether to attend an industry exhibition. We can't choose whether
to have relations with publics!

The choice is between allowing these relationships to be unplanned,
unmanaged, arbitrary and 'come what may'. Or having controlled, managed relationships which are planned and purposeful to the benefit of the
company.

Which of course, as most companies have sensibly realised, is really no
choice at all! As a result, an enormous amount of effort is now invested in
managing relationships with these key groups. In the particular case of
investors, this is reflected, of course, in thorough preparation and rehearsal
for the reporting calendar. As many boards know, a moment akin to the
regular trip to the dentist.

Nevertheless this is life. The relentless pressures and fears of the reporting calendar can very easily paralyse a company's board. In this sense,
'what shall we tell them?' isn't just an academic topic for pleasant debate
but more akin to a terrifying exam question.

For some companies, corporate communications is sometimes dominated by the (normally) twice-yearly pressures of financial results, as well

as other associated corporate accountability triggers, such as the Annual Report and AGM. And between these official reporting dates and triggers, companies invest considerable further time and effort in maintaining close relationships with fund managers, brokers and analysts.

But I wonder whether this, what one might call 'managerial' or 'process-driven' model of corporate-communications relations, which many companies are committed to, is at all adequate. It is a common complaint among many companies in the UK that the City is notoriously short term in its thinking. The claim is that there is an obsession with short-term performance or short-term prospects and insufficient appreciation of 'real' value. But I sometimes think that the complaints might be misjudged or, at the very least, futile.

The fact is that both the rate of return and the speed of return are measures of perceived risk. It is self evident that as time goes on, so risk, quite properly, is perceived to increase. From the point of view of investors this is reasonable enough when evaluating what cannot be directly controlled, for example, markets, regulators, the actions of competitors, capital markets, economic cycles and geopolitical factors.

How investors judge this risk will vary over any defined time-window for the risk. Simply saying that they must sit and commit to the long term is not really an adequate response on its own to the dynamics of the situation. Why should they wait and why should they commit? After all, a risk never stands alone. It has to be judged against other comparative risks which are open to the investor. The best PR wordsmiths in the world can't plaster over this basic crack.

Assuming this to be uncontroversial, I would rather ask a more interesting question and it is this: do companies usually get the shareholders and customers they deserve?

If any of us believe that the investors or other key external audiences are short term, how many of us have the courage not to give in to our own short-term frenzy by the way in which we conduct our own corporate communications?

The need for vision

Above all, it is perhaps the 'vision thing' (as President George Bush once called it) which is most lacking in the managerial, process-driven model of investor relations. Putting aside sophisticated financial analysis, many investors have a gut feeling of whether a company's senior management knows what the company stands for and where it is going. They also have a feeling for consistency – of messages; and, most intangibly but most influentially, of values.

This isn't just guesswork. We know from a number of research studies that there are two attributes seen as far more important than any others in determining investment decisions: the first is strategy and the second is leadership.

What implications can we take from this for the way in which we communicate and conduct our corporate communications? I think there is an interesting lesson here for those responsible for investor relations – and it doesn't come from the City. It comes from the hallowed tradition of brand management. Brands are long-term. Like super tankers, they are difficult to turn around quickly, but once they get going, they acquire a powerful momentum all of their own. It's worth pointing out that seven out of the top ten brands in the UK in the 1930s are still in the top ten today.

Market conditions will change, strategies will need to be constantly evolved. But there are certain fundamentals of corporate communications which must stay constant over time if we want our businesses to be truly understood by our audiences. And the biggest fundamental of all is a senior management which is seen to know where it's going and communicates a consistent vision and mission to prove it.

Moreover, the character of a company's long-term vision; the goals of its corporate mission and how it defines shareholder value, can often all be seen implicitly in the way and style with which the company communicates with its other audiences, such as its customers.

Not just external audiences either. British Airways' internal 'Putting People First' culture-change programme in the 1980s was arguably as influential to its investment positioning as it was to improving customer service. More recently, Archie Norman at Asda is another example of a CEO who understands that demonstrating dramatic internal culture change and effective employee communications are critical to investor communications.

A recent joint report from the Institute of Public Relations and the DTI offers us an interesting fact with which some of you may already be familiar: over the last 15 years, a company's tangible assets, its goodwill, have on average grown to represent 70 per cent of its balance-sheet assets during mergers and acquisitions. This makes your company's reputation potentially its biggest asset.

It is a statistic which may not be expressed in quite the poetic way in which Othello delivers it, but the same point is made: building reputation is critical; losing it is disastrous. But while the light of reputation can be switched off suddenly, it is less easy to switch it on straightaway.

Clear vision, relentless consistency of communication and careful definition of wherein lies shareholder value is the best way to get the shareholders we deserve. In that mix lies management quality. And I hope it almost goes without saying, but I'll say it anyway: what we tell 'them out there' should be what we believe ourselves.

exceeding expectations

CHARLES BARKER

public relations

4

Corporate Communications: The New Agenda

Roger Hayes
President, International Public Relations Association, and Director General, The British Nuclear Industry Forum

I have always argued that corporate communications is a discipline in its own right, from the early days when public relations was embryonic to the present time when there is a whole raft of specialist fields under the public relations umbrella, although some don't call them PR. But that is another story.

But in those days corporate communications was a poor relation to consumer PR and business-to-business and even now is the subject of confusion by being labelled just the sum total of investor, media and government relations. In my view, particularly based on my in-house (as opposed to agency) experience (where work tends to be compartmentalised) corporate communications is greater than the sum of its parts; the total mosaic, embodying the 'inclusive approach' to all stakeholders in a holistic way, as recommended by the RSA's Tomorrow's Company Inquiry.

Where there is a corporate brand, it can be valued, total reputation matters, and what happens in one part of the business affects the rest. In that sense the corporation is a system, and corporate communications a general-management function embracing both external and internal staff and line functions, and requiring access to the top management, especially the Chairman and Chief Executive. It is, therefore, strategic, involving not only a message-distribution relationship between the corporation and stakeholders, but anticipating their expectations, as well as reacting to events.

But corporate communications is only just coming into its own, firstly because of its importance to global-communications strategies and programmes, but also given the changing environment out there and the corporation's changing role within it. This is what I mean by the New Agenda: part prediction, part reality.

The rise of the stakeholder

The nuclear energy industry, for example, like other controversial industries, must earn its 'licence to operate'. With the decline of deference and greater accessibility to information, stakeholder expectations are higher and companies have to deal with *all* stakeholders, not just some – as Shell found to their cost with Brent Spar. However, the more recent kind of stakeholder, the single or multi-issue pressure group such as Greenpeace, learned to its cost on that occasion that 'sound-bite' politics, even if it appeals to people's emotions, is no substitute for informed public debate. Issues such as the environment are complex, long term and global, requiring reconciliation of a whole range of stakeholders. Corporations have rights as well as responsibilities and just because pressure groups like Greenpeace have filled a vacuum created by the fault-lines appearing in the political system, it doesn't mean they can behave as if only they had rights. Citizens, and increasingly 'netizens', demand accountability of all stakeholders, including themselves. For example, research reveals that citizens as a whole believe it isn't the fault of governments or business that waste is caused; there may be some blame attributable, and certainly the media fuel the flames, but people recognise that society as a whole must solve these problems.

This is an opportunity for business, not only to fill the vacuum created by the loss of political leadership (how many CEOs or their corporate PROs are really prepared?), but to become part of the solution, rather than constantly being, or being perceived to be, part of the problem and always on the defensive.

The 'Fat Cats' debate, begun with the Chief Executive of British Gas, meandering through the privatisation of water utilities, and reaching fever pitch recently, is a corporate communications issue! Society really has to make up its mind whether chief executives of Britain's corporations deserve what they are paid compared to their staff or customers, or to other careers, such as pop stars and footballers. Is the chief executive of Britain's most important exporter worth more than all other British chief executives, etc?

Apart from the issue of package transparency and performance against pay, it behoves the media, and indeed, institutional investors and their watchdogs, to behave responsibly. However, it really is up to the chief executives and their corporate PR and other advisors to anticipate public opinion rather than plead surprise when different stakeholders complain. The more difficult it is to explain what a CEO does (other than sitting in an office all day or lunching at the Savoy), the more important it is to do so.

Some of my colleagues in public relations believe corporate PR is just about articles in the *Financial Times*. In practical terms that's not a bad assessment in my view, although fundamentally it is much more, as I'm attempting to argue. The more chief executives and their top management teams can be interrogated not just about their earnings or their sales, but about their strategy, beliefs and vision, the more stakeholders and public opinion generally will come to understand the role of CEOs and where corporations fit in society.

With the growing cost and complexity of everything, governments and international government organisations are increasingly unable to pay the tab. With their skills-base, technology, global tentacles and, above all, access to capital, corporations should be able to turn around their generally poor images. Yet the management of reputation still doesn't command the same respect as the management of money or keeping the company out of the law courts.

Nowhere is this whole business-and-society approach more important than in emerging markets, where the international corporation can play a key role in assisting a whole range of local stakeholders in the transition to developed economies and, in some cases, democracies.

All of this requires trust based on dialogue, building long-term relationships with all stakeholders rather than the transaction style of the greedy 1980s. Indeed, sustainability will be impossible, especially in fledgling democracies, unless the private sector plays a key role. This is an environment in which public relations can flourish as our involvement in privatisations attests.

The way forward

Corporate communications, therefore, means that internal cultural matters should be integrated with external dialogue on the company's strategy and position on issues; that the PR people feed back attitudes and expectations early enough so they can be fed into the strategic-planning process; so that issue management replaces crisis, and anticipation replaces reaction, viz British Gas, Brent Spar, the water companies, and the nuclear industry in earlier years.

No longer can corporate communications remain the poor relation, a sideshow to where the real action is, because the *new* agenda requires a *new* nexus of relationships among a whole host of stakeholders that wasn't expected before. 'We-know-best' communications has been replaced by the need for all actors on the stage to reach consensus before decisions are taken.

We live in a new era where people and communications are centre stage. But are we in the key meetings; are our views and research plugged into the decision-making process; have we latched onto the company's changing role at home base as well as internationally, or are we afraid to tell the truth for fear of being the shot-messenger? Corporate communication has to be consistent, co-ordinated and coherent to be credible. If so, it impacts the bottom line – operational ability and sustainable success.

5

Corporate Identity in a World of Constant Change*

Johnnie Seidler
*Account Director, Enterprise Identity
Group, Sampson Tyrrell Enterprises Ltd*

'We are not just offering people a style. We are offering them a message.' So Nicolas Hayek once said of his success in building the Swatch watch brand from zero.

In a world of constant change and instant communication, cycles of product improvement and imitation have shortened to the point where for many businesses it is no longer feasible – in terms of either time or money – to rely for success on the strength of products alone. It is the intangibles of brands that have often become companies' most durable assets. But identifying what these are, how to protect and nurture them and to communicate them effectively is no easy task. Corporate identity, at its best, rises to this challenge.

What is identity?

Such intangible assets will only be durable if they are rooted in reality and if the message is both believable and sustainable. As Collins and Porras wrote in their book *Built to Last*, 'The crucial variable is not the content of a company's ideology, but how deeply it believes its ideology and how consistently it lives, breathes and expresses all that it does.'

An effective identity strategy should, first and foremost, be firmly based upon a company's corporate strategy, which sets out its ultimate goals. But between one and the other lies a third crucial element: the company's positioning. This defines the combination of characteristics through which, uniquely, the company is seeking to position itself and its products versus its competition.

Only through clarity of long-term objectives and a medium-term definition of the battleground is it possible to define a company's unique 'message' which will serve to achieve the real ambitions of the business. Traditionally, identity has been seen as a visual device defining corporate symbol or logo, colours etc. But if the set of corporate clothes is going to suit the company inside them, we need to go much further. A broader definition would include guidance on the way in which a company communicates verbally, be it through the media or in below-the-line material; and, above all, in the way in which it behaves. Stories are legion of companies whose 'brand promise' was time and again shown to be empty by the gallingly contradictory behaviour of their staff.

Who does identity talk to? If behaviour is the third element of any successful identity (along with the visual and verbal), it follows that an identity's audience is much broader than the organisation's customer base alone. Employees represent an army of 'message' bearers and every single contact with a customer is an opportunity to communicate the essence of the brand. From an internal perspective, and particularly for staff with no customer contact, 'identity' can also serve as a strong motivating force.

While John Egan (now Sir John Egan) was rejuvenating Jaguar Cars in the early 1980s, one of his key actions was to re-establish the use of Jaguar's famous symbol internally. Staff later attributed to this small act a greater resurgence of pride and loyalty than came from many other management decisions.

The third important audience for an identity will be other stakeholders, including, in the case of a public company, its investors. Particularly for a public company, a strongly managed identity may be the closest visual expression of a management team's competence that investors will see.

The role of identity

Put another way, a company's visual identity may be the only experience that a financially oriented investor may have of what type of company it is.

The identity in this sense conveys the company's personality and is the medium by which the company can communicate at an emotional level with its audience – whether this be investors, staff or customers. Virgin Group's red symbol is a strong example of this. Given that most of us are driven far more by our emotions than our rational minds would care to admit, the right emotional message, communicated effectively, represents a powerful weapon.

However powerful the weapon, it will only be useful if it shoots straight. Even the strongest identities will fail unless they are properly managed. An unmanaged identity will quickly fall into disrepair, most commonly fragmenting under the varying pressures of the business or through compromising its integrity by being poorly applied. But nor do the rigid visual identity manuals of old lend themselves to today's increasingly decentralised corporate management structures.

Visual identity systems have been responding by concentrating more on the spirit and less on the letter, epitomised by none better than Castrol's 'Framework for Imagination'. Concentrating on the core elements of Castrol's identity, this system allows Castrol's local brand managers to apply them in a way and at a level of sophistication appropriate to their individual markets around the globe.

The role of identity is thus to meet the needs of a company's structure and culture (unless the express intent is to change either or both), one measure of success being whether that message is coming across at the right volume in each situation. But it is also the role of identity to ensure clarity, not only of purpose but also of branding structure.

Several unsuccessful hostile takeover bids and declining market share forced Gillette in the US to re-evaluate its corporate and branding strategy, where product identities had been allowed to subsume the masterbrand. By rebalancing these elements so that the Gillette name once again became the primary communication across the product range, clarity of 'parentage' was restored in the minds of the consumer. The company's falling market share was halted and substantial improvement was seen in the bottom line.

In summary, the benefits of strong identity management are twofold. It ensures a consistency of message, whether visual, verbal or behavioural. One hymn sheet: as McDonald's know, customers love it. Secondly, by its focus on positioning, identity management can achieve and sustain clear differentiation. Not just cosmetically, but also in genuine behavioural terms.

Identity and corporate change

There are no greater examples of the power of identity, in its widest sense, to make or break deals than are provided by the experience of firms after merger or acquisition. Historically, prior to completing transactions, managements have typically concentrated on the figures – frequently giving scant thought to the implications of merging two very different corporate cultures. By 1986 the British Institute of Management had concluded that this was a major contributory factor to post-deal failure of mergers and acquisitions. As a managing director of the Halifax Building Society said, 'The key to a successful merger lies not in rigid controls ... but in broader issues such as a shared vision of how the business will develop.'

Conversely, addressing these issues head on at an early stage can reap high rewards. Developing (or imposing) one vision and a common set of values may be the easy part; agreeing an identity and branding strategy may also be accomplished without great pain. But the hardest task is more likely to be the winning of employees' hearts and gaining of their commitment to the new order. These are, again, emotional issues and, unlike other managerial actions, cannot be accomplished by diktat. Communication at the emotional level may not come easily to all senior managers, but ducking it can undo the best financial engineering in the world.

Who's got it right?

So which companies deserve our admiration for being models of great identities? Maybe we should seek answers to this question from both our minds and our hearts. In the case of the former, studies have been made identifying the world's most powerful brands. One such study calculated the premium of a brand's value over those of other companies in its sector and, unsurprisingly, names such as Microsoft, Coca-Cola, Gillette, Braun, Levi's and General Electric scored highly.

As for our hearts, we admire companies that we understand. This is often because we feel the company has shared its philosophy with us and practises what it preaches. In the UK the Virgin Group is capturing the hearts of its target market (which, due to its positioning, is not all of us). And its bold, freestyle identity is a genuine reflection of its original, anti-establishment corporate personality – and that, of course, of its founder.

At a less singular level, American Express powerfully conveys its brand message in all its communications – 'the trusted global companion for financial and travel services', based on its core values of heroic customer service, worldwide reliability and individual initiative. There is a continous thread between its vision, its values and its behaviour. Finally, it jealously guards its visual identity, which has become a powerful representation of American Express's business.

What all these companies have is a vision, and it pays. Some have it from a visionary leader or from an inherited tradition. Others seek external advice in helping them to define it. But if it's right, decent and the whole company lives it, such firms prove to be the long-run winners in a world of constant change. They make more money, they are more resilient in adversity – and stock markets seem to know this. Research by Collins and Porras shows that visionary companies as a group in the USA in the last 60 years outperformed the general market by no less than a staggering 15 times.

For this élite group, the old cliché seems to be true: success breeds success. Rather than being resented for their profits, their customers are ardent, emotional fans. Nicolas Hayek of Swatch fame put it like this: 'The people who buy Swatches from us want us to win.' Alleluia!

Part 2
New-Media Communications

6

The 21st-century Company at Work

Peter Cochrane
Head of Research
and
Mike Lyons
Head of Business Modelling Group,
BT Laboratories

The accelerating development of technology is placing increasing strains on the old vertically integrated industries. Those unwilling to change are now experiencing difficulty in operating, competing and surviving. To be successful in the twenty-first century, companies will have to alter their structure and mode of operation drastically.

The world is undergoing a major globalisation with a restructuring of the Fordist production process across national boundaries. Realising an integrated structure will require telecommunications systems to provide the 'glue' essential for global co-ordination. As a result, companies are coming under increasing pressure to rethink their operations in order to position themselves in the new competitive era. This means a faster on-demand delivery of better products of increasing sophistication at lower cost.

Common features of the evolving industries are:

- shorter product cycles – a faster response to market and technological change;

- increasing development costs for new products;
- greater risks, but the potential for greater rewards.

As the competitive environment reduces reaction times, faster decision making is essential, requiring the intelligent processing of more data. This has to be underpinned by advances in IT within the legislative and policy frameworks which may allow or restrict such advantage. Telecommunications is thus critical for all sectors of the global economy.

Technology

With the convergence of IT, entertainment and telecommunications, a new world of opportunities is emerging, including:

- telepresence displacing travel;
- increasing telecommunications mobility;
- natural language recognition and machine speech input/output plus conversation;
- automatic language translation;
- humanised interfaces to machines – everyone will become computer literate;
- integrated terminals for work and pleasure – hi-fi, TV, VR, PC, mobile IT;
- the super computer on your desk – by 2010 the PC will be up to one million times more powerful than that of today;
- computers you wear – communication and computing on the move;
- intelligent office with data sorting, visualisation, filtering, decision support, search–find–classify–anticipate–war games/simulation support;
- mobile medicare – real-time monitoring of your health metrics – is your job, office, work, company killing you?

Value networks

The emergence of an integrated global economy will play havoc with old markets. Existing value chains will become less static and disordered value networks will take their place. These will be dynamic, with many complex features, such as cross or floating links, reflecting the evolving market structure. These will be made even more complex through greater cultural mixing of business and management styles and the need for new forms of taxation for global companies.

Telecommunications will play an essential role in enabling companies to respond effectively in a dynamic, real-time economy in which the unifying managerial resource is information. The vertically integrated company, characteristic of older industries, will become less viable. One process leading to the demise of older structures is the inability to retain strategic information as the convergence of industries necessitates increasing collaboration. We already see companies collaborating in one sector while competing (with different partners) in another.

Virtual organisations

The new companies will be product and service based, with different organisations contributing complementary skills. Unified companies may disappear and become primarily contracting organisations with manufacturing, R&D and marketing run as separate profit centres, offering services competitively to parent or rival companies. Departments brought together to produce a specific product form a 'virtual company' linked, not by geographic proximity, but by intranets which permit the low-cost transfer of ideas and knowledge. This mode of working is already evident in the leading sectors today.

As the virtual company becomes more common, specialised companies may dominate. Those employing a small core of workers may wield tremendous financial power in the design, planning and manufacturing capacity of the planet. This could be particularly important as the means of production shifts from the owner of production tools to the owner of the knowledge to control those tools – the information worker.

One of the stages towards this more integrative but distributed global operation is the transition to flatter and more fluid organisations with multidirectional information flows. Such structures may only be temporary as the market becomes more chaotic (in the mathematical sense); it is unclear what types of organisational structure will be viable under such extreme conditions. It is also unclear what regulatory and legislative frameworks will best suit the requirements of this global economy.

Impact

The impact of these radical changes is profound. As global competitiveness stimulates the atomisation of companies and institutions, it counteracts the cohesive processes, such as co-operation between companies and nations. It therefore places an increasing emphasis on business ethics. Where businesses fail to meet these needs, they will be faced with increased environmental regulation and governmental control.

Such cohesion can be enhanced through:

- more rational/democratic self-regulation of companies;
- communication referenda, televoting etc.

This globally competitive environment, reliant on interworking networks, will depend critically on co-operation between competitors. New ground rules for operation in the marketplace will evolve, perhaps exhibiting many radical changes. However, there are certain attributes which successful players will have to develop:

- engineering of competitive edge through applied creativity;
- ability to assess and take advantage of opportunities and risks.

These changes will affect the lives of individuals, who will no longer expect or be provided with jobs for life, as companies make increasing use of contractors. The future working environment will demand people who are prepared to continue learning and developing throughout their lives. Individuals will have to develop their own strategies for coping with this demanding environment in which multitasking will become commonplace. Many may become simultaneous employers and employees.

Conclusion

The world is going through a deep-seated transition which is affecting all aspects of society. The major characteristics are a compression of time and distance coupled with the removal of delays through telecommunications and IT. While the scale is principally evident on the open market, it is clear that all systems in society are having to adapt at great speed. However the changes will allow a new post-industrial society to emerge, but only if the opportunities offered by the widest spectrum of available IT are exploited effectively.

7

Media Techno-Trends: Opportunities – and Threats – for Advertising

Charles Dawson
Managing Director, Neomedion Ltd

Newly empowered by digital technology and the interactive command button, are audiences set to wreak a terrible revenge on advertising, callously zapping commercial messages from their screens? This article, based on a paper in *Admap*'s 'Digital Revolution' edition, offers some quick checks to see whether the advertising industry will be dead on arrival in the promised land, as many have predicted it will be. The writer sees signs that there is plenty of life in the old dog yet, though it faces a pressing need to learn new tricks.

Converging industries

One overriding megatrend provides the context for the media-technology shifts we are already witnessing, and many which are not yet visible. Three massive divisions of the global communication business – computing, telecommunications and television– continue their inexorable mutual approach. In time, they are set to emerge as divisions of a new composite industry based on the propagation of information in digital form. *The Economist* recently dubbed this 'the bit business'.

This in itself should be no big surprise. The three industries have all been approaching the limits of their intrinsic growth potential. Each is suffering from increasing internal competition. Each has begun to realise first that together they would be bigger than the sum of their parts, and next that they probably need each other to progress, even to survive.

The TV medium as we know it always claimed to be part of the so-called communications industry, but in reality it wasn't part of anything but itself. Until now, TV and video have been cut off and protected from the world's mainstream communications businesses, telecommunications and computing. One reason was that TV's 60-year-old analogue signal conventions were technically incompatible with the digital signals of the other two businesses. This provided an invisible protective 'ring fence' around television's little world.

Digitisation merges and integrates those signals with other communication forms, freeing TV from the prison of its original narrow role, but simultaneously exposing it to competition from vastly bigger forces. When TV talks the same language – a digital language – as computers and telephones, it will for the first time find itself operating in the communications mainstream. We will see in a moment that this has enormous implications for advertising-related industries. Convergence will end the comfortable fiction that the little world of conventional media is somehow separate.

The next phase of development in the communications industries will be costly. Because of their sheer size, telecoms are arguably in a unique position to plan developments over long periods at the required scale. Certainly today's TV industry could not even contemplate it alone. At this level, the logic behind convergence becomes virtually unanswerable. European legislation may slow down the telecoms' counter-move into broadcasting, but it will certainly not stop it.

Computing is also an essential ingredient. We are no longer talking just television. The new services, and the software that makes them happen, will require a network of linkages, much bigger memory capacity, plus faster and more powerful processing; computer power, in fact, although it may not immediately be recognised as such.

With ever bigger and faster chips – the cost of computing power continues to fall by around 30 per cent a year – computing will play an essential role in making the offerings on the TV screen accessible and attractive to the audience. Delivering hundreds of services in digital form is one thing, but computer power is needed to render them user friendly. The definitive set-top box, when it arrives, is likely to be a powerful PC in all but name.

Whether the TV of the future eventually takes the form of a smart television set, a set-top box or a home computer scarcely matters. Either way, viewers will use easy 'point-and-click' software conventions to navigate through a kaleidoscopic choice of programming and services. General anxieties about life may be on the increase, but media 'techno-fear' already seems to be a vanishing threat; indications are that around half of adults and 90 per cent of young people are already regularly using computers. The move to 'smart TV' seems a short and easy step.

Predicting the present

Although not necessarily in their final forms, most of the significant elements for transition are already in place and in use. If we can read the signs right, we will find that to a large extent we are 'predicting the present'. We should look at things which are already happening, then imagine their success rate when they converge and improve twentyfold in accessibility, visual appeal and ease of use.

All the following phenomena are already with us:

- *Yellow Pages* and *Talking Pages* and the use of touch-tone phones to navigate multiple information offerings;
- premium channels on satellite and cable TV;
- home banking services such as First Direct and remote-access financial services such as Direct Line Insurance;
- teleshopping services such as QVC;
- relationship marketing of TV channels;
- on-screen information services such as Teletext;
- interactive advertising;
- Internet and the World Wide Web.

Getting involved

Passive consumption of TV has not disappeared, nor is it ever likely to, any more than will the concept of 'peak viewing'. But it is increasingly an active choice of things which we then watch passively.

Audience characteristics are increasingly full of paradoxes such as the active/passive conundrum. As consumers of the media, we are no longer consistent. We vacillate between active appetites and indolence. Within minutes, we switch from wanting a shared viewing experience to a quest for personal gratification. What we want is no longer a single constant.

New interactive facilities mean that some of our viewing will switch from passive to active mode. Just as a music enthusiast can use a CD-player to skip, rearrange or repeat the tracks stored digitally on a compact disc, so viewers will be able to interrogate, edit, repeat, speed up, slow down, enlarge, superimpose or intermix the images and information on the screen. At this point the viewing experience transcends mere reception and becomes two-way traffic.

TV is becoming part of a transactional environment. TV will be putting advertising and other commercial message formats directly in the frame with the commercial transactions they seek to influence.

Problems for advertising

Turning to TV advertising itself, serious arguments have been advanced that conventional TV advertising is in terminal decline. As the *Wall Street Journal Europe* has commented, 'It is hard to believe that in a digital, interactive world, anyone will sit for numbing repetitions of intrusive jingles, or unrewarding 30-second spots'. The key word is of course 'unrewarding' and the key technique will be getting the viewer involved.

The complete Armageddon scenario of TV advertising zapped out of existence seems fundamentally unlikely. Direct mail, price promotions and sponsorship were all feared as communication forms which would 'eat advertising'; they have all taken share, certainly, yet advertising continues to grow (not least because these newer communication devices themselves need to be advertised).

The key principle here is the all-important difference between ads we see involuntarily and the messages we ask to see. Interactivity means commercial messages for which the consumer actively goes looking. Things shown to us with our active and willing participation make a much bigger impact on us than messages we never asked for in the first place.

This will be the media expert's stock in trade: knowing what viewers want and need, and what they will probably do next. The task will be to respond to interested viewers with tailored messages, and with context-relevant prompts and information, arranged sequentially. This requires a special kind of vision; how, for instance, to 'cluster' like-minded viewers and talk to them so that they each feel like the only one participating in the dialogue – in fact, how to conduct mass-communication at an individual level.

This does not necessarily mean they all have to receive different messages: campaigns can still be planned on similar lines to mass communication, with a limited number of message variants. The response patterns of large numbers of people are likely to be broadly similar. They will just feel as if they are getting personal treatment.

If consumers are persuaded by the first contact willingly to enter the advertiser's carefully prepared array of interactive messages, they can be invited through a methodical 'filtration system', with a chance of the process culminating in a sale, transacted on the spot, before the customer leaves the advertiser's orbit. Commercial communication must learn to flow with the viewer's impulses, providing commercial 'prompts' and 'gateways' to information, promotions and offers at appropriate points in the process. The 30-second spot is no longer an end in itself. It is the beginning of a longer, more complex and vastly more productive process.

A maze of possibilities

That process will involve mastering a post-proliferation offering of available message vehicles. The bewildering labyrinth in Figure 7.1 on the following page shows that there are potentially already over fifty different ways of delivering a message.

Some of them, like TV, radio, cinema, print and Teletext, are already with us, and long established. Others are still in their early stages, from advertiser-funded TV programming production on the far left, to the customised electronic newspaper on the far right. And we will soon be able to use any of them, in any combination which we think makes sense.

However, the ones we pick not only have to work in their own right. They have to work in combination, linking together in complex relationships, and referring consumers from one element to another.

In this bewildering maze of possibilities, we are going to need a route map. Perhaps it will look like Figure 7.2.

For each composite communication task, we will have to pick our media options for their penetration, their accuracy, their efficiency, and their relevant communication power individually. Then we will have to string them together so that the result is coherent and we don't get lost. (If we as communicators are lost, what hope is there of the consumer out there receiving a cohesive and persuasive message?) Advertising people will have to learn 'joined-up communication', as it was cleverly described at a recent *Admap* conference.

Advertising agency and media specialist groups must provide the cartographers who can draw 'route-maps' for advertisers, guiding them through countless options for message association to those which will clinch successful transactions. This is the only thing which will allow us to look at the totality of an advertiser's communications programme in the way the customer sees it: as a composite flow of information from sources which can barely be told apart.

Paying the cost

There is one major issue left to address. Who is going to pay for all this?

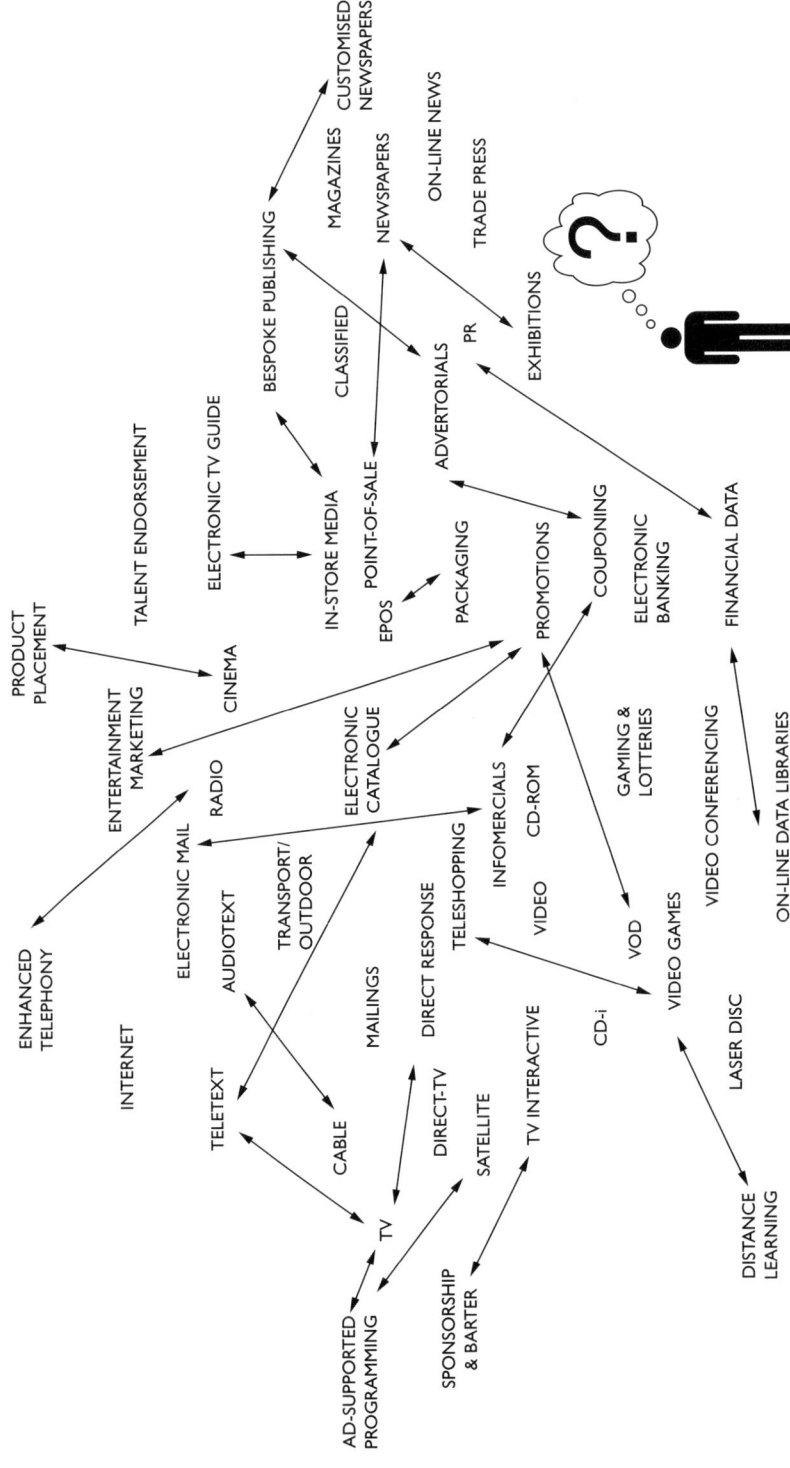

Figure 7.1 For coherent communication …
© Neomedion 1996

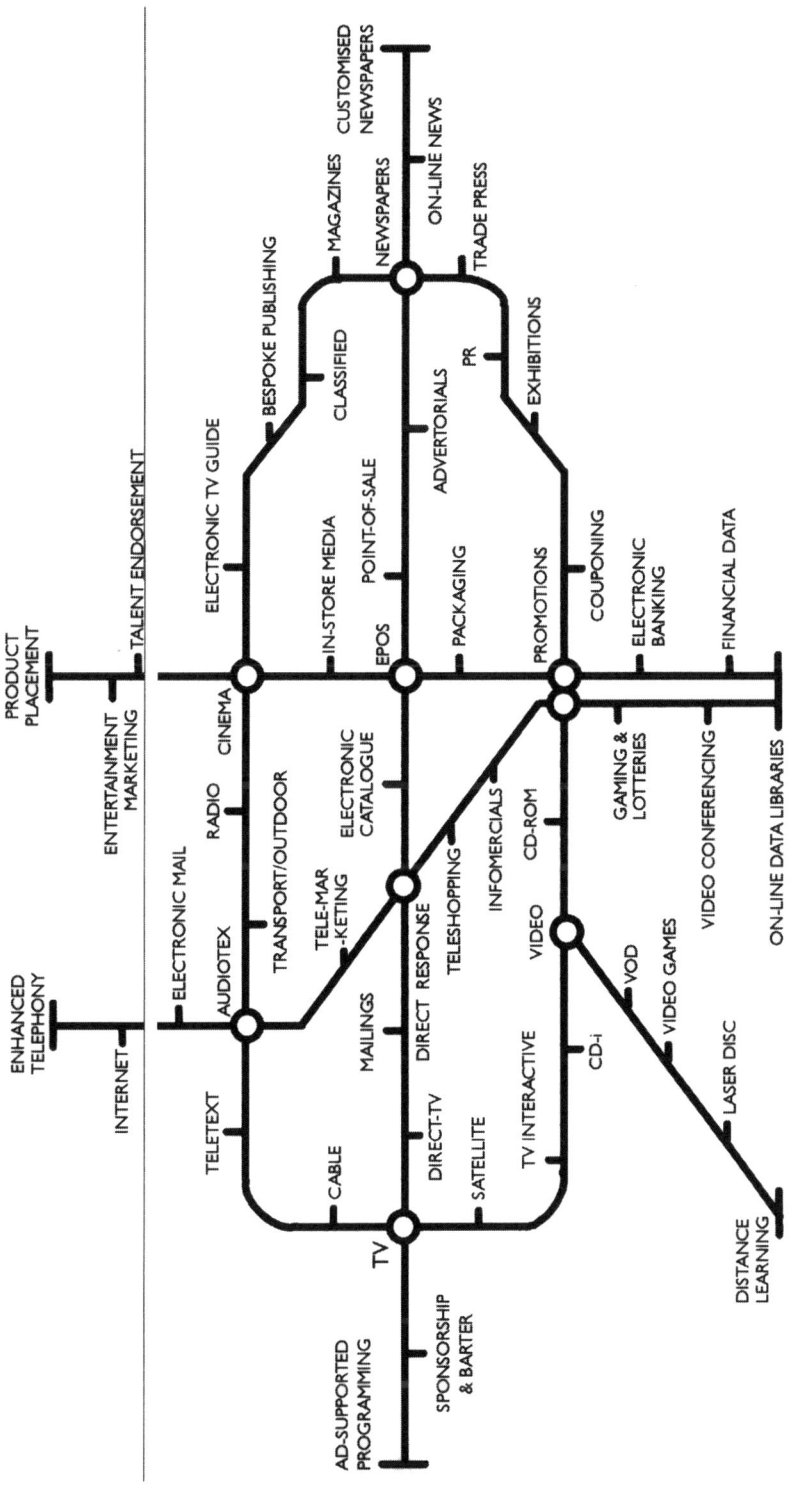

Figure 7.2 ... an advertiser needs a route map

© Neomedion 1996

Some people look to pay-TV in its various forms. Others look at the advertiser. Who will pay the bills? For the hardware? The software? The delivery systems? The programme content? The complex electronic transactional environment? Clearly, the new media age cannot be entirely financed by advertising. But it might not have to be.

In a world of electronic transactions, vast savings can potentially be made by the utilities, financial institutions, insurers, educational foundations and public departments providing services alongside the televisual ones. (In reality, these businesses have nothing to do with our traditional concept of TV; but convergence means they will be using the same two-way signal delivery systems as television.)

Lured by the attraction of dramatically reduced operating costs, these bodies have a solid reason for investing, directly or indirectly, in the new infrastructure which provides them. Public funding, EU subsidies and the like will also be available, since governments at all levels are anxious that Europe and its citizens should not be left behind in the global communication revolution.

As a result, media services can have reasonable expectations of an 'indirect subsidy' for their delivery channels from other, far bigger industries. If this does not amount to a free ride, it will be the next best thing.

Summary

These are unsettling and bewildering times. There is much reason to be worried. The bad news is that the conventional advertising industry could atrophy and dwindle, both as an employer and as a force in the European communications marketplace. The good news is that it has a unique opportunity to reinvent the profession. But that will never be achieved if attitudes do not change to meet the new reality.

In the glory days of their profession, ad agencies traded comfortably on the proposition that 'The answer is a 30-second spot on network television. Now what's the question?' We can do better than that. New media, new message forms, and new ways of binding them coherently together offer an unprecedented opportunity to use creative flexibility in solving advertisers' problems. But it requires involvement at all levels.

Perhaps advertising should try a different proposition. Something like: 'The answer is "Yes". Now, what was it you wanted to achieve?'

8

TV Leads New Media Impact on Public Relations

David Davis
Senior Vice President International,
Medialink Worldwide Inc

After a long-running, on-and-off love affair with information technology, the public relations community is now moving swiftly into the New Media Age, optimistic that they have their best chance yet to put to rest the tag of being the 'poor relations' in the communications business.

By harnessing their cultural instincts and strategic thinking to established media such as television and radio, as well as all the new electronic wizardry such as the Internet and its corporate offspring the intranet, PR practitioners now have the power to control their own destiny and also, for the first time, to gain:

- access to vast amounts of information at great speed, giving them the tools to develop information quickly, rather than relying on instinct-based PR strategies;
- the capability to implement these strategies and to reach and influence highly localised as well as global mass markets with equal ease and effectiveness. By any criteria, television is the most effective method for this job;
- the expertise to research, evaluate and analyse the impact of their

efforts to underscore the value and worthiness of the return on client investment in public relations.

The power of information

At the heart of most effective public relations campaigns is the need to receive, distribute and discuss information. For example, long gone are the days when reading the newspapers was enough to find out what was going on. The PR practitioner can now check into a global goldmine of on-line information databases covering every conceivable topic from the abacus to the zebra. With such power at their fingertips, they can brief clients, raise issues with the media and effectively develop new business opportunities.

Distributing information is equally easy, given that Britain has more than its fair share of PR service companies, led by Two-Ten Communications, a subsidiary of the Press Association, the national news agency; it has computer-to-computer links with its clients for the transmission of press releases to the media via fax, newswire, messenger or the post.

The method of delivery is selected on the basis of the timeliness and scope of the information. The most recent research suggests that the media prefer to receive releases by fax, newswire or straight into their editorial computers.

The Internet offers serious competition and enterprising companies have already established on-line distribution services for reaching the press. They work on the 'push-and-pull' principle. One type of service, created by IPMG Newsdesk, is based on a sophisticated bulletin board, to which registered journalists can go to download company information and photographs; another directs the story to a predetermined list of e-mail media addresses.

Using the Internet to broadcast live, sound-only press conferences, analyst meetings, presentations to doctors and the like is relatively inexpensive and technically acceptable; and when technology catches up, in the next two to three years, it will be possible to distribute and download broadcast-quality video from the Internet which will challenge the efficiency and cost of satellite distribution.

Reaching global mass markets

Global mass markets were generally out of the reach of public relations until the 1980s, when Medialink harnessed the twin technologies of satellite transmission and video. What emerged was the video news release

(VNR) – the video equivalent of the text press release. Since then, the VNR and its 'big brother', the video press kit, have become standard-practice public relations tools, first in the United States, followed by Britain and the continent of Europe and more recently Asia and the Middle East.

Broadcasters around the world have accepted the legitimacy of the VNR, which is produced by journalists in a news format which they can use to build their national and regional news bulletins. In Britain the state-owned BBC and its independent counterparts, both of whom have their own journalistic criteria for handling VNRs, regularly take in Medialink's daily news feeds and a large proportion of the footage finds its way on to the television screen.

Technology drives the Medialink VNR service around the world:

- Television-news-trained journalists produce the VNR from rushes to the final edited version.
- A high-speed newswire and multifaxes advise broadcasters about the story and when they can record it, free of charge, from the satellite.
- Usage by broadcasters is monitored instantly using electronic tracking technology, so that Medialink can quickly report to clients when, where and how many people watched their VNR on television.

Throughout the process Medialink works with its network of affiliated partners in more than 19 countries around the world to contact local broadcasters and gain greater knowledge and understanding of their specific needs.

Satellite Media Tour (SMT)

SMT is an equally popular technology-driven PR tool. From a single location, spokespeople are 'fed' live to any number of predetermined television stations anywhere in the world for one-to-one interviews, which are either broadcast live or recorded for later use. The SMT is the ideal support for a new-product launch, sales promotion, medical breakthrough and, in a crisis, where speed and consistency of message are vital.

Media research and evaluation

The most recent wave of IT innovation to hit the PR industry created the burgeoning business of media research and evaluation. Previously, media evaluation was a simple issue: count the column inches, add an advertising value and multiply by any factor you chose to underscore that editorial publicity is more valuable than advertising because it gave third-party and independent endorsement to clients' messages.

The computer changed all that. Rather than simplistic number crunch-ing, nowadays firms such as Carma International and Impacon have cre-ated in Britain a new and refreshing professional approach to evaluating the effectiveness of media exposure. Medialink has set up a specialist divi-sion as the most significant new entry to the field of media research and evaluation.

Corporations, trade associations, government departments and political parties employ such firms with research and evaluation skills to identify and track trends, monitor competitive activity, highlight potential dangers and opportunities, and contribute generally to a client's corporate com-munications and marketing strategies.

Media evaluation and research is today one of the fastest-growing and most competitive segments of the public relations business in the UK, with more than 20 companies actively in the market; on a per capita basis, there are more such companies in this country than there are in the US.

How things have changed since the most important task in most PR agencies was to tot up column inches of publicity to justify their existence to clients!

PR telecommuters

The public relations profession is a prime candidate for telecommuting, working from home remotely instead of going into an office every day. Computers, mobile telephones and faxes, plus e-mail and other innova-tions, have enabled some established agencies to restructure their tradi-tional organisations to gain more productivity; new agencies have been set up without the pressure of daunting overheads, and independent consul-tants are now able to conduct their business more efficiently and certainly more cost effectively.

For employees, the obvious benefits are the ability to work free from office distractions, and a better balance between personal and professional commitments.

However, a survey of Fortune 1000 companies completed earlier this year by the information clearing house Telecommute America found the majority of responding executives citing several other benefits, including improved morale, reduced office space costs, lower employee stress, improved employee retention, lower absenteeism and higher productivity.

'No meeting' meetings

It is difficult to imagine, but technology now exists to research, plan and implement a public relations programme virtually without leaving the office or even meeting the client in person!

Interactive video conferencing is on the increase among PR practitioners, adding a new and time-efficient dimension to multisite planning meetings, press conferences, medical meetings, investor seminars and sales presentations.

Multiple teleconference calls are replacing meetings of groups of people from different locations, saving expensive executive time and travel costs. One public relations agency, Burson-Marsteller, has set up its own internal closed-circuit television network linking offices around the world for staff and client meetings.

There are other innovative approaches, such as Shandwick uses working on intranets that will become a 'virtual' library for multinational client programmes and new-business development.

Investor-relations managers are also turning to technology to enhance the effectiveness of their work. According to a 1996 survey in the US by the National Investor Relations Institute, 73 per cent of respondents, compared with 61 per cent the previous year, are using conference calls to elaborate on corporate announcements, such as earnings releases.

For audio access, 53 per cent provide a toll-free telephone number; 32 per cent provide a toll number, and 32 per cent provide an audiotape on request; with respect to an Internet home page, 55 per cent have one now and 29 per cent have one in development.

Internal communications

Management's increasing recognition that greater employee empowerment is good business practice has promoted internal communications to the top of most corporate agendas.

In its wake, the role of human resource managers has grown in importance. New recruits are now being sought with skills and experience beyond traditional people-management, to include information technology and communications. They will be vying with their counterparts in management information systems (MIS) and public relations for control of their company's intranet for on-screen distribution of corporate news and information. Each has a justified contribution to make and shared responsibilities may well be the end result, leading possibly to delays and confusion.

Business communicators in the United States are predictably ahead in

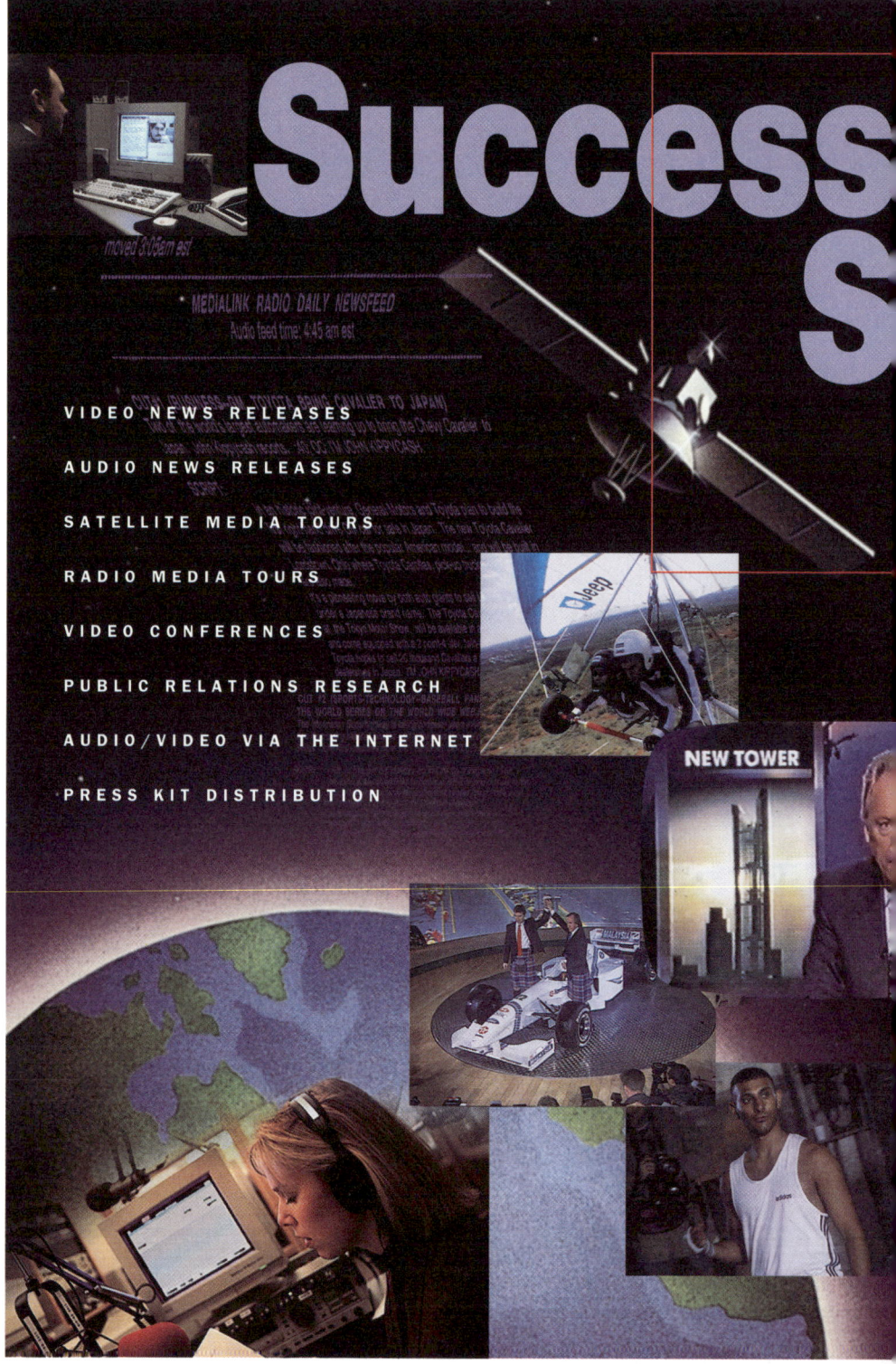

Success
S

moved 3:05am est

MEDIALINK RADIO DAILY NEWSFEED
Audio feed time: 4:45 am est

VIDEO NEWS RELEASES

AUDIO NEWS RELEASES

SATELLITE MEDIA TOURS

RADIO MEDIA TOURS

VIDEO CONFERENCES

PUBLIC RELATIONS RESEARCH

AUDIO/VIDEO VIA THE INTERNET

PRESS KIT DISTRIBUTION

NEW TOWER

the IT stakes. A survey conducted by Cognitive Communications among major US corporations on behalf of Xerox, 'The Document Company', concluded that using technology produced quicker, cheaper and more effective communications.

Professional corporate communicators looking for software more reader-friendly than e-mail and which can prioritise messages, carry graphics and be more interactive have turned to alternatives such as E*News, distributed in Britain by ION International Ltd. Created specifically for internal communications, E*News automatically creates and distributes text into a newsletter, with columns, headlines, resizable type, turning pages and a polling function for employee audits, reader surveys, and market research.

Where next?

At Medialink, we are planning on the basis that technological innovation will continue to drive corporate and marketing communications well into the twenty-first century and beyond. We have introduced desk-top video services, enabling clients to reach investment analysts on Wall Street, and have staked a claim on the Internet by launching video and audio Web releases. We are now awaiting the arrival of technology to distribute broadcast-quality video; at the same time we are studying new systems for electronic monitoring and data transmission.

In the next three years the advance of technology into the world of public relations will create fundamental changes for the industry. By 2000, industry pundits predict that:

- the paper press release will be as extinct as the portable typewriter;
- the majority of companies will have an 'electronic' newsletter;
- company intranets will be the dominant internal communications system, carrying text, graphics, audio, video, feedback and research;
- the video phone will be in vogue;
- the electronic screen, linked to a dual PC/TV or a combined organiser/mobile telephone, will become the PR professionals' best friend.

And by 2005, the profession should brace itself for even more change and opportunities. It can look forward to the talking newspaper which can be downloaded on to an organiser screen; and a television set which allows simultaneous access to TV programmes and the Internet and will also be used for e-mail. We could even see the first virtual PR agency which will operate from the Internet rather than an office!

The electronic wizards will continue to give public relations practitioners tools which will enable them to provide a greater range of services which are more meaningful, have greater impact on a global scale, can be seriously monitored and assessed, and offer greater value for money.

However, practitioners will still have to provide themselves with the most important ingredients: instinct, creativity, wisdom and, above all, enthusiasm, without which none of the new media tools will mean a thing.

9

Trends in Cable

Mike Hayes
Former Marketing Director, The Cable Communications Association

The cable industry now has an annual turnover of £1 billion. We believe that cable continues to be the most exciting telecommunications and entertainment development to affect our everyday lives. The infrastructure which is rapidly networking the country is the most advanced fibre-optic-cable system in the world, bringing a telecommunications revolution to every street and business park.

Statistics released in September 1996 showed that cable has now been built past 7 million homes. This represents a growth of 575,000 in just one quarter and of 2.2 million in a year. Although still very new, cable is proving extremely popular; of the homes passed so far, 31 per cent are now connected to a cable service.

Television

Television is cable's heartland and it is growing fast. There are now 1.5 million cable customers in total with 40,000 new subscribers on average joining every month. Ten per cent of all viewing in UK homes is now of multi-channel television.

Because cable carries satellite plus cable-exclusive and terrestrial channels, choosing cable, rather than just satellite, would appear to be the obvious decision for customers. Cable is already overtaking satellite, with a 7 per cent higher penetration than the national penetration of satellite. In London, over a quarter of homes take multi-channel television, and of these 55 per cent do so via cable rather than satellite. In terms of future growth, cable's growth is already 200 per cent higher and three times as many people in the UK say they intend to install cable rather than satellite.

The greater choice of channels offered by cable does not encourage a nation of 'telly addicts', contrary to popular belief. If applied in another context, this argument assumes that the more choice you give a customer in a restaurant, the more they will eat. While customers enjoy the choice that cable offers, there is no evidence to show that it promotes excessive TV watching.

On the product side, a popular misconception has grown up that cable just offers re-runs, sport and cheap US imports. It is an obvious point but one worth making, that unless the cable industry offered a good product (ie a range of channels that really do appeal to viewers) it would not grow. Cable subscribers choose from a wide variety of high-quality programming from big brand channels such as the Sky Channels, The Disney Channel, MTV, Carlton Food Network, Nickelodeon and UK Living. Judging by the number of new subscribers taking cable every month, the industry is getting its product right and it's getting better all the time.

Among the original programming offered on cable, one of the exclusive and most marketable offerings will continue to be local programming channels, such as Channel One and LIVE TV. Channel One provides local news and features for London, Bristol and Liverpool, and LIVE TV covers Westminster, Birmingham, Liverpool and Edinburgh. Local programming, as opposed to just regional, is regarded by the ITC as a significant selling point for cable in future. The ITC's own research has found that 58 per cent of consumers think that local programming is one of the best features of cable television while 89 per cent said they enjoy seeing people and places they know on local programmes. Incidentally, Channel One is also a good example of pioneering TV production methods. Videojournalists, as they are called, single-handedly write, shoot and edit their own films, dramatically cutting the costs of production without sacrificing quality.

Cable is uniquely placed to offer video on demand and interactive television, which are expected to become more widely available over the next five years. Many of the programmes, involving phone-ins and voting with audiences, currently on terrestrial channels, will be far easier and more sophisticated on cable.

Within the next five years, there will be an explosion of TV choice with the advent of digital formats. As cable's fibre-optic network is the most widely available, cable will be best placed to bring this new technology to consumers and businesses. Digital is a massive opportunity for cable – an opportunity which can only be threatened by BT and the BBC, who currently do not have the infrastructure to offer it.

Telephone

Telephone services are another great success of the cable industry. There are 1.7 million residential cable lines and 60,000 new customers are switching to cable every month. Cable offers major benefits to consumers including significantly cheaper phone bills (up to 25 per cent lower in some areas) and better line quality, due to the capabilities of fibre-optic technology.

Home telecommunications

The Internet market in the UK is the fastest growing in Europe. The number of Internet addresses has increased from 120,000 to 350,000 in one year. More and more people are getting PCs at home to use for their children's education, and their own personal and business use; sales of PCs were higher than any other consumer durable last year. A single cable connection whether originally for phone or TV use can also bring the Internet into the home. The cost is cheaper because the line rental and call charges are cheaper. Indications are that more people will begin to work from home, so this is another significant growth area for cable.

If we regard cable as a technological supermarket, we can say that multi-channel television, telephone service and multi-media access are already on the shelves, but many more new products are on the way. Video on demand, home shopping and home banking, which were all just sci-fi visions of the future, are already a reality and there's much more to come.

10
The Information Superhighway and Multimedia

Dr Roger Till
Chief Executive, Electronic Commerce Association

The Internet and the Web

The Internet is essentially a global network of networks which allows computers located anywhere to communicate directly with each other. It provides connections for sending electronic mail messages, transferring files, linking to other computers and accessing information available in a variety of different forms, such as bulletin boards for people with common interests or electronic product catalogues.

It has been estimated that the Internet has anything from 20–40 million users on over 10,000 linked networks. It all started in 1969 as a way of the US Government Defense Agency sharing information with its research projects. During the 1980s its use spread to academics and only as recently as 1990 did it become accessible to all. Since then it has been hailed as the world's greatest source of information with an explosion of interest in its potential.

The World Wide Web (WWW) was developed by an Englishman at CERN in Switzerland, but it was only in 1994 that the first 'browser' for looking at, and collecting, information from the WWW was launched.

Today, over one million people each day visit the Web site of Netscape which provides the most widely used Web browser.

Currently the fastest-growing area of the Internet, the WWW, allows information to be accessed by subject matter regardless of its location – a real advantage in a network as vast and complex as the Internet. Users move automatically from one database (or site) of interest to another, using 'hyperlinks'. Increasing levels of complexity enable interactive, multi-media facilities to be developed. Many organisations are busy developing their own Web sites to sell products or to advertise their wares.

The Internet, along with its Web sites, resembles a huge, rapidly growing electronic library with little formal structure and no catalogue. As a result, Web browsers (software for accessing and displaying Web-site information) have grown quickly in importance. 'Search engines' (an electronic content/catalogue searcher) have also been developed to allow users to trawl this huge library to locate the required information.

What of intranets?

A more recent hot topic has been the rise of the intranet. An intranet is the use of low-cost Internet technologies to create internal information networks. More broadly, it spans an organisation's entire information network, including the use of Internet technologies as well as PC-to-host connectivity, mobile communications, client–server networks and integration of data warehouses, for example.

Many large organisations, such as GE and AT&T, are now using Internet technology internally, using an intranet to make information available to staff and to share information between project team members who may be located anywhere in the world. Federal Express has now taken their internal system a stage further; originally developed to allow them to keep track of their packages in transit, the system has now been opened up to their customers. Using the ID number of your package, you can sign on to the Internet and find out its status. You can also order your next pickup – and over 50 per cent of customers now do that!

Starting out

So what does it cost an organisation to start using the Internet? Firstly, you need a PC and a modem. Then you will need to pay a service provider to obtain access to the Internet. To begin with you are likely to sign up for e-mail and to be able to 'surf' – that just means using a browser to access WWW sites.

Your shopping bill, based on what the Electronic Commerce Association spent to set up its own Internet access, will be:

PC (high performance)	£1,000–1,200
Needs plenty of memory (at least 16 mb RAM) and hard-disk space (at least 200 mb) to handle systems	
Modem (28.8 kbps)	£100–150
Telephone charges – local calls signing on to a service provider	£25–50 per month
Service provider's usage/access charge	£10–15 per month

After getting to know the Internet a little better, you may well wish to set up a Web site for your organisation. Again, this is not too expensive, especially if you get an expert to develop and maintain it for you. The key to any Web site is to make it attractive, easy to access, simple to download information (keep the graphics basic!) and make sure the information is kept up to date. You will probably want to register your company name as your Web site address to make it clear and easy for people to find you. The cost:

Registering your domain	£100
Developing a Web site	£3–4,000
Monthly site maintenance	£500

At a later stage you may consider taking the work on your Web site in house – a much more expensive process, as with any full-scale system development.

Doing business on the Internet

Organisations are beginning to make creative use of the Internet for business in a fascinating variety of ways, as the following examples illustrate. The 1996 'BT Awards for Innovation in Electronic Commerce' featured for the first time a new 'Business on the Internet' category, sponsored by the ECA. Each of the three finalists was making innovative use of the Internet in widely differing industries.

National Express (www.nationalexpress.co.uk)

Developed to enable passengers to check bus routes and timetables and then book and pay for tickets, the payment procedure is secure, linking directly to the credit-card companies so that National Express does not see or keep any of that information. The Web site offers a new way of marketing to its customers (many of whom are students), and relieves pressure on its telephone booking services.

Shoppers universe (www.shoppersuniverse.com)

Great Universal Stores (GUS) is extending their established mail-order business opportunities by addressing new market sectors through their on-line shopping mall. They are also looking at replacing the traditional paper catalogue with electronic methods. Hi-tech fashion label trainers are the bestsellers!

AMP of Great Britain (www.connect.amp.com)

AMP, which specialises in electronic connectors and cables of all sorts, have used the Web to set up a revolutionary electronic catalogue. Their customers can sign on to this catalogue and obtain technical information, pictures and advice about their range of over 10,000 components. Customers now have access to an easy-to-use, up-to-date catalogue, replacing many paper-based versions.

Other retail Web sites

Retailers have been among the first to explore the potential of this new medium. Like many of the chains, Sainsbury's (www.j-sainsbury.co.uk) have a Web site from which they sell only flowers, wine and chocolates. The majority of people visit the site to download their excellent recipes!

More unusual is a Scottish contact lens manufacturer Scotlens (www.route-one.co.uk/route-one/scotlens) which makes technical information and calculation procedures available to its customers, the opticians, via a very useful Web site.

A beautifully presented site is Fergusons Irish Linen (www.franklins. co.uk), the only makers in the world of double damask linen. Worldwide orders have leapt since they set up this marketing and ordering site.

Many retail outlets opt to join one of the virtual shopping malls. Barclay Square (www.itl.net/barclaysquare) has many household names on it, although sales are still low. Argos, for example, quoted 20 sales in 10 months (including a Wallace and Grommet alarm clock!), probably largely because the profile of Argos customers does not match the typical Internet user's profile.

On the other hand, Blackwell's bookshop, with a more specialist clientele and an existing mail-order infrastructure in place, claims to have made significant (over £350,000) sales worldwide in the first few months.

The Media Village

Although perhaps not amongst the leaders, the media/advertising industry is beginning to make significant use of the Internet. Visiting Media Village, their comprehensive UK site (www.mediavillage.mediatel.co.uk)
shows a wealth of information.

AGB Television Systems has replaced paper subscription-based services
with a fully interactive service. The British Market Research Bureau shows
its products and services, including top-line sample data. Euroquest gives
details about the group and provides information about its research, country by country. The Institute of Practitioners in Advertising includes a
searchable, central list of all IPA-member agencies. Mediatel offers a subscriber database of media information and gives details of its business
information services. The National Advertisers' Benevolent Fund provides
details about the charity and its events. The National Readership Survey
provides top-line information on line, together with subscription details.
The Periodical Publishers Association provides a list of all magazines and
has 'hot links' to some sites. For example, look at the *Economist* and its free
weekly news summary services.

As well as some other consultancies, the Media Village also has Media
Pub for on-line discussion, a Village Post Office (a sort of yellow pages for
the media industry), a Careers and Training Centre and General Store for
purchasing any publications or research reports.

Conclusion

As the above examples illustrate, creative uses of the Internet are growing
across many sectors. Growing numbers of organisations are using the
Internet for informal e-mail communications and then moving on to
setting up Web sites. Many of these are focusing on PR and marketing
activities. Just by being there and being interesting, the site raises the profile of the organisation concerned, although it must be said that badly
designed, difficult-to-use and out-of-date sites do equal damage to their
owners!

New businesses are developing, such as the book and CD shops which
have no physical premises. The use of the Internet for selling, both to
organisations and the individual, is growing fast. This is especially true
now that the concerns about security for financial transactions are being
addressed. By using the standards that have now been defined, it is a safe
place to buy and sell.

This exciting new communications medium is already starting to change
the way we conduct both our business and leisure activities. In the near

future, the Internet and WWW may well revolutionise whole industries. Its impact cannot be denied and its growth is inexorable – communicators cannot afford to ignore it.

11

How to Make (or Lose) a Fortune On-line

Alfred Glossbrenner*

Here's the secret to using the electronic universe to make a fortune. There's actually no mystery to it. The way you succeed on-line is the same as in any kind of business: You put the customer first! That's called 'taking the you-approach', and it applies whether you make pizza, planes, or prams. The companies that thrive are the ones that are constantly asking themselves, 'What do my customers need today, and what will they need tomorrow?'

For such companies, the best use of technology is to help answer those customer-related questions and to help deliver what the customer wants – faster, cheaper, and with a higher quality than ever before. That's the you-approach.

Too many me's and me-too's

The problem in the on-line world is that so many firms have opted for the. 'me-approach'. They view technology in general, and the Internet in par-ticular, solely as a way to cut their costs and boost their profits.

There's nothing wrong with either of those goals, of course. It's just that when cost-cutting and profit-boosting are your major aims, you tend to see and apply technology differently than if you are driven by anticipating and satisfying customer needs. A 'me-approach' company looks at the Internet

*Alfred Glossbrenner is the author of *Making More Money on the Internet* (McGraw-Hill).

and says, 'Terrific! I can get rid of half of my sales force!' A 'you-approach' company says, 'Great! The Internet can help me and my employees serve our customers even better, to say nothing of reaching out to gain new customers.'

The technology is the same for everyone. But the way you apply it – and the results you obtain – depend on your point of view. Keep it in mind as you explore the Internet and the World Wide Web. As you visit an on-line location ask yourself whether the site has been prepared by a 'me-approach' company or a 'you-approach' company. Does the site appear to exist primarily to make things easier or cheaper for the company? Or do you sense that whoever set things up was really trying to be of help to you, the prospective customer?

In our experience, the biggest mistake of all is to assume that large numbers of people are interested in regularly shopping on-line. Yet that is the siren song sung by promoters of on-line (yes, it has become a noun) and the Internet. It goes something like this:

> 'All you have to do is put your product catalogue and order form on the World Wide Web and just sit back and wait for the money to roll in. Why pay to write, design, print, and mail a catalogue? Why pay for advertising or marketing? Get yourself a Web site and all you'll have to do is sign on a few times a day to pick up the orders.'

This is complete and utter nonsense. But it's a classic 'me-approach' notion, to wit: 'I can cut my costs and boost my profits enormously by getting a World Wide Web home page.' And, of course, the company you'll hire to create your home page will encourage you every penny of the way. These days, you no longer have to spend tens of thousands setting up a Web page, although some companies do. Now you can get by for a thousand pounds, or even several hundred pounds.

And we certainly aren't saying that people won't or don't shop on-line. We're just saying that you're setting yourself up for a big disappointment if you believe that all it takes to produce a pot of gold is to establish yourself on the Internet. At the very least, you've got to work at giving your customers a good reason to visit your on-line location.

Where does the Net fit in one's daily life?

You can prove this to yourself by asking a simple question: Where does going on-line to 'surf the Net' or 'browse the Web' fit in my typical customer's day?

After all, going on-line is anything but quick and convenient. You must turn on the computer and wait for the operating system software (Windows, DOS, Macintosh, or whatever) to load, click on an icon, wait for the browser (Netscape, Explorer, etc) to load, wait for the modem to dial, and then wait some more for the software to log onto a system. And then, if it's a good day, pray the system won't be so overloaded that it runs at the pace of treacle in January. It can often seem like the wait of the world is on your shoulders.

So when do your customers make time to do this? Certainly, kids and students have plenty of time to log on and surf. But most don't have credit cards or money to spend. Your customers probably spend their days at work, where they may or may not have access to the Internet. (Many managers see the Internet as an even greater threat to productivity than the Solitaire game Microsoft included with Windows 3.1, so they block employee access.)

How many users?

A published figure of 11.4 million consumer-on-line-service subscribers in the USA in 1995 is really quite soft since it was derived by simply adding up the subscription numbers reported by the leading consumer-on-line systems. That seems like a logical approach, but what most people don't know is that in the on-line world, there are no standards for calculating and reporting subscription. For example, at GEnie, the on-line service started by General Electric, the policy for many years was to count everyone who had ever subscribed to the service. Those who had cancelled their accounts were simply considered 'inactive subscribers'. Prodigy, by contrast, calculates subscribership the way a magazine estimates its readership. Just as the publishers of *Time* or *Newsweek* assume that more than one person in a household reads each issue, Prodigy assumes that each account is used by more than one family member. Thus, when Prodigy claims, say, two million subscribers, that does not mean that there are two million people paying the monthly fee. According to some analysts, the actual number of accounts may be closer to half the number of subscribers that Prodigy reports. CompuServe's and America Online's numbers are pretty solid, since they count subscriptions and apply no 'multiplier formula'. But even the numbers CompuServe and AOL report cannot be accepted without adjustment when calculating the total number of subscribers in the on-line industry. That's because an unknown number of people subscribe to more than one system and are thus counted twice or more.

And what about the Internet?

The soft-number problem is not limited to the world of consumer on-line services. It also applies to the Internet overall. You've probably heard estimates that there are as many as 30, even 40 million Internet users. Well, listen to Bob Metcalfe the inventor of Ethernet, founder of 3Com Corporation, and columnist for *InfoWorld*. In the 22 August, 1994, issue of *InfoWorld*, Metcalfe reacted to a report by Anthony-Michael Rutkowski, executive director of the Internet Society, that stated that there were between 20 and 30 million Internet users: a weak link in Rutkowski's chain of estimates is the assumption that there are on average 10 users per Internet host computer. This is a holdover from when the Internet was made up mostly of VAX UNIX hosts, each of which had many users.

Considering that most computers today are personal, the average number of users is closer to one than ten, even accounting for the few really big ones. So, the Internet might have as few as 3.2 million users!

The 'real' number

Recently, more rigorous efforts have been focused on estimating the actual number of Internet users. In October, 1995, for example, O'Reilly & Associates, a publisher of Internet-related books, and Trish Marketing Systems, announced the results of their survey of on-line and Internet users. According to the study, some 5.8 million adults in the US have direct Internet access and use the Net on a regular basis at their work, at home, or at school. So basically, at the beginning of 1996, there were about 6 million adults in the US with Internet access. For more information, visit the O'Reilly Web site at http://www.ora.com/survey/

Frankly, that feels about right to me. The actual number at the start of 1996 could have been a few million more, but it is simply impossible to believe that it was tens of millions more. The true number of Internet users isn't really the point, however. My point is the huge disparity between 30 million Internet users and 6 million. No one is going to admit it, but we all know that some companies swallowed the 30-million figure hook, line, and sinker, and invested in their Internet sites accordingly. So, please, please, be sceptical of any statistics or figures you read about this field. Invest your time in getting to know what's what on the Net and on the Web before you invest your money.

Think about this: television, radio, newspapers, and magazines are all a form of communication, and all such media carry advertising and marketing information. Indeed they are all supported by advertising and marketing funds. But each is a distinctly different medium. So a TV ad obviously won't work on radio, and a newspaper ad won't fly in a magazine.

The Internet is yet another medium. So why would anybody assume that what works on TV, radio, or in print would also work on the Net? Yet you will find many a Web page that is clearly nothing more than a magazine print ad, with huge graphics files that take forever to transmit and offer nothing of value other than a pretty picture, and very few words explaining the benefits of the product.

The worst mistake you can make is to assume that the Internet and the World Wide Web are like every other communications medium. The second-worst mistake is to assume that lots of people will 'point, click, and purchase' your product on-line just because you are on-line.

You can indeed make money on the Internet, regardless of the product or service you have to sell. But you must go about it the right way.

12

The Strategic Use of Web Sites

Jeremy Keohane
Client Director, UXL Ltd

The business world is always looking for opportunities to develop new markets and exploit emerging technologies to their maximum effect. The drive to introduce extra efficiency in order to streamline operations and increase profit margins is never ending.

With more and more companies embracing the Internet as a valuable tool to achieve these goals, we examine the benefits of stepping out onto the Information Superhighway and look at the key reasons organisations that have not yet caught up with this revolution should consider doing so now.

One of the first industries to exploit fully the potential of the Internet as a marketplace for generating increased revenue was the information-provision sector, particularly those businesses specialising in the supply of up-to-the-minute financial data and market reports. Up until very recently, in order to monitor the current values of stocks and shares as they changed, traders needed expensive, specialist hardware and software that severely limited those who could afford to have the service installed. Now with the advent of the Internet, it is possible for anyone with a budget PC and modem to obtain the same information at the touch of a button. This has helped to open up the once mysterious world of share dealing to a much wider audience of potential private investors.

Putting corporations on the Superhighway

An excellent illustration of this principle is the Electronic Share Information (ESI) Web site <http://www.esi.co.uk>. Developed by an in-house team in conjunction with expert designers from UXL, this site recently won the grand prize in the BT & *Sunday Times* Superhighway Awards.

Customers pay a monthly subscription fee that allows them access to the full facilities available through the site. Indeed not only are there numerous pages of financial data available, containing up-to-the-minute information, but shares can also be bought and sold and performances automatically tracked over a period of time.

In fact it is fast becoming apparent that information is the ideal product to supply on-line as it can be delivered direct to the customer, using Internet technology, the moment it is compiled by the supplier. It may, however, be less obvious how the advantages of the Internet can be applied to more traditional industries dealing in more tangible products.

In this case, there are a number of factors which often influence the decision whether to take the step on-line and develop a corporate Web site. The first, and to many, fundamental issue is whether or not the site can directly generate revenue, usually through direct sales of the company's existing product range. This usually involves ordering over the net from a Web site displaying a catalogue of products, at which point the order is treated in the traditional manner and the required items shipped as soon as clearance of any payment is made. Technology has now advanced to the point at which this procedure can be extended to include the automatic and instant authorisation of credit card numbers, allowing money to be transferred from the customer's account to the supplier's account within seconds of the purchase button being pressed on the customer's screen.

There are several immediate advantages to this model. Take, for example, a normal high-street music store selling cassettes and CDs. The shop only need keep a minimal stock level as modern distribution channels mean the supplier can often obtain items to be purchased as and when the order is placed and still ship them within a couple of days. There are also no shop floor to maintain and no expensive shop fittings. But perhaps most impressive of all is the fact that because a Web site has no geographic location, one branch of the shop can serve the entire global marketplace whereas to do this with traditional outlets would require huge investment in a chain of shops with one in every town and city on earth.

Southern Studios Ltd, the parent company for a large number of UK and international record labels was forward-thinking enough to take the bold step of investing in a large website development project almost three years ago. Perhaps the competitive nature of the music industry, with its fast-changing trends and fashions explains why it has been almost univer-

Who are UXL?

UXL are a New Media company with a difference

Your Marketing or Corporate message
+
UXL's New Media ability
=
SUCCESS

Our Clients include

ICV/Datastream, (Primark Group)	Computacenter	Deloitte and Touche Consulting
ECA International	The Dti	Parity Solutions Ltd
Mobile Communications International	Business Link	OFGAS

What do our clients say?

'...delivered on time and to budget'

'...a young exciting and innovative New Media company'

'...our business has been totally transformed'

'...initially sceptical we are now Internet converts, brilliant!'

Call Richard Sutherland
Tel: 0171 593 3319 email: rs@uxl.co.uk

CBI European Business Handbook

A COMPREHENSIVE REFERENCE HANDBOOK ON BEST BUSINESS PRACTICE IN EUROPE

The economic and social development of the EU, and its possible expansion to the east and south of the continent, all have important implications for European business. This essential reference book aims to keep the business community up to speed.

The CBI European Business Handbook is the definitive reference guide for all those involved, or planning to be involved in European business. The handbook provides comprehensive information on the political background as it is expected to evolve in 1997, as well as practical advice and guidance on best business practice for trading with all 15 members of the EU and the 15 nations aspiring to membership.

- Fully updated for 1997, compiled by international experts and members of the CBI and CBI equivalent organisations across Europe
- Practical advice on how to trade in all European markets
- An up-to-date survey of local economies and business conditions in the countries of the European Union and Eastern Europe
- Investment and trading opportunities in the EU and East European countries
- Sources of further information

£35.00 • Paperback • 0 7494 2088 X 516 pages • Order ref: KT 088

Leadership

Philip Sadler

Philip Sadler examines the ever popular topic of leadership in this highly readable guide. He equips the reader with tools for understanding why leadership is important in business and for recognising different styles - including their own.

Leadership looks at:

- Well-known role models - Roddick, Thatcher, Harvey-Jones and recognises what lessons can be learned
- How to select and develop future leaders
- Cultural differences in styles

Philip Sadler was principal of Ashridge Management College from 1969 - 1990. He is also the author of Designing Organisations and Managing Change, both published by Kogan Page.

£13.99 Paperback ISBN 0 7494 2124 X 192 pages March 1997

More information on these and other titles can be found in Kogan Page's comprehensive *Catalogue*.

To request a copy please phone or fax the marketing department on:

Tel. 0171 278 0433 Fax. 0171 837 6348.

Kogan Page's books **can be bought from good booksellers or direct from Kogan Page's customer services department on 0171 278 0433, quoting the reference number for the title and your credit card details.**

Payment can also be made by pro-forma, or by cheque made out to Kogan Page Ltd and sent to:

Kogan Page, 120 Pentonville Road, London N1 9JN, England

KOGAN PAGE

sally adopted as an important marketing tool by nearly all major record companies.

John Loder, managing director of Southern, identified very early on that direct sales of CDs to customers via the Internet would dramatically reduce the costs currently associated with distributing through the traditional high-street system. With the extra savings and increased revenue generated by cutting out the middle man, the company could supply its products to the consumer at a reduced price whilst actually increasing the margin of profit per unit. Programmers now working at UXL were commissioned to develop the first ever major Web-based retail system in the UK and now the on-line division of Southern's mail-order business <http://www.southern.com/southern/shop/> is outperforming even the most ambitious of forecasts made when it was initially devised.

Loder comments:

> 'The great thing about our on-line shop is that we get really big orders. People don't just buy a single CD like they might in a branch of HMV, but many are spending upwards of £100 on a single order! … When we initially decided to build the shop we considered it a gamble because the market was unknown, but it's certainly paid off and the best thing is, it's cost us virtually nothing to run since the day it was created.'

Advantage of cost and efficiency

Revenue generation is not the only option however. There also exist scenarios in which companies can exploit the emerging opportunities in advanced communications to increase efficiency or cut costs. Take, for example, a business which publishes a large volume of literature and reference material which is key to supporting its primary product range. The costs involved in printing and distributing this paper-based information can quickly mount up, especially if regular updates are required. If this valuable resource was supplied electronically using a Web site, however, not only are there no printing and distribution costs, but customers, or indeed remotely located employees, can receive their new documents the moment they are published (and they can always print them out themselves if they require hard copy).

Enhancing the company profile

Finally, investing in a Web site can significantly raise a company's profile not only in terms of advertising and marketing the organisation but also informing customers of important information related to the company and its services. For example, calls to certain customer helplines can fall dramatically in the case of companies that choose to publish answers to common queries electronically, allowing the customer to browse and find answers to their questions at their own leisure instead of being held in long queues listening to annoying hold tunes.

Still need convincing? According to management consultants Datamonitor, by the year 2000 it is predicted that 10 million households in the UK will have access to on-line services. Remember, that's households, not individuals! So, are these predictions justified? Well, with the exponential growth of the Internet in the past year, there is no reason to doubt them. So, now the question to ask yourself is no longer 'Can you afford to invest in the Internet?', but rather, 'Can you afford not to?'

Part 3
Managing Communications

13

Managing Communications

Gloria Walker, ABC, MIPR
*President, UK Chapter, International
Association of Business Communicators
(IABC)*

Communications excellence describes the ideal state in which knowledge-able communicators assist in the overall strategic management of organisations, seeking symmetrical relations through management of communication with key publics on whom organisational survival and growth depends.

The above statement is taken from *Manager's Guide to Excellence in Public Relations and Communication Management,** a 1995 book which reports the findings of a $400,000, three-nation study of public relations and communication management sponsored by the International Association of Business Communicators (IABC) Research Foundation. The study sought answers to two questions:

- What are the characteristics of an excellent communication department?
- How do excellent communication management and public relations make an organisation more effective, and how much is that contribution worth economically?

*Both of the studies mentioned in this article are available from the UK chapter of IABC. Please visit our website: http://www.iabc.com/chapters/euroafrica/uklondon/

The book cited details the answers to these questions and demonstrates that there is a greater return on investment for those organisations which demonstrate communication excellence. But the most important finding from the study is the documentation of three related factors or spheres which represent the essence of excellence in communication. The first or central sphere is the knowledge base of the communication department.

The second or middle sphere represents a set of shared expectations about communication between top communicators and senior managers in the organisation. These shared expectations create linkages between the communication department and those powerful people who run organisations and make strategic decisions. One linkage is the demand for communication excellence from senior management; the second is the delivery of such excellence from the communication department.

The third or outer sphere is the organisational culture in which the core knowledge and shared expectations exist. Generally, participative cultures based on teamwork and broad-based decision making tend to nurture communication excellence.

Taking the *Excellence Study* as a guide, in 1995 the UK chapter of IABC funded a study of more than 200 directors and managers of the communication function. As an organisation concerned with promoting the role of business communications, IABC/UK wanted to learn what business communicators themselves are actually doing in their roles – core knowledge – and what the business communication function is trying to achieve within organisations – the shared expectations or goals. The main findings are detailed in this chapter.

Core knowledge or roles

It is clear that the role of the communicator is growing and becoming ever more complex. Many new roles are having to be taken on. However, the function of business communication is not growing at the same pace in perceived value within organisations.

- Corporate communication includes a broad range of communication activities and planning, much of which affects the way business is conducted. As yet, however, integration of the various communication functions has not been a major concern of practitioners.
- In particular, the relationship between internal and external communication aims and tasks is not seen as that important. Many activities are shared or jointly conducted with other functions, which may prevent the development of clear communication objectives within the organisation.

- There is still too much emphasis on the unrealistic notion that communication equals information. Some managers are recognising that communication is what provides people with a comfortable context for their work. This requires a particular approach to managing communication activities and systems.
- Technology applications are being hailed as providers of solutions to the problems of 'communication breakdown' and 'lack of communication'. This contrasts with the fact that any employee ever surveyed prefers to receive information face to face from his or her supervisor.

Shared expectation or goals

All too often communication seems to be carried out 'on the hoof' rather than as a properly planned and managed process within organisations. There is support from the top, but this often proves to be no more than lip service since senior managers do not recognise the added value which good communication brings to the organisation. This is a reflection of expectations which are not shared between the communicator and senior management; many times the expectations are in conflict.

- Almost half the organisations represented in the survey do not have a written strategic-communication policy.
- Effective communication management is not yet sufficiently recognised as key to organisational performance. Commitment to pay proper attention to planning and organising appropriate aims and mechanisms will come from the belief that communication is the mode of organisation and management, not the means. Managers will be better able to manage if they adopt this attitude.
- Senior managers within organisations lack a depth of understanding of the nature, scope and purpose of communication. This may be a significant obstacle to achieving co-operative relationships and creative thinking for business performance enhancement.
- Because the nature and contribution of communication is not always recognised – 'communication' is taken too much for granted – there is a prevailing lack of the required investment perspective. Communication is still seen as a 'soft' issue which is considerably less important than more tangible investments, such as telecommunications systems and other capital expenditures.

Managing change

There was overwhelming evidence of major changes in the communication function. A total of 95 per cent responded that their CEO's/board's expectations of the communication function have changed in the past three years, with a majority indicating greater resources and growth of the function.

Other changes have been the establishment or restructuring of an in-house team and an increased emphasis, recognition and acceptance of the need for and focus on managed communication activity, particularly for internal communication. Where this is in evidence, more senior and better trained people have been recruited to take on the responsibilities – improving the core knowledge within the department. So while teams may be smaller, they are producing better work. More active communication and greater use of outside specialists have also increased due to greater awareness of the need to communicate.

Communication channels have been reviewed due to a perceived need to be more discriminating in targeting information. Communication activities are becoming more focused on particular stakeholder groups, often in response to pressure from external audiences such as the media and regulators.

Forces which are driving changes in communications include:

- the desire for greater efficiency and cost reduction through speed and simplicity;
- changes in management needs;
- desire for greater focus and control – especially during growth of the organisation;
- a need for greater openness in the organisation;
- a need for greater flexibility and responsiveness;
- a need for corporate communication to be seen as central to the organisation;
- a need to shift the focus for communication effectiveness to managers.

Contributing to organisational performance

Respondents identified several ways in which communication contributes to an organisation's performance: perception/reputation/image/value management, information for job performance, clearer business aims for people, improves morale/affects attitudes/releases talents/commitment, and aids implementation of strategy.

Communication management may be incorporated in strategic management of the organisation in a number of ways:

- A strategic communication plan is incorporated with all other functional plans into the corporate plan as an integral part of the management and business-planning process;
- Communication objectives are integral to all strategic plans and are included in the corporate objectives, therefore establishing communication as a priority function of the organisation;
- The corporate communication director is part of the strategic management team or board;
- There is a communication slot on the management/board agenda;
- Communication planning is discussed in all management forums.

Achieving excellence

Excellence is not an 'either/or' choice between traditional skills and new expertise. Excellence is a matter of 'both together', the organic integration of the old and new. No programme is purely one-way or two-way. No communicator plays the manager or technician role exclusively. In the textured, multilayered complexity of real-world practices, one-way and two-way models of communication work in tandem. Most communicators play both manager and technician roles to varying degrees each day. In excellent communication programmes, strategic planners work side by side with highly skilled specialists.

To quote from the IABC *Excellence Study*:

'Communication excellence will not be achieved by simply improving how you do things right. Excellent programmes integrate "doing things right" with "doing the right things".'

By having communications professionals with the requisite management and technical skills in the department; by communicators and senior managers working together to determine their shared expectations; by establishing or maintaining an organisational culture supportive of communication, every organisation can achieve excellence, which simply means doing the right things right.

14
Knowledge Management

Iain McLeod
Managing Director, Easy i Ltd

Knowledge? I know what that is! Don't I?

Data, facts, intelligence, information, the low-down – it is all crucial to business and it's gathering momentum all the time. Are you using it? In this ever-changing, fast-moving world, information is all around us and yet quite often it is all too inaccessible. We all know how crucial information is, yet how many organisations really put it to work and proactively develop knowledge and understanding within their business? How many of us can truly benefit from the results of other people's knowledge at work? Sadly, not many.

So, if the old adage is true that 'knowledge itself is power', how can you ensure that all the knowledge contained within your organisation is making you, your people and your business powerful? Have you harnessed the power of your information? Do the right people know the right things? Have you realised the true value of information?

A new piece of consultancy jargon has begun to be used in recent times to describe the proactive management of information within business. Behind the jargon lies a common-sense attitude to ensuring that a key business asset is not wasted.

So, what is knowledge management?

Where should you start? Perhaps a good point is one step back from the beginning – what is knowledge management? Taking a dictionary definition, knowledge management is the process of administering information within an organisation.

Managing the information and knowledge within your company and then communicating the information internally is an important issue. It is imperative to make the most of the information within your company by making sure that it is available to the right people and ensuring that people know where to go for information.

Often the most undervalued asset of any company is the information and knowledge stored within the company. Very few companies realise the true value of information until something goes wrong, and going wrong can be as everyday as somebody leaving – perhaps taking with them intimate knowledge of specific systems, procedures or customers that have not fully been captured within the organisation's 'knowledge base'.

Every business which is set to enjoy continued success must learn as it goes and have in place an integrated knowledge system, with both an architecture and distribution system to ensure that any independent islands of knowledge are brought together. Information in this sense can be anything from staff-development schemes and new legislation to new advertising campaigns and customer-care procedures.

A company's development plans need to take into account changes in markets, communication systems and the way in which their business is conducted. All that in place, it is the people within the organisation who determine its success. Their ability to access and use information and their knowledge within the organisation are important criteria in ensuring productivity and success. Communication, information and knowledge systems must not be ignored or undervalued. Winning companies take action proactively to protect, enhance, build and utilise this asset.

The company which can effectively manage internal communications, efficiently organise and distribute knowledge and information, as well as maximise staff productivity, will have an advantage over its competitors. If all of this can be combined with simplicity, ease of use and cost savings, the advantages are significant.

Successful knowledge management will have a positive effect on the bottom line of your company. A company without an integrated knowledge-management system is ignorant. In time, it will fail. Can you afford to ignore ignorance?

Everyone on the team knows, does everyone in the company know?

Shared information within a company is a very important resource. The combined knowledge of every person within a company – from specific product configuration details through to a list of client contacts (and even what football team they support!) – is fundamental to how that company operates.

Information flows should be designed around the needs of those receiving it. What do people need in order to do their job well? People have to understand enough about the company to be a productive participant and to be motivated and interested in the organisation of which they are a member.

Many more businesses are now recognising that knowledge rather than data is key to competitiveness. With this recognition comes an awareness that a traditional approach to managing structured data is not enough to build a culture where information of many different types is shared. This replaces the old misplaced assumption that corporate information was too valuable to be distributed internally within an organisation.

Making such information available to all areas within a company is an important change in corporate culture. This type of open corporate culture has many advantages. Having taken that step, the biggest issue is having the vision to share information and knowledge with the outside world – ie key customers, important suppliers, key distributors etc.

In today's highly technological commercial world, an integrated knowledge-management and distribution system within an organisation can still have selective access protection where necessary. Simple access control mechanisms and firewalls with controlled access to externals are an easy and effective solution.

How can we solve the information issue?

There are many traditional means of distributing and communicating information internally. Workshops, team meetings, memos, newsletters, bulletin boards – they are all tried and tested, but do they still have a place in today's commercial world and how effective are they?

Regular meetings and workshops might be a highly effective means of communicating a message to a large number of people, but what is the real cost in terms of productivity – especially if they need to be run on a regular basis? Memos, newsletters and bulletin boards – old fashioned, steeped in hierarchy, effective? It depends: they probably all have a place, but they are unlikely to be the most efficient way of ensuring that information is communicated effectively – and they don't allow the user/recipient to get involved, to ask or to probe.

Embracing new technology is the key – making the most of the exciting media given to us by the advent of time and cutting-edge technology. But there is a catch!

To implement an integrated knowledge-management system success-fully, using the plethora of new technologies available, presents its own challenge. Organisations can choose from video, CD-ROM, interactive multimedia, Internet/intranet, groupware, document management – the list of new solutions goes on and on.

Many organisations already have different information databases, direc-tories and programmes in different media and are beginning to realise the benefits of integrating them into a company-wide knowledge programme.

Packaging and linking all of the relevant information in the right way are vital, as are structuring and designing an overall corporate information tool which will provide maximum flexibility to handle all relevant corpo-rate information. The best tool is the one which works with existing IT and organisational or corporate infrastructures, and will vary from organisa-tion to organisation.

The most common objective for a newly integrated information system is to pull together most, if not all, of the data, information and knowledge within a company so that they can be shared and used by others. For exam-ple, this involves providing employees with information that is otherwise unavailable or difficult to access, improving understanding of the organi-sation's activities, goals and values.

Everyday practical information which is already available also needs to be managed and integrated – from internal telephone directories through to staff handbooks. Although often overlooked and considered somewhat mundane, ensuring that such information is instantly accessible and searchable from any department, office or branch, confers enormous busi-ness benefit.

Even with simple integration of corporate information, there are imme-diate benefits in specific areas:

- *For staff induction* – enabling all new starters (and existing staff where necessary) to have a complete and consistent understanding of the company.
- *In business presentations* – enhancing sales, marketing and general busi-ness presentations through effective knowledge distribution.

Managing the knowledge path forward

Effective and efficient knowledge-management systems are crucial to the future success of British commerce and industry. Knowledge affects all companies and businesses, regardless of their size or structure. Every company must employ both formal and informal internal communications for the successful adoption of a knowledge culture.

As with all key issues, it is important that knowledge management becomes an issue for the board, not just any department who will take responsibility for it.

In order for companies to continue to flourish, the issue of knowledge management must be aired and acted on. Common sense dictates that there is no cryptic science behind the words knowledge management – it is just a plain, simple, practical approach to business communications. What is also very clear, however, is that it really is the only way ahead for organisations to achieve the kind of results they want, using the most appropriate media for them.

Data, facts, intelligence, information, the low-down – it is all information and it is gathering momentum all the time. It is too important to ignore any longer.

Information Society Initiative: Programme for Business

The ISI Programme for Business (ISI PfB) is a partnership between industry and government to help the UK thrive in the information-based economy. Its aim is to help UK businesses, particularly small and medium-sized enterprises (SMEs), make the most of the opportunities offered by information and communication technologies and thus help the UK become a world-leading information society.

There are opportunities for business to develop new products and services and to adapt to new ways of manufacturing and marketing; for people to structure more flexible working environments, eg teleworking; for consumers to improve their quality of life with new electronic products and services. And there are opportunities to strengthen education and healthcare. UK industries are well placed to take advantage of the information society – we have significant strengths which put us ahead of most other European countries – but considerably more needs to be done to build on our strengths and sustain competitiveness in a tough global marketplace.

The ISI PfB is a substantial DTI programme comprising many different strands and individual projects, from grants available to companies and individuals with imaginative or ambitious projects to support for exporters; and from help for the uninitiated in coming to terms with new technologies to the promotion of pan-European programmes that will take these technologies even further. DTI is making available up to £35 million in extra funding for the ISI PfB over the next four years – and looking for a similar level of industry investment.

The ISI PfB is targeted at SMEs in the manufacturing, service and creative sectors and is based on a framework of support and awareness programmes. It will also provide practical help for business through a network of 50 local support centres giving businesses access to local advice and valuable opportunities for hands-on experience. It provides a coherent and comprehensive package of programmes and activities based on close partnership between government and industry and aims to provide a national framework for progress in this key area for the economy.

Doing Business in the Information Society booklet

When it comes to technology, jargon is a major problem for small firms. Many businesses are missing out on the benefits that technology can bring simply because they cannot get past the technobabble.

To tackle this problem, the ISI Programme for Business has produced a new 56-page jargon-free guide on how firms can apply new technology to their businesses to increase profits and improve competitiveness.

Doing Business in the Information Society covers every aspect of business, from sales to marketing to customer-service training. It explains clearly how firms can use new technology such as e-mail, the Internet and CD-ROM to operate more efficiently. It is available free of charge from the ISI Business Infoline on 0345 15 2000 or by e-mail to <info@isi.gov.uk>. The ISI PfB website is on <http://www.isi.gov.uk>.

15

Agency Selection and Agency Relationships

Nick Phillips
Director General, Institute of Practitioners in Advertising

The business partnership between a client and his or her marketing communications agency or advertising agency is one of the most important relationships to that client. A successful partnership can help turn products and services into brands: the joint effort creates, develops and sustains brands over a long period. These brands are critical to the profitable growth of the client company.

Selecting an agency

Long-term relationships benefit the health of a brand. To take as the starting point the selection of a new agency, a systematic 10-stage process is recommended, in order to optimise the quality of response and the likelihood of selecting the ideal partner. The process is jointly recommended by the ISBA (Incorporated Society of British Advertisers), the advertisers' trade body, and the IPA (Institute of Practitioners in Advertising), the equivalent body for the advertising agencies.

Preparation

Consider the role of advertising and other marketing communications and the potential contribution of the agency and work out an initial outline brief. This should help determine the type of agency required (for example in terms of size relative to budget, location and specialisation). To gain ideas on a suitable agency you could study the trade press, identify relevant existing advertising which you rate highly or talk to colleagues in other companies. You may seek credentials information from a number of selected agencies who match the criteria in your outline brief. Note, however, that you may not wish your search to be widely known. In this case you can approach ISBA and IPA for confidential information and detailed advice; the two bodies can also direct you to other professional, objective and confidential sources of information. You can then sift all the information against your checklist.

Short listing

The advice from both ISBA and IPA is to decide on a positive list of up to three agencies only (four if the incumbent agency is invited). Competing agencies should be aware of the number on the list.

Written brief

All the competing agencies should have a precise but thorough written brief covering items such as company and brand history; research on the target market; the nature of the competition; and the history of marketing communication. You should make clear all the aspects in which the agencies' presentations will be judged – for instance, do you want strategic proposals alone or are some creative ideas or even a full creative pitch required? You should state the nature of the services which you expect to use and outline your preferred contract terms and proposed remuneration. Agencies need to aim at a reasonable level of profit after covering all costs, including overheads. Nowadays a number of remuneration systems are employed, including a commission related to the size of the advertising billing, a negotiated fee, an amount dependent on agreed criteria of success and various amalgamations of these.

Allow time for response

You should prepare a timetable for the total pitching process and stick to it. Allow sufficient time for constructive ideas between brief and presentation. At least four weeks is suggested for work to a full creative pitch; after all, in an ongoing relationship proper proposals may take weeks or months to develop.

Financial contribution

The advertiser has to decide whether to make a contribution to the pitch. Both ISBA and IPA advise that some financial contribution (announced upfront and the same offer to all agencies in the short list) shows the commitment and seriousness of your intent. The objective is to motivate the agencies; the contribution is not likely to cover all the third-party, staff and associated costs.

Share information

The advertiser should be willing to share, on a confidential basis, market data and other relevant research and allow agency personnel access to people in the company with whom they would work if appointed. There should always be a specified senior member of the advertiser's company to handle all enquiries and to meet requests of the agency (to ensure consistency of response). You should ensure a level playing field by allowing the same rules of access to all those pitching; but don't underestimate the time involved in having a senior person fully available.

Evaluation of the pitches

You should ensure that all the decision makers have been fully briefed and that they are present at each pitch. There needs to be an objective evaluation system for assessing each pitch – for example weighted scores for understanding of the market; positioning the role of marketing communications; creative strategy; media strategy and buying expertise; financial arrangement; and personal chemistry. This last implies ensuring that the agency presentation team includes people who will actually work on the business. Again, allow sufficient time for the competing agencies to present and ask questions and for all the decision makers to discuss the presentation.

Business disciplines

Both ISBA and the IPA emphasise that it is essential to discuss the business side (contracts and remuneration) before an appointment is made and each offers help in this area.

The decision

As soon as possible after the presentations (normally no more than a week) the advertiser should decide on the winning agency. There should be a firm procedure for notifying both the successful and unsuccessful agencies of the decision, on the same day.

The aftermath

Losing agencies should have the courtesy of a full 'lost order' meeting. Any losing agency must return all confidential information provided for the pitch to the advertiser. Conversely the advertiser must, on request, return the losing agency pitch presentation.

As for the previous incumbent, the agency's contract must be honoured, particularly with regard to the agreed notice period and payment of outstanding invoices. The incumbent must co-operate fully in a handover to the new agency and ensure that all materials belonging to the advertiser, in accordance with the contract, are handed back.

That leaves the winning agency to be welcomed into the start of a long-lasting and mutually satisfying relationship.

The ongoing relationship

We have seen that from the start there should be a clear written contract and agreement on the method and amount of remuneration. These business disciplines, however, are just the essential backdrop of a dynamic business partnership whose goal is the creation and management of advertising that is designed to give sustainable competitive advantage in the marketplace. The brand is the focal point and effectiveness is the goal.

From the description of the ideal pitch process, it is clear that the advertiser will not want to go through the process very often! So the partnership must flourish. This will partly be through insistence on rigorous disciplines of objective setting, control of processes, and regular mutual appraisal of advertiser and agency.

But more particularly, the partnership will flourish on true motivation, an acknowledgement of the different roles and skills of client and agency, and a firm commitment to effective communication that has measurable success in the marketplace and is key to the development of the client's business.

One service organisation or several

The communication needs of the brand, be it product or service based, may require skills in market understanding, strategy development, advertisement creation, media placement, direct marketing, sales promotion, public relations etc. The client needs to be sure of the range of needs and then be rigorous in enquiring about the skill base of different companies. Some organisations are able to provide a range of interrelated skills under one roof. Some are unashamedly specialists in one of the marketing communication disciplines. You must decide what you want; but remember that the different communication disciplines require co-ordination and consistency at some point, so if you multiply the number of different service companies, don't underestimate the co-ordination time needed at the client end.

In order to be effective, advertising or marketing communication agencies will continue to cover in the one organisation strategic marketing advice; creative strategy and execution; and (shared) responsibility for outcome, ie manifesting an effectiveness culture. So far as media activity is concerned, a high proportion is now bought by specialist companies (in order to achieve the necessary critical mass, technology and skill to cover a complex fragmented market). However these specialists, whether dependent on an agency grouping or independent, have to work very closely with the agency responsible for the strategic and creative work; it's very much the same value chain. Increasingly, too, agencies are having to learn the skills of direct marketing and the management of databases for continuous relationships with customers. Some other services such as public relations or sales promotion are more commonly carried out by specialist companies within or outside the group of agency companies.

The changing relationship

A successful client–agency relationship can last for decades: decades of partnership and trust and working together for the betterment of the brand. Research in the field seems to indicate that agencies may be hired on qualitative criteria such as understanding, insight, inspiration and originality; however, they are fired when the relationship goes wrong due to much more down-to-earth factors such as slow delivery, routine errors, weak administration etc. Perhaps, however, these are just symptoms of a relationship that has lost its way. If this sad point is reached, it is to be hoped after several fruitful years of joint endeavour, then the client may turn the full circle back to selecting an agency with a view to making it a very close business partner in building up the business through effective marketing communication. And this brings us back to the 10-stage selection process.

16

Tomorrow's Communications Professional

Steve Cuthbert
Director General, The Chartered Institute of Marketing

As the world shrinks – or should it be downsizes? – and methods of communication become ever more sophisticated, the challenges faced by communications professionals continue to grow. More and more companies are fighting for their 'share of voice' in a busy marketplace, and increasingly use specialist agencies to undertake activities such as direct marketing, design, corporate identity, advertising and public relations.

That, in itself, places pressure on the communications manager to ensure that all of a company's communications are integrated. Everybody in an organisation, and all suppliers, need to convey the same message. It needs to be 'one company – one voice'.

Tomorrow's communications professional will need to be better qualified, with a greater understanding of the management process, new technology, the importance of internal communications, and the need for a customer-focused culture throughout the entire organisation. They will need to demonstrate measurable and quantifiable skills, such as possession of The Chartered Institute of Marketing's Certificates or Postgraduate Diploma and NVQs in relevant subjects.

Corporate communications is no longer merely an option; it is a business priority. Effective communication is at the heart of marketing, and marketing is at the heart of any successful enterprise.

Marketing is all about meeting a customer's needs and desires, and research into the financial services sector, commissioned by The Chartered Institute of Marketing and carried out by London Business School, shows that the more successful a business is at satisfying the customer the more profitable that business is likely to become. To quote the Business School's Assistant Professor, Gordon Swartz:

> 'Companies whose cultures truly focus on the customer beyond lip service, beyond just saying that you are customer oriented, are more likely to achieve customer satisfaction goals ... A happy customer is a profitable customer. Companies which focus on customer satisfaction tend to achieve higher than average performance in terms of profitability.'

Although that research was confined to one sector of business, few people question the validity of the argument for any organisation. There is no doubt that the best communicators in business understand that the communication loop begins and ends with the customer, their needs and their desires.

At The Chartered Institute of Marketing's Annual Conference in 1996, CIM President Sir Colin Marshall, told his audience that to be successful:

> 'Business must make the shift towards enhanced competitiveness which makes customer choice and preference the common denominators of every commercial equation.'

That competitiveness must be global, and within the context of the European Union, if Britain is to compete with the economies of Asia and North America.

New forms of communication are becoming available through advanced technology, and tomorrow's communications professional will need to understand and use multi-media such as CD-ROM, digital image-bank systems for down-the-line transfer of photographs and illustrations, and of course the ubiquitous Internet. But they must never forget that the technology is the medium, not the message.

One way in which the modern manager can keep up to date with these advances is through the Institute's Continuing Professional Development scheme. This is an integral part of a member's career progression – vital in ensuring that practitioners are equipped with the skills, knowledge and competence professional communicators need in an increasingly complex and dynamic marketplace. Communications managers should be members of CIM and other related professional bodies which set down a professional code of conduct for members to follow.

Their job descriptions will undoubtedly include the expression 'integrated communications' as it becomes far more important than ever that marketers integrate their internal and external messages.

It also becomes more challenging as outsourcing of communications activities continues to grow; some 350 listed CIM consultancy practices already advise companies on all aspects of sales and marketing. All outside agencies must be given an accurate and clear written brief, to ensure that every aspect of an organisation's methods of communication, from letters and phone calls to television advertising campaigns, are totally integrated and, therefore, synergistic.

Motivating your workforce

The communications manager also has to make sure that the whole of a business's workforce – not just the marketing or public relations department – is involved in understanding consumer needs and delivering customer satisfaction.

The motivation of colleagues is crucial if customers are to get the service and value they are increasingly coming to expect. Where companies offer similar services, good internal communications might just tip the balance in favour of one against another.

Employees have to understand and believe in a company's mission in order to fully support it, but managers must never forget that what employees want to know is sometimes a little different from what management wants to tell them. It's all very well communicating a company's new global strategic direction, but that message has to be directly linked with the question that's most important in the employee's mind, which is 'will I still have a job?'

So a new-style job description for the communications professional will undoubtedly demand a more internationally focused, technology-friendly, custodian of communications who not only believes that the customer comes first, but also has the conviction and ability to ensure this belief is adopted throughout an entire organisation.

What The Chartered Institute of Marketing can do for you

At The Chartered Institute of Marketing we are helping communicators to achieve that objective. We are the largest specialist marketing, sales, strategy and management training organisation in Europe, training some 9,500 executives each year.

The Institute has also developed a wide range of residential training courses. These are offered at the Institute's headquarters at Cookham in Berkshire, with a wide choice of one-day seminars at different locations around the UK. One of the most popular is 'Marketing Communications Strategy for Senior Management', which targets marketing policy-makers who have to build communications into their marketing strategy. New technology is catered for in courses such as 'Using the Internet as a Marketing Tool'.

The Institute also designs over 400 company-specific training programmes each year to cater for organisations requiring specific training courses to meet their individual needs.

Together with City & Guilds in England and Wales, and SCOTVEC in Scotland, the Institute is developing a range of National Vocational Qualifications (NVQs) in sales and marketing which will help to put tomorrow's communications professional into the vanguard of a fundamental change in business strategy. The first were NVQs in Sales and Sales Management. Now there are also NVQs in Marketing, Customer Service and International Trade and more are about to become available; these include the NVQ in Export Sales which is to be launched in 1997 and an NVQ at level 3 in Telemarketing/Selling which will take telephone selling to a more advanced level.

Communications has come a long way since cavemen painted the walls of their homes, or native Indians sent smoke signals across the prairies. It's not a job for the enthusiastic amateur. Today's communications professional needs to be highly educated, highly qualified, technologically aware and customer-focused. Get that right and both the individual communicator and the company which employs the communicator are likely to flourish.

17

Outsourcing – Is it Working?

Caroline Bainbridge
Consultant

Outsourcing, the buying-in of goods or services from outside suppliers, became topical in the 1980s when, after a period of growth and acquisition, companies re-focused on core competencies. The decision to outsource can be driven by both operational and strategic considerations. Operationally it allows access to specialist skills, and the ability to cope with fluctuating needs. PA Consulting Group in their 1995–96 International Survey on Outsourcing, described successful outsourcing as a strategic decision, and 'a significant element in the business planning of most major organisations'.

Outsourcing in communications is not new; companies have used external agencies for all or part of their communications for decades. In August 1996, *PR Week* surveyed companies' use of outside suppliers for communications and found that just under half (48 per cent) outsource communications in some way.

What are the options?

There are three common outsourcing options: using large agencies who provide a range of services; using smaller specialist suppliers to provide distinct 'products'; and using independent consultants or freelancers.

Table 17.1 Outsourcing communications functions

	%
Use any external supplier	48
Media relations	29
Strategic consultancy	17
Literature production	15
Financial relations	8
Internal communications	6
Lobbying	5

Base: 106 companies
Source: *PR Week* 23 August, 1996

The large agencies

While use of large agencies is widespread, there are variations in the extent to which the agency is considered part of the communications decision-making team. Philips caused a stir in June 1994 by outsourcing all corporate communications to Lowe Bell, transferring the entire communications function, including staff, from Philips to the PR agency. Two years on, this relationship is still working successfully. Roger Woods, the director of corporate affairs, who led the move, says that although several companies have enquired about the experience, he is not aware that any others have yet adopted this wholesale outsourcing approach.

More common is a high level of openness between senior clients and senior agency staff, but this does not always extend to full openness or sharing of information among the entire communications team at both agency and client.

Over time, specialisation within corporate communications has given rise to distinct 'skill areas'. Table 17.2 shows fee income for the top ten agencies across the main corporate communications disciplines.

Table 17.2 Corporate communications: Fee income 1995, top 10 agencies by sector

	£m
Financial relations	40.29*
Corporate communications	33.94
Government relations	22.86
Crisis management	7.02
Internal communications	6.67
Total	110.78

*includes some personal finance PR
Source: *Marketing* 6 June, 1996

According to Suzanne Finch of the PR Register there are clear trends in agency selection. Firstly, companies generally keep consumer and corporate PR separate, with big companies preferring big agencies for corporate work, despite being happy with smaller agencies for brand support. Similarly, many clients separate internal and external communications, as the former often takes a back seat if both are handled together. When selecting a new agency, companies' three priorities are:

- strategic input;
- good media knowledge;
- creativity.

While some companies change agencies through dissatisfaction, many corporate accounts are subject to regular reviews, generally on a three- to five-year cycle. As communications moves up the management agenda and, increasingly, has board status, some companies are considering outsourcing for the first time, thus increasing the size of the overall market.

Specialist suppliers

Few figures are available about companies' use of small agencies and specialist suppliers. *Hollis UK Press and Public Relations Annual 1996* lists 2,000 PR agencies, 95 per cent of which have fee income under £350,000. There are hundreds of specialists offering such communications 'products' as event management, staff newsletters and annual reports. Table 17.3 shows a rough allocation of clients' expenditure against these specific items. Much of this is likely to be outsourced rather than handled in-house. Companies using specialist suppliers tend not to look to them for strategic input, but to commission specific work to an agreed brief. The relationship is more likely to be that of purchaser and supplier, rather than a consulting or partnership relationship.

Freelancers and independent consultants

Communications has always been considered a 'people business' and the emphasis on individuals' expertise, contacts and skills has traditionally led to a large number of independent operators. Many freelance or consultancy projects are arranged through personal contacts or by word of mouth.

In recent years, however, the marketplace has grown and become more formalised, with specialist placement agencies developing. Stop Gap Marketing is an employment consultancy specialising in freelance staff. Gaynor Egan, the founder, sees two kinds of freelance outsourcing in corporate communications: interim management, where companies need additional help for a specific period of time, perhaps maternity or holiday cover, and consultancy, where specific skills are required. She says that while freelance numbers increased during the early 1990s as companies and agencies were shedding staff, redundancy is not the only reason for freelance life. The relatively high proportion of women in communications means that there are large numbers of skilled people who are keen to work on a flexible basis to balance work and family commitments.

Charles Russam of Russam GMS, a consultancy specialising in interim management, believes that some people are better suited than others to freelance life. Those who are successful tend to have a clear skill area, the ability to promote themselves, and the emotional make-up to cope with working outside an organisation.

Table 17.3 Budget allocation

	%
Design and print production	17
Conferences/exhibitions	6
Sponsorship	5
Annual reports	5
Corporate advertising	4
Corporate hospitality	3
Research	3
Press mailings	3
Media training	2
Corporate video	2
Press clippings	2
Advertorials	1
Evaluation	1
Business TV	1

Base: 106 companies
Source: PR Week, 23 August, 1996

Is it working?

Industry figures indicate that communications outsourcing is increasing. In communications agencies, after a lean patch in the early 1990s, both staff figures and income figures are increasing, growing by 10 per cent and 15 per cent respectively year-on-year. Meanwhile a recent *PR Week* survey of in-house expenditure reported that one in five companies had suffered a drop in budget and, of those reporting an increase, growth averaged between 3 per cent and 7 per cent. This suggests that more money is being allocated to outsourcing of communications.

This does not mean, however, that there is total satisfaction with outsourcing. *PR Week* asked companies using outside agencies about their main criticisms. More than one in five respondents criticised suppliers for failure to deliver, while a similar number criticised them for overpromising. One in six felt that agencies lacked knowledge of their business and one in eight complained of budget overruns. Staffing levels were also a source of complaint. Other criticisms of outsourcing in general are that it can lead to a loss of internal expertise and increased reliance on outside suppliers.

Considerable time must be invested in maintaining a level of relationship which allows the contractor to function as effectively as an internal department.

Future prospects

There is every reason to believe that outsourcing of communications will continue to grow. Companies are becoming increasingly aware of the importance of communications and prepared to invest in it. The trends are for that money to be invested in outsourcing.

There are indications, however, that the structure of the market is changing once more. The large agencies are growing again and investing in specialist staff and expertise; there is some speculation that growth in staff numbers may be limited to availability of staff, particularly at middle and senior levels. At the same time, smaller agencies and consultants, having grown in the early 1990s, seem now to be decreasing in numbers. Figures from Barclays Bank suggest that, in the last year, 57 per cent of owners of small business start-ups across all sectors have moved back to paid employment.

My own research suggests that several factors can make communications professionals return to paid employment. Regular income is one factor but, more importantly, people are accepting employment for tactical reasons; the opportunity to build new contacts, to develop in a new direction and to gain additional skills and experience.

At the other end of the scale, however, there are some freelancers who will not wish to return to paid employment. The benefits for the individual who can make a success of self-employment are considerable: flexibility and the opportunity for time management, coupled with opportunities for achieving income levels at least equal to those from permanent employment.

Part 4
Measuring Communications

18

Measuring Communications

Dr Jon White
Consultant

Why measure communication?

Management depends on communication. It would be impossible to set direction, build support for management objectives and encourage work towards them without communication. Equally, communication with groups outside the organisation is important, as organisations seek the support of customers, favourable treatment from government, and understanding within the community. But managers recognising the importance of communication are faced with the problems of judging the usefulness of communication techniques, assessing the investment they should make in communication, and the results they will get from use of communication.

Practitioners such as public relations and corporate communications specialists are aware of the need to demonstrate the value of what they do. One of their present preoccupations is with finding ways of measuring communication and with the task of evaluation. Some commentators feel that this concern for measurement is related to professional insecurity. In other areas of management, measurement questions may have been answered or the requirement to measure activity is not so acutely felt.

There is a need to measure communications activity in order to:

- improve management of communications;
- demonstrate the results achieved for a given investment;

- judge the work of advisers and staff with responsibilities for communication.

However, measurement of communication is seen as difficult. There are a number of reasons for this. Communication is often regarded as one of the 'soft' areas of management practice and not amenable to measurement; it involves activities which are hard to quantify, and effects which are by no means clearly related to any one cause. For example, poor morale might be one result of poor communication, but it might also be affected by management style or unsatisfactory working conditions.

Results

The manager who is skilful in the management of corporate communications can expect results in the clarity given to organisation mission and objectives. By thinking carefully about how these are to be communicated, they are made clearer and easier for others to follow.

Effective communication involves listening, as much as, if not more than talking, writing or otherwise presenting information. Listening requires empathy and can be measured through checks on understanding. Does the manager's understanding match that of employees? Is there a similarity of understanding at different levels in the organisation, or among members of work groups?

The process of communication itself can be measured, through checks on content, entering, passing through and leaving channels of communication. At present, content analysis is carried out extensively, particularly in public relations practice, in order to check the content of mass media, to see whether or not messages (negative, positive or neutral) are appearing there.

Important though process and output measures are, it is essential that communication be traced through to its effects or impact. For example, are forms of employee communication, such as staff newspapers, or electronic newsletters, containing important messages, having an effect on the understanding, attitudes and behaviour of employees?

As soon as methods other than those involving face-to-face communication are used, feedback becomes much harder to gather. Specific attention must be paid to gathering feedback, using data-collection and survey-research methods. Feedback completes the process of communication, allowing the sender of any message to check that messages have been received and understood.

Measurement methods

Measurement can be applied to communication practice at a number of points. At the outset, questions can be asked about objectives, which are to be supported by communications activities. Are these sufficiently clear, and what would constitute progress towards achieving them? An example might involve voluntary staff redundancies. How many staff might have to be made redundant? Are the reasons for the redundancies set out, in terms that will be readily understood by staff? A programme of communication with staff would aim to win their understanding, support and co-operation. A final measure would be of the numbers of staff coming forward to offer themselves for voluntary redundancy. Measures would be applied to objectives at the outset, the actual process of communication (are messages moving through channels to be received by staff?) and to audience reactions and behaviour.

Techniques for measuring communication (to assess awareness, measure attitudes, and observational techniques) include simple output measures; measures of activity against objectives; content analysis; and survey research methods among members of target audiences. These last measures are used to see if behaviour changes as a result of communication.

Despite likely limits on resources, several measures should be used to assess the effectiveness of communication. Measurement at the outset helps in the development of programmes, while measurement during programmes can be used to make mid-course corrections, to find out what is and is not working. Measurement at the end of a series of activities helps in making judgements about effectiveness and value for money.

Essentially, measurement of communications requires the use of project and programme management techniques, which set precise objectives, relate series of activities to the achievement of those objectives, and allow for measurement of progress and results. What's not being measured?

Measurement is only patchily applied to communication practice at the present time, for a number of reasons. Managers do not generally think consciously about elements in the communication process, such as objectives for communication and encoding or message-preparation issues. In general, they work with a limited concept of communication as a process of telling, and are likely to be uncomfortable with the requirements for listening and empathy.

Communication is judged according to the medium used. For example, an article in a national newspaper may be deemed to have impact, in spite of the lack of any evidence that it has actually had an effect.

In public relations practice, there is an obsession with media content. Some practitioners feel that conclusions drawn from media content can tell them about the impact, and the effectiveness of their work. In fact, content analysis is only one measure among many.

What is needed is a more comprehensive understanding of the communication process, and the part that it plays in management and the achievement of business and other objectives. As the role of communication is appreciated, specific systems from a whole repertoire of measures can be selected and used. This requires a familiarity on the part of managers with the communication process, as well as relevant research and measurement techniques. However, this familiarity is not currently developed in management education and training.

The future of communications management

The importance of communication in management, and of the need to manage the process of communication, is growing, for a number of reasons. Organisations themselves are changing, losing permanent staff and layers of management, drawing more on temporary and contract staff, and making use of information technology to change working practices. They need political support: the willing support of their own members, and important groups outside. They need to present themselves and to minimise opposition to their activities.

In future, success will depend on whether or not management has used communication to build support, sustain its position and prosper in its relations with important groups, such as customers. It is already possible to measure communication. In the future, measurement of communication may take place alongside measurement of productive, competitive and business performance. Before this happens, there will need to be a step-change in the way in which managers as a group see communication as a task of management.

19

Benchmarking Communications Management

Dr Tom Watson
Managing Director, Hallmark Public Relations

What is benchmarking?

Benchmarking, a relatively new and fashionable phrase in the corporate communications lexicon, is interchangeable with the more established term of formative evaluation, the stage of research prior to objective setting. Both terms indicate that the monitoring and management of corporate communications form a continuous process linked to business objectives, not a six-monthly or annual review. It is thus linked to a management-by-objectives approach to corporate communications which is evident in those organisations which take a best-practice approach.

What is evaluation?

When discussing the topic of evaluation of public relations and other marketing communications programmes, there is considerable confusion as to what it means. For budget holders, whether employers or clients, the judgements have a bottom-line, profit-related significance. US academics

Grunig and Hunt have written of a practitioner who justified the budgetary expenditure on public relations by the large volume of press coverage generated. Yet he was flummoxed by a senior executive's question: 'What's all this worth to us?'

In the UK, articles in the public relations and marketing press refer to evaluation in terms of 'justifying expenditure', which is similar to Grunig and Hunt's example. Professor Jon White of London's City University suggests that company managers have a special interest in the evaluation of public relations:

> Evaluation helps to answer the questions about the time, effort and resources to be invested in public relations activities: can the investment, and the costs involved, be justified?

To evaluate public relations effectively, you must be clear on the objectives of the activity. The most effective approach is continually to plan and evaluate public relations and marketing communications programmes. In that way, information is fed back from evaluation and monitoring into the continued development of the programme. This means that you can rapidly change plans to meet new opportunities, problems (a competitor's launch of new products or services) or barriers (legislative changes or production problems).

Media-based programmes

If your public relations activity is mostly carried out in the media, here's how you can evaluate the results:

- Check that the programme's messages are being received and interpreted correctly by monitoring content of media coverage;
- Review which journalists and publications are positive, neutral or negative towards your product, service or organisation;
- Track issues which are relevant to your business or organisation.

Media analysis can be undertaken in-house, but look out for 'observer bias' when interpreting results. There are several media-analysis firms in the UK which use independent reader panels and sophisticated software. Leading companies include CARMA, Infopress Communications and Mantra. One of the leading market-research companies, MORI, has also entered this market.

However, for many companies the cost of using external evaluation companies is too great a burden and increasingly they are using consultants to set up evaluation systems for staff to operate. The consultants return during the year to advise on the interpretation of data.

Attitudinal research is very important in the benchmarking process as it tells 'where we are now' and 'where we have got to'. Ultimately, communications activities must act persuasively to change attitudes and prompt new actions by the target audiences.

Beware the substitution game: media analysis mainly measures the effectiveness of PR output, it doesn't tell of the impact of the message. Awareness of name (unprompted or prompted) does not equate with action. It only indicates receipt of message. For judgements on impact, study the attitudes of your target audience through quantitative (surveys, sales responses, enquiries) or qualitative (focus groups, panels, audits) methods.

In judging public relations and marketing communications, avoid phoney valuations of media analysis data such as Advertising Value Equivalent (also known as Advertising Cost Equivalent). These give a monetary value in terms of advertising space costs as a valuation of editorial coverage, but they have no statistical validity. Essentially, they attempt to give a value to something which would not have been purchased in any case. One US commentator says that it is like 'comparing apples with oranges'.

In benchmarking press coverage, one of the leading international accountancy firms uses a simple + or − 0 to 4 scale to monitor the quality and quantity of media coverage for its management consultancy arm, 0 is for a mention in a listing of firms, while 4 is given to extensive coverage, possibly with a photograph. Unfavourable coverage gains negative points. While lacking in social science finesse, this simple benchmarking exercise gives an indication of trends in coverage and the distribution of material.

Multistrategy programmes

Not all PR programmes are carried out in the media only. Many business-to-business campaigns use contact programmes, seminars and events and corporate entertainment. Lobbying, community relations and publications may be the main strategies in others.

The key evaluation points are:

- Use research to help set objectives;
- Select the key messages you want to put forward;
- Use surveys, audits, media analysis and feedback to judge effectiveness;
- Create an information loop to change and vary the campaign.

Avoiding information clutter

By choosing separate messages for different promotional methods, such as advertising pushing a price message and public relations pulling through the case for expertise or product/service benefits, the relative effectiveness of each method can be tracked. This is known as 'disaggregation' and addresses the main problems facing all evaluation techniques.

Effects-based planning – a new approach

A question often asked is whether success or effectiveness can be measured in a long-term programme. There is a US communications method called 'effects-based planning', which not only helps select objectives, but guides on the attitudinal or marketing effects to be created. By monitoring the effects during the life of the programme, it can be determined whether the programme is on track or not. If not, it can be varied to take account of problems or new opportunities.

My research in the past six years has looked at the way in which PR practitioners work and checked on existing models of PR evaluation by testing them against real-life case studies. By adding effects-based planning, new insights have been found for benchmarking and evaluation. From this research programme, two new models of evaluation have been developed – the short-term model for the typical media-relations-based awareness campaign in support of sales or marketing objectives, and the continuing model for longer-term programmes where attitudinal and persuasional effects are to be created.

Because the two models are based on real-life public relations practice and have been tested extensively as well as being discussed at conferences and workshops in the UK and Europe, they have been easy to apply to public relations programmes. As aids to planning and evaluation, they help practitioners get over the barriers and demonstrate the effectiveness of their work. That helps complete the loop to answer the question of 'What does it all add up to?' and give greater impact from PR expenditure.

Using PR evaluation data

The latest UK research shows that evaluation data are used in five main ways to judge PR programmes:

- measure coverage in the media;
- help prepare reports to clients or employers;

- review effectiveness of activity;
- track issues and attitudes of opinion leaders;
- track attitudes of journalists, as shown in articles and reports.

20

The Communications Audit

Dr Richard J Varey
Director, The BNFL Corporate Communications Unit, The Management School, University of Salford

No one doubts that good business requires real communication. Often, however, employee attitude surveys reveal dissatisfaction and a feeling of mushroom management – kept in the dark and expected to grow! Communication as a management problem to be addressed is nothing new. Often a communications audit is employed in the hope of improving the situation.

Where organisational improvement is sought, the communications audit may be employed to analyse advertising, public relations activity, relationships with customers, the supplies-ordering system, sales and service response, and so on. Typically, it focuses on internal communication among employees.

An internal or external consultant makes a careful and detailed study to measure the effectiveness of existing internal and external communication systems and behaviours, employee attitudes to them, and to identify the factors affecting systems operation. This can provide a sound basis for formulating new communications policies. The audit may be more than an information-gathering exercise – a process of organisational change in which employees are able to participate directly.

A communications audit is a broad-scale, loosely structured examination of communication assets – systems, strengths and weaknesses, and communication styles. Are they compatible with the basic management philosophy of the company?

Why audit communications?

Good management takes control and avoids the stresses and losses of organisational sickness by periodically visiting the 'Well Man' clinic. An examination of communications systems effectiveness and efficiency is particularly relevant and potentially valuable:

- prior to or after large-scale restructuring or rationalisation;
- in increasing motivation of employees;
- when customer complaints are a concern;
- when developing long-term plans and strategies;
- in checking for gaps in attitude, beliefs and knowledge between various groups;
- when large-scale expenditure on new technology is considered;
- when job performance is poor due to lack of relevant information;
- when labour turnover is too high;
- when aspirations for greater organisational effectiveness arise;
- when there is an obvious communication problem.

Theory and experience show that the effectiveness of well-designed and managed communication systems has critical impact on the functioning of an organisation.

To ensure good performance it is necessary systematically and rigorously to assess communication flows and patterns: effectiveness and efficiency; inhibitors and opportunities; quality of content and relationships within the organisation and with external parties. Managers need to identify networks operating (formal and informal) and their effectiveness as well as the impact of new technology. They can then identify gaps and bottlenecks. Essentially they must also take steps to assess the quality of communications management, to assist in the development of improvement plans and activities, and to check cost-effectiveness of channels and methods. They can then develop and evaluate communications policy and practices, and budgets, with benchmarks for the impact of changes and progress assessment.

To prepare for and facilitate change and learning properly, managers should map the cultural patterns of the organisation and define communication as part of management behaviours and styles. A communications audit will help to spread ownership of desired change, including development or restructuring of the communications function itself. Employees will experience involvement and the communication process will provide feedback, so that people and the organisation as a whole are able to learn from failures and successes.

A comprehensive audit schedule

Some informal impressions of communication-system performance can be gleaned by simply taking a look around at how various groups relate to each other – consider the level of co-operation, quality failures, expressions of frustration, employee absence and turnover etc.

More formally, the audit project will be aided by a steering group, comprising senior decision makers who understand how the business works and can facilitate access to various parts of the organisation. The tasks of the project will be executed by a working group of employees from various functions and a project co-ordinator, and may include internal/external consultants/researchers.

A formal audit would typically take up to 12 weeks and a stage approach is preferred to ensure a manageable rate of data generation. The kick-off point is workshops with senior managers to discuss their approaches to employee communication, to build consensus and senior management support from the outset.

The research should then examine communications effectiveness by reviewing key communications performance areas for all employees, and then assess communications efficiency by considering the use of particular channels of information flow in the management process.

The methods used to generate and analyse data must be selected on the basis of the audit objectives and the nature of data required. This will first require that the nature of the problems should be defined.

Most organisations have some data available which can be useful, so the second step is to examine all existing studies, measurement against business performance indicators, annual attitude surveys, personnel records, customer complaints etc.

Next, the auditors should collect samples of all written communications media and descriptions of all formal/organised communications methods. Interviews and group discussions then focus on issues identified.

Next, a survey of employees might be required, using a tested questionnaire, to examine how well the organisation communicates with its own members:

- Do they understand the organisation's objectives?
- Do they understand their role in achieving the objectives?
- How well do they feel the organisation communicates its objectives to them?

- How could communication flows be improved?
- From where is information received?
- What are their preferred sources and channels?
- What are their information needs and desires?
- How useful are current information flows?
- To what extent is there necessary inter-department/division co-operation/information sharing?

The auditors should seek to provide managers with an understanding of how employees identify with the company, division, department or other group. The nature of relationships that exist between individuals and sub-groups can be assessed through network analysis and communication diaries.

The audit should also look at 'motivation to contribute' and the level of satisfaction with employment and work. It must also ask what are employees' interpretations of company values and objectives – how does this differ in the subgroups of the organisation? What are employees' expectations and aspirations for the future?

Communication with other stakeholders can be reviewed by examining product and corporate literature, trade directories, advertising, sales force reports etc, and through focus-group discussions. Comparison should be made with materials of competitors and benchmarked with examples of good practice.

As a result, it is essential to review communication policy and strategy thoroughly to ensure that it is relevant and comprehensive, as well as cost-effective, and that it tells employees the what and how of communicating with the various key groups which can influence the operation of the business.

Finally, the findings should be used to derive recommendations which can be related to the wider management system, with a clearly worked-out set of action points, including a programme of long-term training and development.

How does an audit work?

Expressions of communications problems can often be a sign of much deeper-seated difficulties. By systematically mapping and evaluating communications activity and attitudes, the health of the organisation can be assessed and improved.

The audit generates data which can provide a better understanding of the flow of information in the organisation. But to secure the maximum benefit, more is required. While specific improvements in communications

BNFL Corporate Communications Unit

As the only large scale research programme in the UK in the emerging field of Corporate Communications Management, this is a unique opportunity to pursue PhD, MPhil and MSc degrees by research.

The MSc in Corporate Communications Management is also offered on a part-time basis by The Management School along with other specialist degrees.

Researchers from the Unit are engaged in projects as part of the GEMISIS 2000 partnership between the University of Salford, the City of Salford, and NYNEX CableComms. This programme of research aims to use the information superhighway to serve the local community.

Researchers are also available to undertake research and development work on various aspects of communications management.

Research proposals and course enquiries should be addressed to Dr Richard Varey, Director, BNFL Corporate Communications Unit, The Management School, University of Salford, Salford M5 4WT. Tel. 0161 745 5884.
E-mail: R.J.Varey@business.salford.ac.uk
Web site at http://www.salford.ac.uk/man-sch

THE UNIVERSITY OF SALFORD IS COMMITTED TO HIGHER EDUCATION, TEACHING AND RESEARCH behaviour and attitudes are sought, the communications audit should be a positive and motivating exercise. For many employees, an audit is the first real consultation process they experience.

Anything other than the most formal of communications flow along channels of friendship, in which trust enables freely communicated content and generally accurate perceptions. As people have differing goals and value systems, it is important to create understanding about needs and motives. The free flow of innovating ideas is often stifled, however, by feelings that credit will not be given where due or that ideas will be hijacked by someone else.

A carefully planned communications audit can catalyse change. It may indicate the need for changes and will raise expectations that things will improve. Careful preparation is essential. Employees must be made aware of the impending work, its objectives, its progress and eventual findings.

Successful audits place communication on the agenda of management issues for regular monitoring and periodic assessment. The evolving communications needs of managers and other employees, of customers and of other stakeholders, can be addressed in a changing environment. The management system gets a 'health check' from time to time. Serious breakdowns which adversely affect performance can be prevented, and serious flaws can be repaired and effective and efficient business restored. Managers can expect to achieve improved staff morale, greater efficiency and higher productivity.

The communications audit process should be repeated as soon as steps have been taken to remedy identified shortcomings. This will demonstrate the improvements achieved.

Do communications audits make a difference?

Communications audits are often, unfortunately, undertaken as an end in themselves, often because managers feel an urge to be seen to be doing something about 'poor communications' or to boost low morale. The audit is altogether more constructive and less likely to create frustration when it has been designed as part of the organisation's managerial communication process, and managers have a clear plan for using the results and for meeting the expectations for feedback which will inevitably be raised.

Organisation development can result from:

- improved communication flow;
- enhanced organisational effectiveness;
- change in behaviour;
- greater integration between communication functions.

In a divisionalised engineering company there was a decision to rationalise public relations work to a single agency. A communications audit was commissioned and this revealed that the real major problem lay with communication between managers and shopfloor workers, and a general lack of co-operation between departments. As a result a number of strategic management-development workshops were run, a new IT system was commissioned and the business groups were reorganised.

During a period of merger and reorganisation, a public-sector organisation experienced growing complaints about a lack of communication. The senior management team was perceived by many to be aloof and remote, and many were suspicious of hidden motives for changes. A great deal of insecurity about jobs was evident. A number of immediate changes in communication channels and methods were made and a communications audit was commissioned. It was important to publicise the project as the start of a serious effort to improve internal communications. Procedural information was made more accessible through IT systems and the employee newsletter was redesigned with a new intent to be seen as more informative and less of a mouthpiece for a few senior management figures. The result has been a greater flow of information to help employees do their jobs and much more of a sense of the corporate view and linkage up from local-level effort and innovation.

A service organisation identified, through its communication audit, a number of issues which were leading to communication blockages. The results were major restructuring of communication channels and the initiation of a skills and attitude development programme for managers. Now communication strengths and weaknesses are firmly on the continuous improvement agenda for the business.

21

Justifying the Media Mix: What's Out There?

Kate Lynch

European Media Research Director, Leo Burnett, and Member, Research Committee, Media Research Group

The traditional job of the media department in an advertising agency is to ensure that a communication is:

- seen by the right consumers;
- in the right context;
- at the right time;
- at an acceptable cost.

This practice used to be quite straightforward in the UK, when the main media choices were limited. The media marketplace has, however, developed at a rapid pace over the past decade worldwide, and this development is certain to continue for the next decade. We have witnessed an enormous proliferation of media channels and a fragmentation of audiences, which is affecting how advertisers now reach their consumers with their messages.

Table 21.1 details the change in the last 14 years in the availability of just TV and print media in the UK.

Table 21.1

	1982	1996
Commercial TV channels	3	50+
National daily and Sunday newspapers	34	27
Business press	2872	4934
Consumer magazines	1656	2452
Regional press	1300	1925

Why is it changing?

There are several reasons for this prolific change, technological improvements, economies of scale and the deregulation of the media industry:

- Technological improvements in the printing industry have allowed publishers to launch, expand and modify magazines and newspapers at a fraction of the previous cost;
- The development of high-powered satellites has enabled broadcasters to launch satellite channels cost-effectively across large multicountry areas and improvements in digitisation and fibre-optic as well as coaxial cables have allowed cable companies to offer cheaper telephony with the supply of a variety of cable channels to individual households;
- The opening up of communications within Eastern Europe and the other former Communist states, as well as across mainland China, has also encouraged large media owners to expand their total coverage and develop localised versions of their most popular channels.

These vast increases in the supply of delivery systems mean that the consumer has more channels, programmes and publications to choose from; audiences therefore fragment into smaller, and more tightly defined groups.

This fragmentation fundamentally affects the three main components of the communications model – the media owner, the advertiser/marketer and the consumer.

The reality is now that consumers in nearly one-third of the homes in the UK have a choice of over 50 TV channels, nearly 200 radio services and over 164 newspaper sections each week. The vast majority of these new media services are commercial and can be used by advertisers to reach their target audiences. For example, a lager advertiser trying to target 'young male drinkers' is now able to use channels such as Sky Sports 1 and 2, Granada Men and Motoring, supplemented with the sports sections of *The Times*, the *Express* and the *Independent*. Advertisers trying to reach children have seen their choice of TV channels increase from just one, ITV, in 1991, to seven in 1996, with still more expected before the turn of the century.

How do you decide what to use?

In order to justify the mix of media which is used for a brand-advertising campaign, the media planner must first understand the marketing objectives, the advertising objectives and then the communication task. Only by following this procedure can the media planner be sure that they have developed the right media strategy and are choosing the correct mix of media vehicles to deliver the message for the client.

For example, if the marketing objective, say for an airline, was to increase share of business among existing customers by 10 per cent, the advertising task might be to increase loyalty among current customers. The communication objective would be different to the case if the marketing objective was to gain new customers. The target audience is different and the media chosen different.

What do you look for?

The vital questions are:

- What size of target do you want to reach, 10 million or 0.5 million?
- Is there more than one target?
- How many times do you need to reach them?
- Do you want to reach them at a specific time of the day?
- Will the environment in which you reach them matter?
- Does it matter when during the year you reach them?
- Does it matter where they live?
- How quickly will they respond to the message?
- How quickly will they forget the message?
- Are the targets interested in the message?

The most effective media mix chosen depends on the answers to all the above, in relation to the target audience which the advertiser is trying to reach. The steps which a media planner will go through from start to finish are detailed in Figure 21.1.

Previous experience with the advertiser is also useful. Most advertisers are not new, they will have run campaigns the previous year using some media, possibly TV or magazines, and will have some understanding of how it worked.

Media owners and agencies will also have invested in their own proprietary research to study media effectiveness, what media work best and more importantly how each medium works.

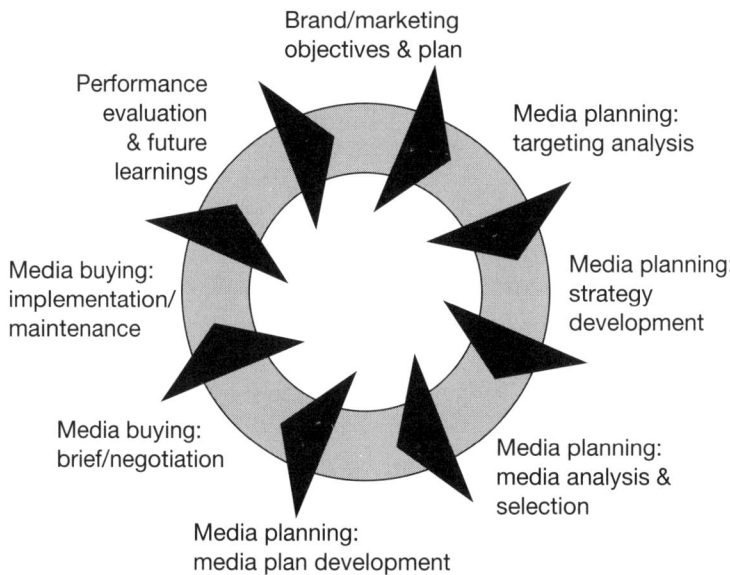

Figure 21.1 The media process

PR plays a crucial role in developing your key corporate **M**essage but it's always difficult to measure its effectiven**E**ss in a quantifiable manner. Strategic Media Measurement (SMM), the only international on-**D**esk PR evaluation system currently available, has changed that. SMM is different because **I**t analyses specific messages in an article within the **A**ctual context in which they are written. The result - pinpoint

WE WILL FIND ALL YOUR MESSAGES

accuracy of interpretation. Which **M**eans you're not relying on one person's general view on the favourability of an articl**E**. So you don't get an overall tone or feel for an article, you get a cle**A**r, individual analysis of the constituent parts so that all hidden messages and comments are revealed. This **S**ystematic approach to PR meas**U**rement allows you to benchmark your current portrayed image, examine the importance of specific individual messages and **R**einforce or change your current messag**E**. Furthermore, it gives you the ability to compare your media image against that of your co**M**petitors in a truly quantifiable fashion. As a company Media Measurement has grown 300% in the past two y**E**ars which bears testimo**N**y to the success of SMM. **Don't wait for your competitors to get in first call us today for a demons T ration.**

M E D I A   M E A S U R E M E N T

Media Measurement Ltd 62 High Street Stony Stratford Milton Keynes MK11 1AQ
Tel: 01908 265011 Fax: 01908 262455

What would make you change the mix?

Cost efficiency is probably the most often quoted reason for changing the media mix, but others include effectiveness, the desire to dominate a medium and a keen eye on what the competition is doing.

Table 21.2 provides an overview of the typical media mix of several advertising categories.

Table 21.2

Charities	
Outdoor	10%
Print	38%
Radio	12%
TV	40%

Jeans	
Cinema	26%
Outdoor	13%
Print	10%
TV	51%

Credit cards	
Cinema	1%
Outdoor	11%
Print	20%
Radio	0.5%
TV	67.5%

Soft drinks	
Cinema	2%
Outdoor	9.5%
Print	1.5%
Radio	12%
TV	75%

22

Media Measurement Standards: Whose?*

Mike Monkman
Mike Monkman Media

To evaluate all the considerations in media selection, the planner needs a great deal of information about the nature of each medium's audience; the pattern of exposures it offers; and how it can contribute to an overall advertising schedule.

The primary purpose of any media research is to provide the very basic currency of exchange between buyer and seller. For any spot, for any magazine or newspaper, the research must tell us how many OTS (opportunities to see) among any particular target audience can be expected. This will aid the media owners in setting their rate card, and also aid both parties in negotiating a suitable rate for particular campaigns.

Further, we will need to know to what extent high coverages of any chosen target audience can be achieved. We would not choose a medium which won't deliver the coverage targets we have set; neither would we want one which won't build up that coverage within the required time span – particularly if we are, for example, advertising a new product and seeking to generate as much trial as possible very quickly.

So the research must describe the medium's audience pattern in detail, and also provide a broad overview of the medium's capabilities.

*This chapter is based on an article by Mike Monkman in *The Media Research Guide*, published by the Media Research Group.

The Joint Industry Approach

Media research must be regarded as acceptable to all parties buying and selling advertising. This has led to the view that they must all have a say in how the research is conducted, achieved by the setting up of Joint Industry Committees, known as 'JICs', to manage the main industry research projects. These JICs typically included representatives of the relevant media owners, advertising agencies and media independents – usually via the Institute of Practitioners in Advertising (IPA) and the Association of Media and Communications Specialists (AMCO), and the Incorporated Society of British Advertisers (ISBA).

Here are the main industry research projects:

- BARB Broadcasters' Audience Research Board. Measures audiences to all television channels, minute-by-minute continuously from a panel of around 4,500 homes.
- NRS The National Readership Survey administered by NRS Ltd. Measures average issue readership for all national daily and Sunday newspapers, and for several hundred magazines.
- RAJAR Radio Joint Audience Research. Measures listening to all radio stations, national regional and local, both commercial and BBC. (But only subscribing stations are reported.)
- JICREG Joint Industry Committee for Regional Press Research. Research into regional and local newspapers.
- POSTAR Previously Joint Industry Committee for Poster Audience Research (JICPAR). Manages a range of research into outdoor media – posters, bus sides etc.
- CAVIAR The cinema and video audience research programme.
- TGI Target Group Index. Unlike all the foregoing, TGI is a commercial venture with no 'joint industry' input at all, other than customer pressure. Many publishers and agencies buy this research which measures media exposure in broad terms, but also measures on the same sample a wide range of product consumption data. The significance of this is the ability it offers to relate these two elements to each other on the same survey.
- ABC Audit Bureau of Circulation. Although not strictly a research project, this organisation is an important source providing independently audited information on newspaper and magazine sales.

Part 5
Internal Communications

23

Managing Internal Communication

Colette Dorward
Managing Director, Smythe Dorward Lambert

The boundaries between internal communication and external communication have never been more fluid. Not just because many more employees now own shares in their own company or actively read the newspapers that report on its activities; a whole raft of social and economic changes are influencing the way people think about their work and the way employers view the need for loyalty, commitment and flexibility from their workforce.

And just as satellite, cable and the Internet are ringing the bell of doom for mass-media broadcasting, so too, internally, the trend is to move away from traditional top-down communication where one corporate newsletter or team-briefing system is deemed to suit all, towards a much more tailored individual approach, where employees are increasingly responsible for the quality of information they receive and generate. In other words, from supply-driven information *push* to demand-driven information *pull*.

Significant evidence of this change is demonstrated by the changing role of internal communication within most large organisations. The role used to be equated with the person, a middle-ranking manager, typically an ex-journalist, whose primary responsibility was to edit and publish the company magazine or produce the annual corporate video. Now there is clear evidence of a more broadly based approach to internal communication, with management teams appreciating the need to make a direct functional link between the business-planning process, marketing, sales and other external communication activities, and the people-management processes driven by the HR function.

Right-thinking organisations keep their need for effective internal communication under continual review, considering three distinct but related headings: information, relationships and change.

Effective information flows

Moving information round today's organisations is a complex affair. Some 'top-down' channels and messages are still needed: common information about the purpose, values and direction of the organisation; its business results; and its strategic goals. So too are appropriate feedback, consultation and involvement processes designed to ensure that individual groups and teams within the organisation are linking with each other in productive mutual dialogue. To manage and assess these activities, the organisation needs to develop a comprehensive communication strategy, integrally linked to the business strategy. Critically, this needs to be agreed by all key managers and functional heads to ensure that it is supportive and supported.

In the context of changing corporate structures, new flexible work patterns and the opportunity for 'technology anarchy' through the wide availability of real-time on-line communication, communication roles need to be clearly defined. In particular, the communication roles of the centre, the operating units and individual functions within the corporate structure need to be agreed, such that the differing influences upon an employee's attention and loyalty are negotiated and agreed. Systems and processes – face-to-face, technology-driven or paper-based – need to be put in place which ensure that key messages from all decision-making activities are distilled and articulated, and their distribution targeted at all those who need to know.

Communication to underpin productive working relationships

However good the internal communication strategy and the channels and processes that support its implementation, not much will change if the people who work in the organisation don't know how to make the machinery of communication work, or if their behaviour conflicts with the communication culture the organisation is trying to engineer.

Working relationships need to be effective at a number of different levels:

- in the workplace: at every level, between managers and employees; managers and teams; teams and individuals; and one department and another;
- between the centre of an organisation and its individual operating parts;
- between the employees of the organisation and its various constituencies: customers; shareholders; outsourced and joint venture colleagues; the community; media; suppliers; and all others influential to its success.

The internal communication strategy needs, therefore, to take account of how awareness and understanding of the organisation's values and desired behaviours can be generated.

On the one hand, this might mean developing communication standards, or guidelines, against which individuals can assess their own behaviour or that of their colleagues, in terms of its fit with the communication culture the organisation is trying to generate.

On the other, typically, it means defining the desired communication competencies and finding ways to make managers and team leaders aware of their own communication styles and how to make these more effective. These competencies and skills, in turn, need to be built into the organisation's human-resource development programmes, such that they are recognised and reinforced through the normal appraisal, reward and performance-management systems.

Achieving successful change

If you've got the right information infrastructure in place and your people are equipped to manage and contribute to a culture that promotes effective communication, what else is needed? Perhaps little except the constant need to refresh and renew the strategy in line with changing needs. Of course, sometimes the degree of change being experienced by the organisation is dramatic and the demands on its collective communication skills are extremely high.

In such cases – corporate restructuring, shifts in strategy, new ways of working, mergers and acquisitions – maintaining productivity and, ideally, heightening motivation are usually critical to the success of the change. A keen focus on communication is required to help top teams clarify or articulate the purpose of the change, but many are still struggling with how to make the experience one of renewal rather than one of paralysis.

Clear messages, effective delivery and feedback processes, and tight project management are needed to:

- Ensure buy-in from the senior teams driving the process and those in the line managing its implementation – both must jointly own the change;
- Create broad understanding of the rationale and processes involved in change among those affected, both internally and externally;
- Ensure those who know most about the area or activity to be changed are sufficiently involved to bring their knowledge to bear on the design and effective implementation of change.

If an organisation's internal-communication strategy takes these three strands into account – information, relationships and change – it will be more capable of challenging and mobilising itself in pursuit of business goals. The communication channels and processes will be used to articulate its corporate voice and transmit the operational information needed to promote its business objectives. For the individual employee, the cultural and performance expectations will be explicit and the level of involvement in tune with the business needs of the day. In short, internal communication has been propelled to the top of the management agenda, playing a critical role in an organisation's success.

24

Communicating Change

Bill Quirke*
*Managing Director, Synopsis
Communication Consultancy*

Lift the lid off almost any business today, and there will be a host of initiatives under way – Business Process Re-engineering, TQM, Customer Service programmes – each demanding scarce time and attention, and all having urgent priorities. Meanwhile, staff complain of initiative overload and pray for a respite from change and a chance to consolidate.

Managing change has become a preoccupation of senior management, but reports of failed change, initiative after initiative, have sobered organisations. Senior management are now trying to get communication right, because they realise in the past they have got it so wrong.

In a survey published by Ingersoll Engineers, poor communication was cited as the single greatest barrier to achieving necessary change within organisations.

> '... managers' apparent resistance to change stems from lack of understanding and the need for more or better communication rather than any underlying wish to oppose change in principle ... Only when communication and understanding of the benefits of change are achieved will commitment be given and behaviour change.'

Organisations need more from communication, but are applying outmoded approaches to employees who are inclined to give less.

* Bill Quirke is author of *Communicating Corporate Change* (McGraw-Hill).

The complexity of work life

While organisations may be shrinking in terms of numbers, and layers may be being removed, life inside is becoming more complex; key timers, outsourced functions, networkers, flexiworkers, sub-contractors, interim managers, franchisees and telecommuters are all alternatives to the traditional employer–employee relationship.

Confronted with change on every front, the typical organisation will have strategic-action teams, cross-functional task forces, supplier-quality groups, and new-product-development project teams galore.

The stretch factor

As more work is now done by fewer souls, people are now more stretched, and the working day has lengthened. There is less time for chat, and the social interactions that used to diffuse communication around organisations. Typically, employees receive 70 per cent of their information on the grapevine, by corridor communication and informal networking. Head-count reductions have damaged these apparently peripheral activities, and have driven social interaction down, eroding the mortar that helps cement different parts of the organisation together.

One organisation found smokers were best informed as, in a no-smoking office, those standing outside smoking crossed all grades, and had the time and opportunity to swap gossip.

Increasingly, organisations are engineering greater social contact between their people to rebuild the social cement. Marks & Spencer, for example, have introduced 'parties with a purpose' to mix business and pleasure and build informal contacts among their staff.

Flexible working brings the danger of greater fragmentation

As companies look more closely at using flexible workforces, and mixing and matching full- and part-timers, the fragmentation threatens to worsen. By the year 2003, it is estimated that 50 per cent of the workforce will be part time, and 70 per cent of those will be women. Part-timers may see the job as only a part of their lives, which has to fit in with other commitments. They will be working short and irregular hours, and it may not be easy to pull them together in one place as a group. Yet they will increasingly come to represent their company to the customer, and it is vital they understand what's going on.

The amount of change has worsened employee suspicion and management's credibility. MORI's norm for the credibility of management is 66 per cent under normal, stable conditions. For organisations going through change, it drops to 49 per cent. Similarly, the norm for understanding of the organisation's objectives is 48 per cent normally, but in periods of change drops to 34 per cent. In times of change, companies have to communicate far more just to stand still.

Information overload

The growing volume of information competing for employees' attention is confusing rather than helpful, and frustration with how communication is managed is on the increase. Each time a new product is launched, or a new business unit is formed, the amount of communication needed to keep everyone informed increases at what seems a geometric rate.

A common complaint is that operating units are on the receiving end of communication sent direct to them, without being first co-ordinated with other functional departments. This lack of co-ordination produces mixed signals, lack of coherence and competition for attention.

From the internal customer's viewpoint, communication seems to be overwhelming and unco-ordinated. Each of the business units busily produces information which it feeds into the communication channels. Added to this, managers engage in 'vanity publishing' – producing updates on their latest achievements and promoting their own favourite initiatives.

The net result of this is information overkill at a local level, with communicators jockeying for attention and time, and creating ever increasing clutter of electronic information, videos and brochures. Meanwhile, the recipients experience information fatigue and put the lot in the bin.

Communication needs to be co-ordinated and orchestrated, with agreed roles between corporate centres and business units, who traditionally compete for employees' 'brain space'.

A lack of understanding of the need for change

In research among chief executives, the most common reason given for the slow pace of change was that people simply did not see the need to change. Worse, they do not seem sufficiently interested in learning about it, and suspect that management is simply crying wolf.

The climate of trust inside an organisation has a huge impact on communication. Where there is a lack of trust, people look for the 'real' agenda and the true meaning of the proposed changes. To do that they use their past experiences to put clues and signals into the context with which they are familiar. Employees opposing any change can see themselves as the 'resistance', or the 'loyal opposition', challenging the data and the interpretations, slowing the advance, and defending the values of the organisation. They are not resisting, they are protecting.

Organisations faced with making changes typically aim to 'sell' the change to their people, and become frustrated when their people decline to buy what they are selling. The lesson to be learned is that often the way change is communicated itself creates the apathy and resistance that was feared. The pain managers feel at the hostile reactions they encounter is often self-inflicted, and caused by their approach to communicating.

Too narrow a focus

Senior managers tend to focus on what they believe employees need in order to fulfil their task, rather than what they need to understand about, and feel part of, the organisation. This mismatch hurts most when those at the bottom of the organisation only receive narrow communication on the specifics of implementing change. The lower down the organisation you are, the less context you have as background to the specifics, the less rationale you understand, and the less sense the specifics make.

The communication collision

Typically at the outset of a change, the board of directors has been through the thought process, and has had the chance to get comfortable with the proposals, evaluating alternatives and understanding why these make sense. The board has the most information and, probably, the greatest level of security, about the implications of change.

People lower down the organisation need some chance to go through a similar process. For people to accept and co-operate, they have to share the thinking. Announcing the conclusions gives them no chance to assimilate the thinking, or understand the context – it is like trying to start a car in fourth gear. The later you leave it, the harder it gets. As you get closer to the implementation of a change, people naturally want answers to their own specific questions. They don't want the big picture, they want the close-up shot so they can see the detail for themselves. At such a stage it is too late to try and explain the business rationale, as employees are now operating on their own personal agendas, and their individual priorities will inevitably be different from those of the business.

Without the context, information does not make sense or have the impact it is intended to. Employees will decode and filter communication from their own position, more often than not anticipating that the organisation is out to do them down.

The stage is set for a collision of interests, and for communication that seems to be pushing the business agenda at the expense of sensitivity to people's immediate concerns. At a time when managers are announcing the new way ahead, people's heads are filled with much more immediate and apprehensive questions about their own future, which makes it difficult to take anything else in.

Share the thinking, not the conclusions

Communication should mirror the thought process that has already gone on within the organisation. In a surprising number of cases, the answers to questions raised by staff have already been considered by the team who first mooted the changes; what is needed is to share the thinking, not simply to announce the conclusions.

Increasingly, businesses are running regular briefings about their business, progress against the strategy, and industry trends. Outside speakers give insights from customers and suppliers, and colleagues provide updates on each other's departments.

Communication needs to be continuous

On average, less than half an organisation's employees know where it is going, and half again get any feedback on progress. Companies are starting to keep their people up to date, running monthly team meetings, quarterly business updates and annual conferences, for all, not just for management. Communication needs to be given time. Because of the pressures of time, managers tend not to explain the rationale or the intention behind specific changes, and neglect to counsel their people, who are themselves feeling pressurised.

Middle managers report that they are caught in the crunch – told by their bosses to communicate, but not allowed the time to do so properly. Increasingly businesses are having to plan-in time for communication – into production schedules, budget allocations and timesheets.

Match the channel to the objective

There is a mismatch between what's wanted from people and the channels used to try and achieve it. Research into the most commonly used communication channels within organisations shows that they are largely designed to distribute messages, not educate employees, or shift their perceptions. Newsletters and videos are fine for creating awareness of issues, but communicating change takes time spent face to face.

While different groups of employees normally receive communication in proportion to their status in the hierarchy, employees' 'right' to communication should be based on their relative importance in the achievement of the business strategy.

Conclusion

Changes in organisations have changed the rules for communicating change:

- Start communicating early – don't wait until you feel you have something to say;
- Where detail is still unclear, communicate probabilities and possible scenarios, describe the timescale, and say when you will communicate specifics;
- Get all communicators – corporate communications, human resources, marketing and operations – to agree a communication calendar, not compete for brain space;
- Involve communicators in early planning of business changes – don't bring them in only when it's time to implement;
- Communicate an umbrella rationale, not a series of standalone initiatives;
- Allow employees the opportunity to vent their concerns, and make it safe to speak;
- Allow managers the opportunity to debate and challenge changes, or their lack of conviction will come across when they communicate;
- Train managers to listen, don't rely simply on good presentation skills;
- Use research to track communication, and publish the results.

The need for change has forced organisations to look at how they communicate and to try and improve it. The world we now find ourselves in has very different rules for communication and, to succeed, organisations will have to learn them.

25

Internal Communications the On-Line Way – Are We There Yet?

Neville Hobson, ABC
Senior Consultant, William M Mercer Ltd

Behind all the media hype about the information highway, a technological and business revolution is in progress, driven by business needs, that will transform the very nature of how organisations conduct business and serve their customers.

Key to this transformation is the organisation itself or, rather, the people who comprise it. Add in four major 'change factors' – increasing competition, new technology, deregulation and globalisation of markets – and it's easy to see that the pressure is on. The need to produce more goods and services faster, and to be more responsive to customer needs, means that every organisation has to change to meet these demands, if they want to survive and prosper.

Throughout Europe, more and more companies recognise the need to move quickly and achieve change in their organisational processes in order to stay one step ahead of their competitors. Indeed, according to research carried out during the past two years, this recognition is fast dawning.

Challenges and change

Electronic Data Systems commissioned a survey in 1996 among 350 company directors of major organisations in eight European countries (Belgium, France, Germany, Italy, the Netherlands, Spain, Sweden and the UK) about the challenges facing European organisations over the next 10 years.

Almost 90 per cent of those surveyed think they will need to redefine the rules of the businesses and markets in which they operate, at least to some extent. Those surveyed said that achieving this will require:

- new and more flexible skills from employees;
- a learning-oriented culture;
- the creative adoption of new technologies;
- new skills from the company's management;
- significant re-engineering of organisational processes.

Three of these relate to human behaviour, indicating that companies are trying to balance the continuing need for process improvement with the need to create flexible learning organisations and develop their people with new skills and knowledge.

In a similar vein, a survey commissioned in 1995 by Oracle Corporation among nearly 300 senior business executives in North America, Europe and Asia/Pacific on the business implications of the information highway produced firm evidence of the impact which new technologies are already having on how organisations need proactively to respond to changing markets.

Into the digital age

Now picture this scene. Your company has 15 branches throughout the UK and 2000 employees who need easy and rapid access to up-to-date information such as product or service descriptions, accurate pricing and customer data.

In the main, such information has traditionally been printed. At best, some but not all employees might have access to computerised versions of perhaps a customer database or contact file. Sure, everyone's on e-mail with lots of information flowing over your computer network. But how can you guarantee that all your people have the right information? How can you be sure they have rapid access to exactly what they need? And how can you ensure that the information available to everyone is up to date?

On the face of it, you can't: unless you give your employees access to the right tools.

The Internet, the World Wide Web and emerging environments such as intranets; e-mail, voicemail, multimedia, television, videoconferencing and added-value public and private information networks – all these embryonic elements of the information highway provide the infrastructure (the right tools) that enables the teams in tomorrow's digital age companies to work together, communicate and share knowledge.

One of the early pioneers in this area is the Ford Motor Company, which some years ago discovered how technology tools can be effectively employed as an integral part of its employee-communication strategies. Recognising that employees are entitled to expect from their leaders a clear and reasonably confident picture of where their business is headed, the company developed an in-house television network both in the United States and Europe that delivers graphic, teletext-style news 24 hours a day, along with the company's own television news and magazine programmes.

Using a combination of satellite, cable and modems connected to Ford's internal telephone systems, the continually updated service reaches employees through television sets installed at more than 300 locations. The daily teletext news is also distributed globally to Ford employees through a bulletin board on the company's e-mail network. New developments under investigation include integrating technologies where, for example, television programmes are distributed to the screens of desktop computers.

While traditional means of communication will not diminish in importance for the immediate future (and personal, face-to-face communication will never be supplanted), the new methods of working to achieve business objectives demand faster, instant means of enabling employees to communicate effectively, as well as establishing clear and open channels to and from those employees and the organisation's leadership. Only technology tools can meet this critical need.

In the new marketplaces, companies will build teams that come together for a particular purpose to meet a customer need. Such teams will be a collaborative effort between employees, suppliers, customers, even competitors, and will be dispersed wherever the team members are physically located, working together across worldwide boundaries. Technology plays a critical role, to enable team members to access, analyse and share information and knowledge, and communicate quickly to exploit fast-changing business opportunities.

'The harmonising effect of being digital is already apparent,' proclaims cyber guru Nicholas Negroponte, 'as previously-partitioned disciplines and enterprises find themselves collaborating, not competing.'

Intranets and business benefits

During 1996, one word captured the imagination of business managers everywhere: intranet. What is it? Compare it to the Internet and then apply that comparison to an individual organisation. In essence, an intranet is an internal Internet that runs on networks within the private and secure 'virtual walls' of the organisation.

What makes an intranet so attractive to many organisations is that it uses open technology standards that are relatively easy to plan and implement at a low relative cost – significant reasons why comparative and proprietary knowledge-sharing tools such as Lotus *Notes* are restructuring their offers.

A classic example of how the successful deployment of an intranet can help radically improve business processes and enable clear communication channels is at Hewlett-Packard, which currently has the world's largest intranet, connecting more than 100,000 personal computers and workstations in its offices worldwide. It transports 1.5 million e-mail messages every day and approximately 7 terabytes of information every month – the equivalent of a stack of paper 350 kilometres high.

With the advent of its intranet, HP is enjoying measurable business benefits, including greater organisational flexibility and an explosion of information sharing among its employees.

Many other organisations see the potential of intranets as a highly effective communication tool. Ford is investigating the introduction of an intranet-based news service for employees, containing news, pictures and eventually video and sound.

Of course, such benefits also apply to smaller organisations – you don't need to be a major multinational to gain the benefits of an intranet.

Tomorrow's world

You'd be forgiven for thinking that all you've read so far paints a rose-tinted picture of a communications Utopia with technology as the universal panacea. Don't lose sight of one essential fact – all of this represents purely the power to achieve things, not the end result. And it's purely a snapshot of what you can already do today.

As for tomorrow, the currently disparate elements of the information highway will come together – 'converge', in the parlance of the IT business – to enable organisations everywhere quickly to take advantage of new ways of working and communicating. In turn, this means they will be well placed to empower their employees with the tools and the abilities to communicate and share information with anyone, anywhere and at any time.

We're not quite there just yet. But we're definitely speeding down the slip road, preparing to join the main highway. It's unlike the typical motorway, and there's no 70 miles per hour speed limit on an intranet. The slow journeys to be found on the Internet due to high volume of traffic don't apply so much on an intranet, because it's a private network, without the variables that affect the public Internet's performance.

More information is available on-line:

- Electronic Data Systems European directors survey – www.eds.com
- Oracle information highway survey – www.uk.oracle.com
- Ford Motor Company – web.ford.com/global/
- Hewlett-Packard and intranets – www.hp.com

26

How 'Investors in People' Helps Corporate Communications

Clive Bonny
Director, The Solutions Organisation

The purpose of this chapter is to highlight the processes and business benefits available to organisations that commit to becoming an 'Investor in People'. The reader will learn the extent of success for this benchmark of quality in corporate communications. This chapter also summarises why organisations use the standards as a yardstick to measure internal communications, the process involved in winning this national award, and what direct benefits result for employers and employees.

What is 'Investors in People'?

IIP is a framework for organisations of all types and sizes, to measure themselves against in order to improve the way they manage their internal communication and training processes. The framework consists of 23 indicators published under the four principles of *Commitment, Planning, Action* and *Evaluation*. These indicators provide guidance on good practice to help managers commit to supporting their people by planning, actioning and evaluating appropriate ways of communicating with, and developing the potential of, their employees.

Within the first five years of its introduction no less than one-third of the UK's entire workforce were employed by organisations who were committed to the IIP standard. This is a clear indication of its success, and there are already numerous case studies published by employers confirming the direct business benefits resulting from their commitment and successful assessment.

Some examples of results highlight the extent of this success:

- A chemist with 54,000 employees and 110 stores increased operating margins from 7 per cent to 11 per cent;
- A retail stationer with 15,000 employees and 500 branches saw a 41.5 per cent increase in profit within two years and a 40 per cent reduction in labour turnover;
- A manufacturer with 12 employees saved 60 per cent on purchase costs and improved customer spend by 200 per cent;
- A solicitors' practice of 45 employees extended its range of services and improved net profit by 45 per cent;
- A borough council with 650 employees achieved higher service levels, despite a 13 per cent reduction in manpower;
- A building group with 1500 employees reduced accidents by 50 per cent and increased market share.

Many of these business improvements began by employers making a commitment to a standard without being able to fully quantify the outcomes. Now that these organisations have completed the 'journey through IIP' and publicly shared their success stories there is no reason why *any* organisation should not follow their example and reap equivalent reward.

How can companies make this journey?

The process begins with an initial 'diagnosis' against the standard. This is available from consultants trained and vetted by the Training and Enterprise Council. The purpose of the diagnosis is to enable an organisation to identify where it does and does not meet the standard. This helps to calculate what is needed to win the award. More importantly, the surveys which are performed as part of the diagnosis accurately identify communication problems and bottlenecks within the organisation at all levels and across all groups.

The survey examines the business plan, and assesses how successfully employees understand the main aims of the organisation, their team's goals and their personal objectives. Misunderstandings of overall vision or mission commonly result in people pulling in the wrong direction. Managers are often unaware of the extent of dilution in the messages as their information travels through others. The combination of written and verbal surveys conducted by an independent IIP consultant can identify the degree to which people understand the big picture and how their own roles contribute.

The effectiveness of communication channels is also audited, identifying the strengths and weaknesses of information being transferred across and upwards. In a larger business this can be particularly important in helping senior executives respond quickly to address more immediate commercial opportunities or problems.

The consultant will usually complete the diagnostics with both a verbal and a written report, and can, if required, subsequently help the management team draw up an action plan to address any issues identified. In doing this, two key points are realised: those affected by any problems can contribute to solutions; and ownership of issues can be delegated 'down the line'.

The consultancy time for this initial step usually ranges from two days (for small businesses) to ten days (for larger organisations), with the Training and Enterprise Council typically funding 50 per cent of the costs. Consulting fee rates are also usually significantly lower than normal commercial consulting rates, enabling a communications audit to be performed in a highly cost-effective manner with very little management time.

Furthermore, the Training and Enterprise Council will often continue to subsidise the implementation of the action plan through to final assessment against the standard. They can offer additional services to improve the communication skills of managers and staff with consequent improvements to customer communications. Their consultants will invariably also share with the client how and why they undertake their diagnostics processes, thereby enabling the clients to replicate them without continually relying on outside help. In many instances the consultant will introduce the client to other organisations which have already undertaken the journey and which can act as a benchmarker. This network of over 25,000 companies in the UK represents a sizeable opportunity for the learning organisation.

Here is a selection of quotes from a few who have experienced the process:

- *'The Investor in People award has given us common ground to become a learning organisation.'*

  Personnel Manager, Brooke Bond Foods

- *'The Investors in People standard is all about having a vision for the future and communicating it to your staff in such a way that they understand what is required of them. Then providing training and development opportunities for*

them so they can help the company move towards its vision by meeting busi-
ness objectives.'

Personnel & Administration Manager, Ciba Agriculture

- *'Investors in People complements very effectively our philosophy of creating a*
  professional and highly motivated workforce.'

Managing Director, Center Parcs

Ninety-four per cent of those organisations that have applied for and have
achieved the standard have stated that they would willingly do it again. To
help these become even better, the standard has recently been revised. This
will make it even more difficult to attain, thereby stretching applicants further and equally improving their communication skills and processes, so
that, as a nationally recognised award, it will continue to act as a standard-
bearer.

Its dramatic success in only five years had led other countries, from the
Netherlands to Australia, to participate in trials to install it. The international business community is already noticing its impact on the bottom
line.

27

How One 2 One Involved Employees in Developing a New Brand Positioning

Annette Allen*
*Former Employee Communications
Manager, One 2 One*

Background

One 2 One, the mobile-phone service which was launched in September 1993, was the third entrant in the UK's mobile-communications industry. That year, Cellnet and Vodafone, the other two contenders, had around two million mobile customers between them, with most bills paid by businesses, owing to the high call charges.

A joint venture between US WEST and Cable & Wireless, One 2 One was determined to be completely innovative and change the market from a business-user emphasis to one where mobile phones were an essential part of consumers' lives.

They launched One 2 One in a blaze of publicity as 'the mobile phone, for everyday, for everyone', with coverage in London's M25 beltway area and a great offer – free evening and weekend local calls for every customer. Despite the phones' prices, £300–£350, people flocked to buy them in high-

* Annette Allen is now Director of Words into Action.

street retailers like John Lewis and Dixons, leading to supply problems. Free calls proved so attractive that people were soon ditching their old BT phones.

One 2 One's customer-services department was contactable, toll-free, 24 hours a day, all year round. The company was inundated with people either wanting to buy the service, complaining their phone hadn't been delivered, or ringing to ask general information about mobile phones. After overcoming its initial supply problems, it managed to attract 65,000 customers just seven months after launch. But the impact of dealing with consumers soon took its toll – in the sheer volume of calls to the call centre and on its systems. One 2 One was a victim of its own success, which affected employee morale as well as customer satisfaction.

Offering free local calls was never sustainable in the long term, as all the pundits predicted. The company had major congestion problems (where customers were unable to make or receive calls) in some parts of London after 7pm, and it was spending millions of pounds to increase the network capacity in these areas.

In July 1995, the board agreed to increase network rollout to reach 65 per cent of the UK by the end of 1997, as poor coverage was affecting sales and market share; and to drop free evening calls forever, repositioning the brand.

In September 1995, two years after launch, a new logo was introduced to communicate to existing and potential customers that the company had changed; it introduced new price plans without free evening calls, while retaining previous customers by preserving their right to free evening calls.

We communicated the change to employees at all sites with an all-employee meeting, supported by professionally produced videos. Everyone took away an information pack and they had a special copy of *One 2 Another* (our internal magazine) later that week. We measured the impact of all this and our people felt it had been clearly communicated. What many didn't like was the new advertising. One commercial showed a man in a loo trying to answer his mobile, and the second some 20-somethings out for a good night in a bar. It made a number of people feel very ashamed of the brand.

Needless to say, consumers didn't respond well to the new campaign and it was pulled before Christmas. Our new marketing director was determined to review all the activity, and put in place a proper positioning for One 2 One, based on a market which by then (January 1996) had 5 million users – 50 per cent greater than in September 1993. In addition, industry growth predictions were becoming more bullish as phone prices and call charges tumbled, with most industry analysts quoting 12 million users by 2000.

By April 1996, the company had six sites and just under 1800 employees, with an average age of 29.

Brand development

Extensive market research was carried out between January and March 1996 to establish what existing and potential customers thought of mobile communications, and just what they wanted from the 'ideal' operator. One 2 One found that they viewed the industry as a 'shark pool' – similar to double-glazing salespeople or used-car dealers. What they really wanted was to be listened to – to have a service from a company that made any contact simple and that took action once it had listened to customers.

The company took the opportunity to involve employees in the research, particularly customer-services people, who heard on a daily basis just what their customers wanted from the service.

The new positioning – that One 2 One listened to its customers, was committed to them and was professional about it – had to be turned into a creative brief for all the marketing-services agencies, and everything had to be in place for the peak selling season in October 1996. It was also crucial for all employees to demonstrate the new brand values to their customers.

Developing the employee communications plan

The challenge was to make sure that the following objectives were met:

- to demonstrate how much thought and research had gone into the new positioning;
- to position it as a credible evolution (it was the third in three years, therefore open to cynicism among employees);
- to persuade managers to see their role in demonstrating the new brand values to their teams.

Within that context, specific segments were targeted:

- senior managers, who needed to be fully supportive of the new brand;
- line managers, who had to become champions for change among their teams;
- customer-facing employees, who needed to understand the new positioning, as well as the detail of the new procedures with regard to their job.

A cross-functional team was established, consisting of market research, employee development, PR and employee communications. The plan was to announce the new proposition to employees first, then brief the external markets. The dates were set for 30 September and 2 October 1996 respectively.

The 1996 employee survey revealed that success was vital, because less than 40 per cent of employees were proud of the company's image. However, employees' level of satisfaction was very high – 74 per cent – so there was a great deal of goodwill to build on.

In the early autumn of 1996, an additional £1 billion was raised from financial institutions and the shareholders further to accelerate the network rollout – to cover 95 per cent of the British population by the end of 1997.

Communications timing

Senior managers were briefed on the process for new brand development in March 1996, and customer-facing employees helped in developing internal views of the existing brand and the new positioning.

A series of workshops about the new brand positioning and its impact on their role was given to line managers during September, while meetings were held with senior managers to consider the impact on future business strategy. Customer-facing people participated in workshops about the new brand positioning and then undertook training on all elements of the new proposition the same month.

Ending on 1 October 1996, 43 all-employee meetings to cover the changes were held in two days and the new brand positioning was announced externally the following day.

Results

Questionnaires were used after the all-employee meetings to gauge opinion. These established that 75 per cent felt very positive about the changes:

- 'This time we have listened to our customers and employees which is extremely positive';
- 'New logo looks clear, hip, and simple – which is how we want to be seen by Joe public';
- 'Well researched … easily stands up to Orange and Vodafone ads'.

Conclusion

This carefully implemented plan has enabled One 2 One to 'mesh' people at all levels in a meaningful, relevant way. Equally, employee communications demonstrated that integrated planning and effective employee communications can make a difference. It is possible to measure 'soft stuff' to deliver concepts such as business strategy and customer focus. In essence, the company succeeded in humanising business strategy.

The communications department benchmarked its performance through the annual employee survey. In 1995 and 1996, One 2 One had come in the top three for 'effective communication' among a group of 'best in UK' companies, including organisations like the AA, BA, BT, 3M and Rank Xerox.

Part 6
The Media Business

28

Trends in UK Advertising Media

Bob Wootton
Director of Media Services,
The Incorporated Society of British
Advertisers Ltd

Overview

As elsewhere in business, the underlying trend in the UK media scene is towards rationalisation, synergy and the resultant economies of scale. Bigger media companies are getting bigger, absorbing others so as to be ready for a time when six or seven players are expected to lead the global media industry, though the debate continues to rage over whether our current regulatory regime prevents indigenous media companies from achieving sufficient critical mass to compete on the world stage.

This process of consolidation is already accelerating in anticipation of the Broadcasting Act (see Chapter 31), which got on to the statute book in late 1996, and whose provisions pave the way for some further shakedown of ownership of the media. Advertising and media-buying agencies are also consolidating, with over 80 per cent of all television advertising bookings now being placed through the top 25 buying points.

Advertisers are clear in their desire for a vibrant media scene, offering strength and diversity of communication channels through which they can reach their target customers, but are also keen that the market continues to be well-regulated, as past evidence suggests that media companies can be quick to overexploit strong trading positions.

Overall Trends

Figures 28.1 and 28.2 show trends in UK media spends over the last five years, with projections for the next five. In broad terms, Broadcast continues to grow at the expense of Graphic media.

Television now accounts for 33 per cent of all adspend and is set to grow further as digital technology allows many new channels to air, providing both new targeting and entry opportunities for advertisers.

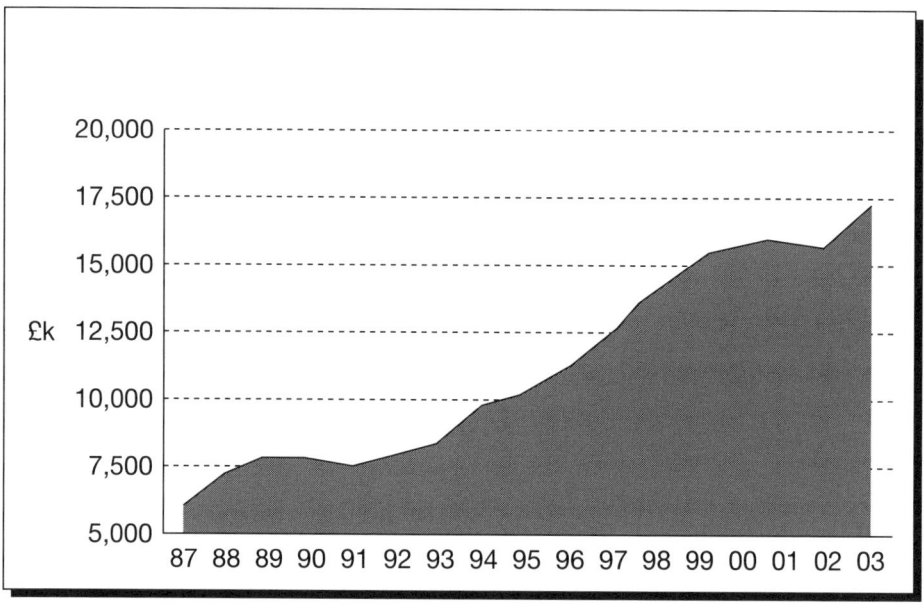

Figure 28.1 Growth in total advertising mediaspend 1987–2003

Television

The UK is unique within Europe in that almost half (currently 43 per cent) of all TV viewing is of channels which are funded by a licence fee and carry no advertising – BBC 1 and 2. This has implications for advertisers, as the lack of access to a large proportion of the viewing audience serves to raise the price of reaching people through the available channels.

The average UK home has at least two television sets, with 20 per cent having three or more. More than three-quarters of homes have a video, and a quarter receive satellite or cable – a figure which is expected to rise to 45 per cent by the year 2000.

But the advent of successive new channels – Channel Four in 1982 and over forty satellite stations since 1985 – has not served to increase the com-

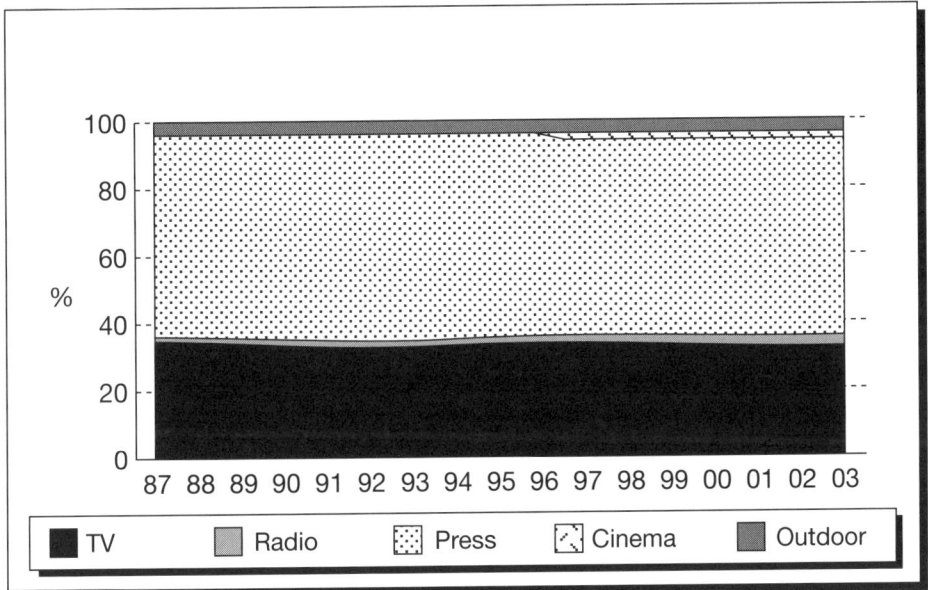

Figure 28.2 % share of adspend by medium 1987–2003

mercial viewing audience significantly. Rather, it has merely tended to fragment it. Against this, it is hoped that the advent of the new near-national Channel Five service in early 1997 will help to draw viewers from the BBC's channels into an environment where they can be reached by advertisers.

Nor has the awarding of ITV licences to the highest bidder, which took place in the last franchise renewal round of 1990, served to improve ITV companies' output as measured by the audiences they achieve. The 1996 Annual Report from the Independent Television Commission (which is responsible for regulating UK commercial television) shows that while programme investment is static in real terms, the ITV companies' profits and shareholder dividends have risen steeply.

Inflation in the cost of reaching their target customers is running well ahead of RPI, and is thus a major concern among advertisers. This is seen in particularly stark relief by those who also operate in other European markets, where they are seeing the cost of advertising static or even falling as new channels come to air.

The near future will see the start of digital broadcasting, which offers the opportunity to fit many more channels into the existing terrestrial and satellite wavebands. Rupert Murdoch's British Sky Broadcasting has already stated its intention to broadcast up to 500 new channels, many of these being used to run movies starting at 15-minute intervals to maximise audience. (This is known as 'Near Video on Demand.')

Further off, we will see the much-vaunted convergence of broadcasting, computers and telecommunications becoming a household reality. As the television screen becomes a multi-purpose item in the home of the future, capable of accessing many channels, some offering interactive services, some downloadable programmes (true Video on Demand) and some very narrowly-targeted, so the range of communication channels available to advertisers will burgeon, but so will the fragmentation of audiences.

National press

Whereas many other countries are characterised by stronger regional press media, the UK has a very strong national press, though circulations are in long-term decline as newspapers gradually give ground to new, usually electronic media.

The market is also characterised by fierce competition between a few powerful media owners. Price promotion, first exploited when News Group cut the cover price of *The Times* to 10p in 1994, has proved to be a powerful and sometimes enduring method of building circulation and readership share, albeit at considerable cost. Only players with deep pockets can afford to play at this table!

The 1980s saw the arrival of several new titles, notably in the Sunday Market – the *Independent*, *Independent on Sunday*, *Sunday Correspondent* and *News on Sunday*. The first two still survive, though both experienced difficulties which resulted in their being acquired by Mirror Group Newspapers two years ago, evidencing the consolidation and even closure that are characterising the national press in the 1990s.

This trend was given further weight in 1996 when News Group finally pulled the plug on *Today*, the ailing mid-market tabloid it had bought from its founder, Eddy Shah, back in 1987.

Yet amidst this turmoil, 1996 has seen the launches of several new titles – maverick Tom Rubython's *Sunday Business*, which is understood to be circulating less than 100,000 copies each week at the time of writing, and the *Planet On Sunday*, which holds the record for the dragonfly of the media world, only lasting for a single launch issue before its backers withdrew support!

Sections continue to proliferate, often launching and then closing at will; the UK's 19 daily and Sunday newspapers currently appear as no less than 100 sections.

Magazines

Despite increasing competition from other media, principally broadcast, the magazine industry is buoyant. The number of consumer magazines has risen 20 per cent to about 2,200 in the past ten years, while cover price increases continue to outstrip inflation.

Over the last five years, an entirely new sector has grown from nowhere to cater for the young men's market, and EMAP plc, previously a publisher of regional newspapers and specialist magazines, has become one of the country's largest consumer magazine publishers.

Publishing technology and low entry costs maintain healthy competition in the market as new players constantly enter at the bottom end to challenge existing titles. This fierce competition forces publishers to keep close to their readers – those that do, succeed, while those who lose touch atrophy, and are absorbed into others or scrapped.

Radio

Commercial radio stations have been broadcasting in the UK for just over 20 years, and the medium has recently shown signs of maturing. Its revenues have climbed sharply, and the share of total advertising spend it achieves has breached 4 per cent for the first time.

Much of this success is attributed to the Radio Advertising Bureau, an industry-wide generic marketing body which aims to facilitate the use of radio by removing all the barriers to its purchase.

There are presently 174 stations of very different size and editorial complexion across the UK; from the national stations like Classic FM to small local stations such as Bay FM in Blackpool, from general entertainment stations such as Capital in London to dance specialists like Galaxy FM, based in Bristol. The dominant player in the field is Capital Radio plc, which is both one of the largest owners of radio stations and, through its MSM subsidiary, also controls nearly two-thirds of the market for national airtime sales.

The last London-wide FM licence before digital broadcasting arrives on the scene is about to be awarded, the favourite contenders being music-based stations which promise to cater for a younger, independent music-oriented audience. At last, some would say.

Cinema

Cinema has enjoyed a renaissance over the last decade, with almost every year reporting admissions higher than the last. 1996 admissions are expected be about 126 million.

This is attributed to two things: the movies themselves, particularly ever more spectacular (and expensive) Hollywood blockbusters and surprise successes, like the British hit 'Four Weddings And A Funeral'; and the refurbishment of cinemas, usually in the form of multiplexes – multi-screen centres with parking and restaurant facilities.

Carlton, holders of the London weekday and Midland ITV franchises, have recently diversified into cinema by buying Cinema Media, the sales house responsible for some 80 per cent of all cinema airtime. This is seen as a 'good fit' as cinema's strengths against the young may enable them to strengthen their overall sales proposition, given that ITV is relatively weaker in the Southeast and against younger audiences.

Outdoor

Although it is still the medium of 'men up ladders with bills and pots of glue', the major outdoor site contractors have risen to the competitive challenge presented by other media by upgrading the quality of their plant and the way in which it is presented.

Much of this, it must be said, is due to a French invasion. Both J C Decaux, who operate precinct sites, and Havas Avenir, owners of roadside contractor Mills and Allen, have brought a new professionalism to the market which the other players have been quick to emulate. Two sizes now dominate the field: 48-sheet (20-foot by 10-foot) roadside panels and 6-sheet 'adshels' (illuminated bus shelter sites). More 'ultravisions' – sites comprising rotating prisms which show three different subjects on the same (usually premium) site – are also appearing, indicating that the revenues they can generate far outweigh their higher initial capital cost.

New media

If media were ranked not by revenue but by the column inches of coverage they receive, the Internet would currently be the biggest medium of all! Yet beneath the vast hype, the medium is, nevertheless, growing almost exponentially – there are now over 200,000 UK-based web sites alone – and is truly both international and cosmopolitan.

It also provides challenges to advertisers wishing to exploit it successfully, as it offers its audience the opportunity to edit not only its contents but its very appearance. Advertisement content and placement alike thus have to be reconsidered from the ground up, making new demands of advertisers and their marketing-services suppliers.

Computer games have become significant advertising media for those targeting youth, while screensavers are now widely used to target domestic and office environments, and are particularly popular in a business-to-business context.

New-media consultancies are burgeoning to capitalise on the opportunities presented by these 'new' media, and the first media sales house which facilitates advertiser access to genuinely relevant sites has recently been launched.

Conclusion

The UK and indeed the global media scene is experiencing more change than it has ever seen before, and this rate of change is further set to increase.

Yet as has been observed in the US, the major established media 'brands' continue to enjoy the bulk of audience patronage – for example, the networks still take about 70 per cent of all TV viewing, while ever more channels compete for the rest. This model is likely to show the way forward in the UK for the next few years at least.

Sources for all data : Industry sources/Zenith Media

29
Global Media Trends

Daphne Luchtenberg
European Marketing Manager,
Shandwick International

A networked computer is no longer just a wordprocessor; it is a gateway to the world, they say. And that's not all. Accelerating technological change means that we will soon be able to say the same about our telephones, videos and much more besides. They are all gateways to the world.

A latter-day Rip Van Winkle who dropped off to sleep a decade or so ago – when newspapers, phone companies, broadcasters and computer manufacturers kept themselves pretty much to themselves – would wake up today to a multimedia world where nothing is quite what it seems.

Suddenly, companies are marketing via computer, phone companies are broadcasting TV channels and niche markets are increasingly made up of single individuals who take decisions themselves to look at an Internet site and then move on.

Information is everywhere. But paradoxically, the more information becomes available, the lower its quality. We increasingly fail to take in the whole picture, and the little we do absorb consists mostly of opinions about the facts and not the facts themselves.

The result is that prejudices tend to increase rather than decrease. There are more controversial views about more controversial subjects, which is why PR people who deal with public opinion – especially across international borders, like Shandwick – are increasingly busy.

This is only one of a range of paradoxes which seem to govern the fast-changing media world: more information is available, but less of it is useful. More money is spent to market to niches which are increasingly narrow. And then the key paradox of all: although the cliché of the shrinking world has never been so true, there is a corresponding interest in the local, in the familiar and in cultural traditions.

These two trends – globalisation and localisation – are the keys to understanding the new media world which is emerging.

Globalisation

The globalisation story is hardly new, but during the 1990s it has reached a fresh chapter. Stories about a European company, for example, can appear in the *Financial Times* in London at breakfast – and simultaneously in FT editions published in the USA and Asia. What's more, the editions are printed locally.

CNN has changed the nature of television news: you can watch the same pictures on TV sets in any one of 100 countries at the same time.

There are also a spiralling number of people in financial institutions, business, government and the law who have Bloomberg terminals – or something similar – which keep them instantly up to date with news around the world.

This new globalisation has spawned the following trends:

- *More interactive news:* while fewer young people are watching traditional television news, there has been an explosion of news on-line. The world's top newspapers – from *The Times* to the *Wall Street Journal* and *Le Monde* – now have Internet sites. CNN and the big three American TV networks now have their own news Internet sites as well;
- *Fewer outlets:* the media ownership of newspapers, magazines and broadcasters is being concentrated in fewer hands;
- *More competition over news:* at least six business-news channels have been battling for European viewers. CNN and BBC Worldwide are now head-to-head across the world;
- *Fewer players:* the arrival of digital television will mean that BSkyB, for example, will be able to broadcast 150 TV channels simultaneously. The global media conglomerate News International is first in the field with a digital 'box' decoder in the UK, which has led to fears here that one company will be able to dominate the TV delivery system;
- *Tabloidisation of the news:* the four serious British 'broadsheet' newspapers devoted as much as 1752 column inches to the liaison between actor Hugh Grant and a Los Angeles prostitute. Chat shows, talk radio and other new television concepts are increasingly popular. The Amer-

ican talk radio host Rush Limbaugh can command an audience of up to 20 million.

Localisation

PR professionals have been talking about global PR for years, but there is something about the phrase which is a contradiction in terms.

When the American congressman Tip O'Neill said that 'all politics is local', he might just as well have been talking about public relations. Getting it right on the ground, understanding the dynamics of each world market and what to emphasise where, is how PR has always worked.

Fears of media domination by Microsoft or News International, or fears that global brands will drive out local identities, are driving a corresponding interest in local diversity, in underground or traditional culture, in the religious, cultural and faddish.

These trends are conspiring to make sure that the world does not end up homogenised, and they are driving some of the following:

- *Increasing political pressures to back local culture:* Hungary's TV privatisation requires guarantees of high levels of local programming. European Union rules are similar;
- *More narrowcasting:* publications, cable TV outlets – not to mention Internet connections – focus increasingly tightly on narrow niches. Organisations can scrutinise, say, the performance of semiconductors or pharmaceuticals in depth as they happen and make their perceptions instantly available. This has a corresponding impact on the global audience;
- *Local marketing:* Disney has been buying local US sports teams to plug its brand name directly into local culture.

Technology

The impact of electronic mail, groupware, mobile communications and the Internet has changed the way we all work forever. It has also changed the speed at which decisions can be made and the way organisations can collaborate and communicate.

A new set of global alliances has been forged between telecommunications and software companies to drive these changes further. Microsoft in particular has hammered out strategic alliances in almost every emerging market. Its link-up with MSNBC has enabled it to get into TV broadcasting. Another alliance with Hughes Network Systems Direct PC/TV means

American personal computers will be able to receive up to 175 satellite TV channels.

While 23 million people worldwide are now surfing the World Wide Web, nearly twice that number are using the same technology for e-mail. More Britons are currently hooking up to the Internet than are subscribing to satellite or cable television. There are nearly 700,000 Internet users in the UK already. A similar growth is going on in Internet advertising: $37 million worldwide in 1995, probably over $310 million in 1996 – and it may be more than double that by 1998.

The explosion of technology looks set to drive some of the following trends:

- *Convergence of media:* increasingly the media will become part of a single digital 'platform' including television, telephone, CD players, radio and computer – although this will mean major investment by the entertainment broadcast industry;
- *Converging sales functions:* advertising, sales and marketing will increasingly become part of the same effort – targeting a personal message to narrowly defined individuals;
- *24-hour commerce:* world commerce will increasingly compete round the clock, 365 days a year, constantly updating and retargeting its messages.

We have been in the forefront of using these new technologies to communicate to key audiences. The new field of 'Net relations' is already playing an important role, where we began successfully promoting our own complete Internet package, Spiderworx. Even before it was launched in November 1995, Spiderworx had attracted clients like Northwest Airlines and Polaris Industries.

Advertising agencies had been providing Internet home pages for their clients, but – until Spiderworx – the full communications possibilities of the Internet were barely being fully thought through, let alone exploited. Then it became clear that Shell might have been able to anticipate its problems over the dumping of the Brent Spar oil rig, if only it had read what was being said about it on the Internet.

Our own home page – <http://www.shandwick.com> – was launched in 1995. It went one step beyond its rivals by including interactive features to attract the attention of browsers and to build relationships with them – like 'SourceFinder', which provides contacts to journalists, and 'Doing Business with Shandwick', which allows potential clients to brainstorm PR problems by e-mail for free. All the trends which are driving the new world of media – globalisation, localisation and new technology – are coming together in the way the big media companies are merging, shifting places, creeping outside their traditional markets and jockeying for position.

Disney has launched its own Internet-based shop, selling Disney paraphernalia. TV, film and publishing companies such as Time Warner are battling with telephone companies like Bell Atlantic over cable television investment. Microsoft has relaunched its own Internet network, providing shopping, entertainment and information. Time Warner, which is planning a new TV channel in the UK, already has cinemas here, plus High Street stores and plans for a theme park north of London.

Media competition looks set to spread to other areas like sport. The enormous BSkyB deal with the Premier League will plough as much as £670 million into soccer between now and 2001. After that, there has been speculation that the clubs could launch their own pay-per-view TV channels.

In this way, communication has entered a new world which is reinventing itself every few months. We have to be flexible in our understanding of global and local markets, constantly upgrading skills, services and products. But it also means adapting to the new communication needs of clients: as the boundaries between the different media blur, the message itself becomes increasingly important.

That is why public relations skills, which are all about honing messages, are increasingly vital. That's what the new media world is all about.

30
Regulatory Trends

Arthur Pryor*
*Head of Competition and Regulation
Group, The Public Policy Unit*

A number of challenges lie ahead in the area of commercial communications – the promotion of products and services (or of the image of a company) to consumers and/or distributors through all forms of advertising, direct marketing, sponsorship, sales promotion and PR. This chapter looks at prospective regulatory developments and their implications.

Different UK and EU traditions

The UK has traditionally relied extensively on self-regulation against the backdrop of 'bedrock' consumer-protection legislation, primarily the Trade Descriptions Act. Advertising controls at the national level are mainly exercised through the twin Codes of Advertising and Sales Promotion Practice administered by the Advertising Standards Authority. PR codes are maintained by the Public Relations Consultants Association and by the Institute of Public Relations.

Elsewhere in Europe, a different tradition has often been the norm, with a preference for prescriptive regulation by public authorities. Current examples include formal limits on:

- discounts, loyalty premiums and price discounting;
- advertising of non-prescribed pharmaceuticals and alcohol;

* Arthur Pryor was formerly Head of DTI Competition Policy Division.

- the content of teleshopping or on-line services;
- sponsorship of events and audiovisual programmes.

More generally, there has been a culture of specific regulation to protect aspects of the national interest (eg plurality of the media) or to promote social goals. The picture is nonetheless not uniform across the rest of Europe. Self-regulation has its adherents and there are substantial differences in regulatory practice.

The Commission green paper

The agenda for further consideration of this issue at EU level has been set by the Commission green paper of May 1996 on commercial communications. The Commission is alert to the view (held with particular force by the UK) that, under the principle of subsidiarity, a Community regime should not be imposed on activities which lack a Community dimension and are properly the responsibility of the member states. The Commission has, however, undertaken an extensive comparative review of member-state regulatory practices and has concluded that differences in the restrictions imposed could create barriers to the internal market. This provides the basis for EU action.

The green paper concluded that:

- cross-border commercial communications are a growing phenomenon;
- differing national regulations pose obstacles to cross-border transactions, to the disadvantage of consumers
- this situation will get worse as more such communications flow across frontiers and as Europe moves into the information society.

Since most regulations are not overtly discriminatory between national and non-national firms, the Commission has proposed a methodology for assessing the 'proportionality' of national measures (both existing and proposed). This means making an assessment of the extent to which such measures may go beyond what is strictly necessary to protect a legitimate public-policy interest, and amount to a restriction on the free movement of goods or services.

Next steps in the EU

The conceptual approach of looking at the economic effects of regulation (and self-regulation) from the standpoint of facilitating the opening of EU markets looks preferable to the alternative of promoting 'harmonisation for harmonisation's sake'. But the devil will be in the detail; at the moment, it is not clear how the methodology would be applied within the frame-work of existing EU infringement procedures. The scope for conflict with member states' own views on proportionality is considerable. The danger for the UK is that a common EU position (determined by qualified major-ity) will tend more towards prescriptive regulation than we would wish.

The position of the current (1996) UK government continues to be to resist EU proposals seeking to introduce more restrictive and costly con-trols. The government argues for self-regulation in the negotiations in Brussels on legislation likely to affect advertising, eg of tobacco and alco-hol or toys and anything directed at children.

Regulation in the UK

Looking at the situation in the UK itself, there are signs that consumers and other interests now seek regulatory responses with legal backing rather than relying wholly on self-regulation. The fall-out from the Nolan Com-mittee's report on standards in public life has perhaps encouraged the view that enforceable rules-based solutions have the advantage of apply-ing to all participants in a market, not merely to those who acquiesce in self-regulation. This trend might become more pronounced under a Labour government, although a wholesale attack directed at self-regula-tion is unlikely. Labour is committed to banning tobacco advertising and statutory status may be given to industry codes to ensure that alcohol is not targeted at young people.

Some elements of the UK regime for advertising and sponsorship already contain what might be termed prescriptive elements. The Codes of Advertising Standards and Practice and Programme Sponsorship main-tained by the Independent Television Commission, and the Advertising and Sponsorship Code maintained by the Radio Authority, flow from pro-visions in the Broadcasting Act of 1990 (which itself in part implemented a 1989 EC Directive on TV broadcasting activities). The respective regulators can impose sanctions (although in practice implementation of the codes is largely on a self-regulatory basis). Similarly, the Securities and Investments Board has the power to control advertisements by firms regulated under the Financial Services Act 1986.

Misleading advertising

Misleading advertising was the subject of a 1984 EC Directive, imple-mented in the UK by the Control of Misleading Advertisements Regulations 1988. These empowered the Office of Fair Trading (OFT) to take action against any advertisement calculated to deceive the consumer or damage a competitor. OFT cannot seek compensation or other redress for any complainant; its role is simply to prevent the publication of misleading material, for example by seeking an injunction. But OFT will not intervene in this way unless the case is exceptionally serious and/or other channels (such as the ASA's codes) have been exhausted or are inapplicable. In practice, OFT's involvement is rare: the ASA deals with 10,000 complaints a year and has referred only eight cases to OFT since 1988. In only a few cases has OFT needed to take the initiative itself by seeking undertakings to bring misleading advertising to an end.

Moves have been under discussion for some time to extend the scope of the directive to include comparative advertising. This illustrates the sort of challenge which the UK will now increasingly face. The Commission's aim is to promote the internal market through greater standardisation of the regulatory treatment of comparative advertising, the use of which is currently severely restricted in some EU countries. Some may say that this is not a priority area for EU action, but the UK government and industry have been generally favourable to greater harmonisation if it has a genuinely liberalising effect. Comparative advertising is regarded as an effective marketing tool which stimulates competition.

There is no perceived need for change in current UK comparative advertising controls, which are based on self-regulation and trademark legislation. The question, therefore, is whether a more standardised regime can be secured without obliging the UK to introduce more restrictions (eg by encouraging more legal challenges to advertising claims). Present indications are that an outcome acceptable to the UK may be achievable. Judgements on trade-offs of this kind are likely to become a standard feature of the UK's response to EU legislative proposals on commercial communications.

Role of the European Parliament

A further complicating factor these days is the role of the European Parliament, which is prone to add restrictive elements to proposals even after a hard-won consensus has been achieved at the Consumer Affairs Council. Amendments proposed by the Parliament have, for instance, significantly delayed progress with another proposed directive dealing with distance selling (direct mail, TV advertising and direct response, catalogue orders, fax, electronic mail and telephone selling) throughout the EU. Practical proposals to facilitate trans-border movements (and trans-border consumer protection) will be welcome so long as undue restrictions are not imposed.

Regulation of lobbying

I share the view of many within the institutions of government that lobbying, as distinct from reputation management directed at the system, is not a 'communications' activity. Much of the current concern over alleged unethical activities is underpinned by irritation, on the part of MPs in particular, that they are too often treated as targets of inappropriate PR techniques. Poor – rather than dishonest – lobbying has led to a re-examination of the regulation of professional lobbyists, which currently operates on a voluntary basis. One option being mooted is for Parliament to take a more direct interest by declaring its 'expectation' that third-party advisers should be regulated by 'approved bodies' – which could be the Association of Professional Political Consultants, PRCA, Law Society or Institute of Chartered Accountants – putting the spotlight on those not prepared to offer government and clients safeguards against abuse of the system or negligent advice.

The future

The focus of regulatory activity to date has been largely on advertising and sales promotion; attention is now turning to other aspects of commercial communications (notably in the fields of telecommunications, intellectual property, legal protection of databases, encrypted services, audiovisual services etc). Equally, other initiatives dealing with cross-media ownership and access to the media, and proposals for the conditional access regime for digital television broadcasting, will have implications for those active in public relations and marketing. A close eye should be kept on regulatory developments.

Advertising Standards – A short guide
by the Advertising Standards Authority

Most people are familiar with the well-publicised advertising code that 'all advertisements should be legal, decent, honest and truthful', but the Advertising Code itself is an extensive document which covers everything from advertising to children to promoting cures for baldness.

The Committee of Advertising Practice is a self-regulatory body that devises and enforces the codes in Britain. The Advertising Standards Authority is the independent body responsible for ensuring that the system works in the public interest. The ASA's activities include investigating complaints and conducting research.

There are detailed codes (and legal requirements) governing the promotion of competitions with prizes, free draws and instant-win offers.

As might be expected, the code covering alcoholic drinks is particularly restrictive and includes such directives as 'advertisements should not portray drinking alcohol as the main reason for the success of any personal relationship or social event ... nor should it be suggested that people who drink are brave, tough or daring for doing so ... A brand preference may be promoted as a mark of the drinker's good taste and discernment.'

Slimming claims are similarly carefully proscribed, including: 'Short-term loss of girth ... achieved by wearing a tight-fitting garment ... should not be portrayed as permanent nor should it be confused with weight loss.'

The code also covers environmental claims, motoring, health and beauty, distance selling, list and database practice, employment and business opportunities, financial services and products, charity-linked promotions, trade incentives, free offers and cigarette advertising.

For further information contact:
Advertising Standards Authority
2 Torrington Place
London WC1E 7HW
Tel: 0171 580 5555
Fax: 0171 631 3051

31

The Broadcasting Act, 1996*

Claire Beale
Associate Editor, Campaign

What is the Broadcasting Act?

The Broadcasting Act 1996 is a 194-page document that sets out a new framework for the media industry to take it into the next millennium.

Who created it?

The Act was drawn up by the Department of National Heritage, and was shaped by extensive industry consultation and a lengthy passage through Parliament.

Why did they bother?

According to the National Heritage Secretary, Virginia Bottomley, the Act is designed to give media organisations the chance to expand, develop new services and exploit new opportunities, transforming the broadcasting and communications landscape.

* Reprinted from *Campaign* (30 August 1996). Used with permission. © Haymarket Campaign Publications Ltd.

'We must now move forward to a dynamic, deregulated, flexible and innovative media industry,' declared Bottomley, and the Act 'will allow us to be a major player in the emerging world market.'

When did it come into effect?

The Act received Royal Assent at the end of July 1996. Most of the digital broadcasting provisions came into effect on 1 October and the media ownership provisions came into force on 1 November 1996.

Why should I care?

The Act could potentially have enormous implications for the entire structure of the media industry.

So what are the main points?

There are two main planks to the Act – new rules on cross-media ownership and legislation governing the introduction of digital television.

What is cross-media ownership?

In the past companies have been prevented from having too much power in the media industry by being restricted on the share of a particular medium they can control and the influence they can have in other media.

The new cross-media ownership rules allow greater concentration of ownership in an individual medium and enable companies to expand into other media.

What will be the effects of the new cross-media rules?

Brace yourselves for fevered takeover and merger activity among television, press and radio companies. Many players – big and small – will be swallowed up in the race for synergies across different media, concentrating power and investment into the hands of fewer, larger operations.

So it's all about media concentration, then?

Not exactly. The digital broadcasting provisions will herald an expansion of media opportunities – a host of new channels catering to niche and not-so-niche audiences.

What does the Act say about ITV licences?

TV companies used to be restricted to owning two ITV licences. The Act allows a single company to own any number of ITV stations, up to a limit of 15 per cent of the total television audience.

What will this mean for ITV's structure?

This is the green light that the big players have been waiting for – they can capitalise on their original ITV investment by taking a greater share of the network through snapping up smaller companies.

Who are the major ITV players at the moment?

ITV is already roughly carved up among three big operators – United News and Media, Carlton Communications and Granada Group. These three are expected to consolidate their interests through the acquisition of smaller ITV stations.

What are the opportunities for national newspapers and TV companies to merge?

National newspapers with less than 20 per cent of national circulation will be able to own any ITV or other broadcast licence up to 15 per cent of the total TV audience, and a TV company can control up to 20 per cent of the newspaper market. Newspapers with more than 20 per cent will be able to own broadcasting licences outside of ITV, Channel 5 or analogue radio as long as they do not exceed the 15 per cent market limit.

Wasn't there a tussle over the provisions for newspapers?

One of the most contentious provisions of the Act is the rule preventing national newspaper groups with over 20 per cent of national circulation from owning more than a 20 per cent stake in a Channel 3 (ITV), Channel 5 or radio licence.

The Labour Party argued throughout the preparation of the Act that the 20 per cent limit should be abolished and has now indicated that it will revisit the issue should it come to power at the next General Election. Crucially, this provision means that neither News International nor Mirror Group will be able to expand into ITV territory.

What are the prospects for local newspaper groups?

A similar rule applies. A local newspaper with more than 20 per cent of newspaper circulation in its area will be able to control a national broadcast licence but not a regional Channel 3 licence in the same area.

Local newspapers with less than 50 per cent of local circulation will also be allowed to control one AM and one FM radio licence in their area.

Local newspapers with more than 50 per cent of their market will be allowed to control one local radio licence provided that there is at least one other commercial local radio licence serving the same area.

What about radio companies?

Like television, the numerical limits on local radio licences controlled by a single company have been abolished and replaced by a ceiling of 15 per cent of the total radio market.

Is there much room for growth in the radio market?

Most of the big radio groups have very little room for expansion in their own medium. Emap already has just under 15 per cent of the total radio market, while GWR has around 12 per cent.

In any given area, a single radio company can hold up to three local radio licences, as long as one of them is an AM licence and one an FM licence.

What about cross-media ownership between national TV and radio, then?

The old rules governing joint ownership of TV and radio stations remain largely the same under the new Act. The main change is the provision allowing a regional Channel 3 licence holder to own one national radio licence.

Can regional TV and radio get together?

Regional ITV companies will not be allowed to control radio licences in their area, and vice versa.

What does cross-media ownership mean for media buying?

David Cuff, broadcast director of Initiative Media, says that cross-media ownership will result in fewer negotiations and in deals being done at a higher level. 'Where companies can develop sales strategies across their media holdings they will become very powerful, and will be able to talk to advertisers at a very senior level. They will develop more far-reaching relationships with their advertiser clients,' Cuff explains.

Will media companies need to adapt?

Bigger conglomerates selling across media will be even more powerful around the negotiating table, so buying muscle will remain an important requisite for a media company.

What does the Act say about Channel 4?

Channel 4 has been battling for several years to end the formula whereby any excess advertising revenue it makes is handed over to ITV or put into statutory reserve.

The Act ends payment into the statutory reserve and will phase out the payments to ITV from 1998. The phasing out of the funding formula should mean more money for Channel 4 programmes, making it better able to compete in the TV arena of the future.

What provisions are being made for the BBC's commercial activities?

Any commercial services launched by the BBC will be licensed and regulated by the Independent Television Commission under the provisions set out in the Act. This brings the BBC's advertising- or subscription-funded services into line with the UK's other commercial television channels.

What is digital broadcasting?

Digital broadcasting is a method of compressing the TV signal to allow more signals on to a broadcast frequency than is possible using analogue technology.

Why is digital part of the Act?

Digital broadcasting will revolutionise the media framework by introducing a vast array of new television and radio channels to UK consumers. These new channels will have to be allocated and policed and the Act makes provisions to ensure their smooth introduction.

Will terrestrial channels be invited to the digital party?

The terrestrial TV channels will each be allocated a digital TV licence for broadcasting their existing channels.

How will the other digital licences be allocated?

The 12-year TV and radio licences will be awarded by the ITC and the Radio Authority on the basis of which applicants are likely to do most to promote the development of digital broadcasting.

Will cash bids be involved in digital allocation?

The licences will be free for the first licence period to encourage investment in digital broadcasting. After the first licence period all digital service providers will have to pay a percentage of their revenue to the Exchequer.

What does digital broadcasting mean for advertisers?

Crucially, digital broadcasting will mean more outlets for advertisers to promote their products. These outlets will, in many cases, be more tightly targeted than terrestrial channels, which means less wastage. The digital revolution could also result in more opportunities for advertisers to move into programme supply as the proliferation of channels leads to a surge in demand for editorial material.

How will digital broadcasting affect media buying?

The rapid growth of advertising outlets will require greater understanding of a client's target market and more research of media consumption, often working off very low levels. Planning skills will come to the fore more than ever before.

Who will ensure that programme and editorial standards are maintained throughout this period of change?

As well as the Radio Authority and the ITC – which will monitor licence holders to ensure that they fulfil the terms of their contracts – the Act establishes a new body to ensure that certain standards are maintained. This new watchdog will be formed from the merger of the Broadcasting Standards Council and the Broadcasting Complaints Commission. The merger will create a single forum for public concerns about taste and decency and will monitor violence and sexual content in TV and radio programmes.

What about ensuring that 'national' events are available to everyone?

There has been much concern that the new era of media choice could lead to a bidding war for major sporting and national events, which could result in them moving on to subscription channels and away from general access.

The Act guarantees the availability of live coverage of certain listed events such as Wimbledon to free-to-air TV channels like the BBC and ITV.

Part 7

Marketing Communications

32

Seamless Marketing Communications

Amy Smith
Marketing Director, McCann-Erickson
and
Gerard O'Neill
Member, McCann Strategy Group

Marketing used to be simple. So simple, it could even be left to marketing managers. But it isn't like that any more and this chapter will tell you why, as well as what you have to do about it, while there's still time. Very simply, managing directors and chief executives are beginning to realise that marketing is too important to be left to the marketing department. Of course, it always was, but in the past the marketing task was sufficiently straightforward for CEOs to delegate the task of designing and implementing marketing strategy. Not any more. The business of marketing – namely creating value by managing customer relationships – must be central to corporate management and financial planning. Marketing must be seamlessly woven into every function of those companies intent on getting to the future first. Here we examine why this is happening now, and how some leading edge companies in Europe are already practising seamless marketing.

The 'whole egg'

The fashion, at least among marketing managers, is to describe this process as 'integrated marketing'. Or even 'integrated marketing communications' for those preferring a three letter acronym – IMC in this instance. The concept of integrated marketing has been around for a long time: back in the 1980s, Young & Rubicam called it 'the whole egg' approach to marketing communications. But then, as is still often the case now, integrated marketing really just meant co-ordinated marketing. At the very least, the point-of-sale materials should reinforce the sales promotion drive which should support the direct mailshot which ideally should build on the advertising campaign. Not forgetting public relations. Unfortunately, this tended to become too much, and more often than not, even co-ordination proved too difficult.

Of course, the intention was always genuine, even if the execution lacked finesse. The consequences, however, were rarely fatal (either to sales or to careers), though we could all tell stories about sales promotions initiated by one part of a company which undid in one fell swoop the entire brand-building intent of a major television and press campaign sanctioned by another part. But that was then…

A decade and more into total quality management, zero defects and business process re-engineering, co-ordination is not enough. And a lack of co-ordination is inexcusable. Integrated marketing is not so much an idea whose time has come, as a style of managing that has already become mainstream in all other business disciplines. Marketing is just catching up with the nineties.

More bang for your TV ratings

So what is integrated marketing? The standard definition portrays it as the co-ordinated application of an array of communication tools to achieve a specific set of marketing and sales goals. Integrated marketing, therefore, recognises that different marketing tools have different applications for different audiences. Above-the-line advertising and PR should create awareness and develop the product's or service's positioning; direct marketing should turn that awareness into interest; while sales promotion should convert interest into actual purchases. Audiences should include not only customers but also employees, suppliers and shareholders. The challenge then is to apply the appropriate marketing tool to the appropriate task, spending the marketing budget wisely in a manner that is more effective and more efficient. At least, that's the theory.

Too often, however, so-called integrated marketing has been used to:

- reduce the overall communication budget and to switch a greater part of what is left below-the-line;
- abandon brand support and positioning campaigns, replacing them with sales promotion efforts;
- push product at the market, rather than invite customers to reveal their preferences.

The result is not so much integrated as frenzied: substituting activity for strategy. And it works ... for a while. But just as the drug addict needs higher doses over time in order to get the same effect, so the frenetic marketer needs to send out even bigger mailshots and offer even greater discounts in order to get the same, temporary blip in sales as the last time.

Practised thus, integrated marketing is unsustainable. Practised as it should be, integrated marketing could actually transform the ways companies think about and relate to their customers – a transformation that will pay enormous dividends over time.

So how should it be practised? Before we answer that, let us take a brief look at integrated marketing from the customer's viewpoint – such is supposed to be the perspective of marketing anyway. After all, the dynamics now shaping our customers are the real drivers of the movement towards seamless marketing.

I want it all and I want it now

If you want to picture the future, imagine a two-year-old with a credit card, an Internet account and an IQ of 180. As every parent will vouch, toddlers can be very demanding. Unreasonably so, in fact. They are, however, the customers of the future. Today's consumers have grown up with consumerism. They are confident and sophisticated users of a range of media, and they are already literate in all the 'tricks' that marketers use to sell their wares.

They have also become used to being the centre of attention, and they know that their opinions, their needs and their money matter an awful lot to the same marketers. And that's just the parents. If your worst nightmare is predatory pricing by your biggest competitor, wait until you meet the coming generation of predatory buyers out surfing the global cybermall, armed with intelligent agents...

But in the meantime, a dangerous chasm has opened up between many companies and their actual and potential customers, driven by:

- *a decline in trust*   In the marketplace of the late twentieth century, you are, as a corporation, guilty until proven innocent as people see all the traditional icons of authority come tumbling down around them;

- *a decline in loyalty*   Commitment has become contingent, and you are only as good as your last encounter in the marketplace, with every slip up affording your competitors an opportunity to take your customers away from you;
- *an increase in anxiety*   Pressures of time, pressures at work, and pressures in the home are all adding to the high stress levels that people experience, and to a sharp decline in tolerance for anyone who fails to deliver the right product, at the right price, at the right time, every time;
- *an increase in differentiation*   With many markets at saturation, the only viable markets are niche markets, a trend supported by a movement towards consumer pluralism characterised by more diverse needs, a greater variety of behaviour patterns and of circumstances, financial and otherwise.

Add to these the challenges of media fragmentation, information overload and rising communications costs and it should be clear why integration has become such an important theme in marketing practice in the late 1990s.

The message is not the meaning

We have a saying at McCann-Erickson: 'the message is not the meaning'. Which is to say that you should never presume that the message you send is the same as the one that the customer sees (or hears or reads). People interpret, they don't record. Hence our discomfort with the term 'integrated marketing'. Yes, it is necessary these days to ensure the proper co-ordination of marketing and sales programmes across the appropriate range of communications channels. But in our opinion, and in our experience, this is not sufficient. At least not if the goal is to embark upon a sustainable path of marketing communications designed to effect long-term, profitable changes in consumer behaviour.

We prefer to explore with our clients the theme of 'seamless marketing'. In effect, this means 'marketising' the entire organisation from the boardroom to the delivery van. It is, in a nutshell, about nothing less than synchronising – through marketing communications – the values and goals of the company with the attitudes and needs of the customer.

Thus, the management of marketing communications goes well beyond programme and media co-ordination, necessary as this is. Rather, it reaches inwards to the centre of the company, to the core values that imbue the organisation's purpose and practices. It then reaches outwards to the hearts and minds of customers; aligning the two together through effective, efficient and empathic communications. An alignment that will ensure that the right people get the right message ... and that the company gets the right results.

Such results are nothing less than stunning. At United Parcel Services, for example, we worked with our client to develop an external and internal communications programme designed to position UPS as the best express service provider in Europe. A 15-country campaign was designed which not only communicated the UPS offer to key decision makers in corporate Europe, but which also equipped the van drivers themselves with information and handouts designed to bring our client's Europe-wide message, in person, right to the customer's doorstep.

We have developed the Casa Buitoni Club for Nestle (over 100,000 UK members already); designed carelines for companies who previously didn't know the names of their consumers; and engaged Britain's children in 'pea popping' competitions! Examples from work with different clients designed to achieve the same end, namely: the creation of a relationship between the client and its customers that is meaningful for both parties; that provides the basis for win-win growth in the future; and that builds upon professionally co-ordinated above-the-line and below-the-line communications activity. A relationship that exists between the company and the customer: not between the marketing department and the marketplace.

Imagineering

Marketing isn't simple any more. Perhaps it never really was. But now we all know that a new approach is needed in order to survive and flourish in the years and decades ahead. That approach has been called integrated marketing. But hopefully it is clear by now why we don't think that that is the right term to use any more.

Walt Disney came closest, in our opinion, to the essence of the future that we have already begun to explore with our clients. He called it 'imagineering': the combination of imagination with engineering. Seamless marketing is like that. The same need will always exist for creative communications – for 'Truth Well Told' as our founders put it. But that must now be combined with the disciplined management of the communications process, both within the organisation and externally with the customer. We think of it as managing the 'mechanics' – the actual system of communications, as well as the 'humanics' – the actual creative content.

But such a task is clearly beyond the boundaries of traditional marketing demarcations. The challenge of communicating with the future is one that must engage everybody in the organisation, a process that must be led from the top. Nothing less is demanded, while nothing more than a new century of success is promised to those who rise to the challenge.

International Executive Development Programmes

Second edition

Consultant Editor: Philip Sadler

"... this guide will be a valuable source of reference in an area which is central to the success of any global business." SIR MICHAEL PERRY, CHAIRMAN UNILEVER PLC

The second edition of this important international directory is the ideal resource to address the problem of executive development. The directory covers: management development programmes, open learning programmes, in-house company training programmes and a special section on executive MBAs. It includes:

- profiles of training organisations
- an extensive listing of over 3,000 organisations
- a series of practical articles written by leading management experts, business academics and industrialists.

£75.00 Paperback ISBN 0 7494 2257 2   400 pages A4   May 1997

Ethics in Organisations

David Murray

The question of ethics in business has become a major concern for many organisations in recent years. Avoiding the theoretical stance too often adopted by writers on the topic, David Murray shows how managers can approach the dilemmas they face in an uncomfortably complex world. Looking at both top-level policy and the day-to-day concerns of people throughout a company, this book shows how everyone can make a real difference within an organisation.

David Murray is an independent consultant concentrating on the field of business and professional ethics. In recent years he has worked extensively in the post-communist economies of Central and Eastern Europe.

£13.99 Paperback ISBN 0 7494 1592 4   160 pages   April 1997

The Corporate Healthcare Handbook

Consultant Editor: Helen Kogan

In order to comply with government and EU legislation, organisations of all sizes are committing themselves to 'best practice' in corporate healthcare.

Published in association with The Industrial Society, this new book aims to be a comprehensive guide for all organisations who have made this commitment. It provides authoritative and practical assistance on all aspects of health in the workplace, and guidelines on implementing strategies for good corporate healthcare. With illustrated case studies providing greater insight, this accessible handbook is a 'must' for all healthcare managers.

Topics covered include:
- cost/benefit analysis
- risk assessment
- health and safety issues
- health promotion
- work organisation

With a membership of over 10,000 organisations, and a 77-year track record, The Industrial Society has unparalleled knowledge of what constitutes 'best practice' in the management of people and how to achieve it.

£20.00 • Paperback • ISBN 0 7494 2154 1 • 320 pages   Published April 1997 • Order no: KT154

More information on these and other titles can be found in Kogan Page's comprehensive *Catalogue*.

To request a copy please phone or fax the marketing department on:

Tel. 0171 278 0433 Fax. 0171 837 6348.

Kogan Page's books can be bought from good booksellers or direct from Kogan Page's customer services department on 0171 278 0433, quoting the reference number for the title and your credit card details.

Payment can also be made by pro-forma, or by cheque made out to Kogan Page Ltd and sent to:

Kogan Page, 120 Pentonville Road, London N1 9JN, England

33

Brands: What's Happening to Them?

Stuart Crainer*

Brands are an ever-present part of our lives: from the clothes we wear, to the food we eat; from the toys our children play with, to the drinks we consume; from our mobile phones to our cigarettes. We read about brands in our carefully branded newspapers. We are loyal to brands and almost everything appears to be capable of being branded – from turkeys (thanks to Bernard Matthews) to bananas (Geest).

Not only has the world of brands expanded to take in virtually everything that can be made, provided or breathed, it has re-invented its traditional relationships. Small, locally available products have been converted into nationally and internationally renowned money-earners. Sleeping giants – such as Lucozade – have been transformed into commercial success stories drunk by top athletes at every available photo opportunity.

The world of brands has expanded. Once it was dominated by fast-moving consumer goods. Now it is filled with retailers – from Kwik-Fit to St Michael, Dixon's to Benetton – and financial services companies (banking services such as First Direct, building societies and insurers).

For all this activity, the function of brands is fundamentally straightforward. Brands are little more than prompts, symbols and representations; activities which have been used since we started buying and selling things. Brands are marketing shorthand which companies hope will lead us to purchase their particular products.

* Stuart Crainer is author of *The Real Power of Brands* (FT/Pitman 1995), and editor of *The Financial Times Handbook of Management* (FT/Pitman 1995).

Brands have become associated with the hard-selling entrepreneurial superficiality of the 1980s when deals were everything and brands changed hands as readily as stolen watches. The 1990s have brought brands back down to earth. Companies now appreciate that brands are neither frivolous nor a necessary evil, but important, expensive and potentially lucrative investments. That they are now all-embracing is a fact of life, caused in part by the human need for re-assurance, labelling and ease of identity.

Brands are exciting. For business people and consumers, the world of brands appears invigorating and sometimes glamorous. It is the world of Bacardi advertisements and multi-million pound campaigns. But, there is much more to brands than this alluring image. There is also, for example, a comfort factor. Brands may pander to our dreams and aspirations – beaches, sunshine, not a worry in the world and a glass of spirits too – but they also re-assure. We like the idea of a life of excitement and unlimited finance, but settle for having a drink in the comfort of our home. The brand becomes a surrogate for our ambitions and dreams. The successful brands are the ones which we are comfortable with, but which are not complacent. They sell us Caribbean dreams at an affordable price. We know what the brand does, what it looks like and how much it costs, and the best brands continually meet and exceed our expectations.

The brand states ownership

At its simplest, branding is a statement of ownership. Cows are branded and, in the commercial world, branding can be traced back to trademarks placed on Greek pots in the seventh century BC and, later, to medieval tradesmen who put trademarks on their products to protect themselves and buyers against inferior imitations. (Of course, in the modern world people are adept at copying trademarks – whether they are Lacoste, Sony, Rolex or Le Coq Sportif – and producing imitations, which are often highly accurate.)

The brand is a product

In the beginning came the product. Branding was a mark on the product – a signature or symbol – signifying its origin or ownership. The traditional view of what constitutes a brand is summed up by marketing guru Philip Kotler in his classic text book *Marketing Management*. Kotler writes:

> '(A brand name is) a name, term, sign, symbol or design, or a combination of these, which is intended to identify the goods or services of one group of sellers and differentiate them from those of competitors.'

The trouble with older definitions of brands is that they remain preoccupied with the physical product. The product stands alone; the brand exists within corporate ether. The product comes first and the brand does little more than make it clear which company made the product and where. John Pemberton's brain tonic is the product, but the brand is much more.

A more recent definition comes from Richard Koch in his book *The Dictionary of Financial Management*. Koch defines a brand as:

> 'A visual design and/or name that is given to a product or service by an organisation in order to differentiate it from competing products and which assures consumers that the product will be of high and consistent quality.'

Reflecting the emphasis of our times, Koch stresses differentiation, making your product or service different (or seeming to be different), and achieving consistent quality.

The brand provides information

An editorial in *The Economist* acutely observed:

> 'The point of brands is, and always has been, to provide information. The form of that information varies from market to market, and from time to time. Some products make a visible statement about their users' style, modernity or wealth – examples include clothes, cars and accessories. Others purport to convey reliability, say, or familiarity, or something else. Whatever the information, however, the right question to ask is this: does the buyer still need or want it?'

It is easy to underestimate the amount of information a brand contains. There is the physical information – the contents, ingredients, weight, calorific content – and there is the abstract information – the statements about the user, the associations, the memories.

The brand is an experience

With hyper competition and constant change, companies have sought to do more and extract more financial worth from their brands. Increasingly, people's perception of what constitutes a brand is widening. Instead of being sacrosanct and untouchable, the product is beginning to be regarded as just one element of the brand. While in the past the product came first and other elements followed, now the product is a single component of the marketing mix alongside price, promotion and distribution.

Some idea of the complexity of modern brands can be seen by looking at retail brands such as Sainsbury and Marks & Spencer in the UK. The total Sainsbury or M&S brand is made up of not only the store, its location and contents (size of product range etc), but also the quality of service, range of own-label products, price competitiveness and even trading hours. The brand is all-embracing, whether or not the store has an EPOS system is a brand-related issue, as is its layout and the quality of its service.

The product is now recognised as only part of what the consumer experiences of the total brand. Note the emphasis on experience; customers used to buy things, now they *experience* them. We are in a new era, where brands are positioned as having emotional and lifestyle benefits which are transferable across several products, rather than being narrowly identified with a particular product.

In this new era, brands are driven by consumers. They are psychological, as well as physical; brands are about hearts and minds. To look at the product in isolation from the overall package is no longer possible – the simple purchase is perceived as an experience.

In a world of brand profusion the dividing lines are no longer clear. Brands overlap and interact continuously. The category they belong to is not important – what matters is how they add value to what consumers experience and to the organisation.

The brand is delicate: handle with care ...

The world may be increasingly filled with brands of all types, shapes and sizes, but it is also cluttered with expensive brand disasters. Quantity does not usually increase quality. Brands may be big and brash, but they are also delicate: managers and organisations must handle them with care.

... and, the brand is robust

Brands have to be managed sensibly and cautiously otherwise they can fall to pieces in your hands. No one can sit still – even Moet & Chandon is now advertising. But, alternatively, brands can be incredibly robust, defying any notion of product or market maturity. The best brands go on and on, outlasting fads and competitors, proving their competitive worth time and time again.

34

Advertising Trends

Alan Cooper
*Chairman, Account Planning Group, and
Director, Simons Clemmow Johnson*

'To get into best society nowadays, one has either to feed people, amuse people or shock people – that is all.'

A Woman Of No Importance
Oscar Wilde

Since the advertising industry discovered that creativity, rather than simple 'hard sell', was an important ally in promoting a client's product, humour and shock have been used liberally. Leviathan brands such as Hamlet and Heineken have used intelligent humour to great effect since the early 1970s. Likewise, advertising for political parties and for many government 'anti' campaigns over the last two decades have used the tactics of shock. Consumer brands, such as Tango and Benetton employ shock approaches – as do many charities in their advertising.

These two styles of creativity (and there are others) have arisen in response to the mushrooming levels of media availability that have led to people becoming over-saturated with advertising. Many consumers, in particular younger ones, have become highly advertising-literate. Selling messages have to be 'wrapped' with entertainment in order that the advertised brand has the strongest opportunity to be remembered and motivate its audience. The legendary US advertising man, Bill Bernbach, recognised this development as early as the 1960s when he said:

'Nobody counts the number of ads you run; they just remember the impression you make.'

As the millennium approaches three key dynamics are influencing consumer advertising to produce a new trend. The emerging wisdom is that it is no longer sufficient to build a brand by advertising a relevant message in an entertaining way. Brands are becoming successful in the long term by building relationships with their target consumers. Advertising's role is to initiate the relationship and, in tandem with other forms of more direct communication, nourish it. Developing strong consumer-brand relationships adds a further dimension to the purchaser's loyalty: it helps to protect the brand from competitive threats such as new launches and the ever-increasing pace of product technical innovation. The adage that it costs five times as much to recruit a new user as it does to retain an existing one is being put into practice in 'relationship marketing'.

The cost of marketing

The first dynamic helping to bring this about is the closer scrutiny which companies pay to marketing costs. 'Marketing at any cost' during the boom of the 1980s has been tempered permanently into 'marketing with prudence'. However, one marketing cost that continues to enjoy strong growth is the cost of media – this makes direct marketing, an important channel for nurturing consumer-brand relationships, an attractive option for marketeers.

Media fragmentation

The second dynamic is media fragmentation, which helps advertisers practise increasingly subtle and detailed consumer targeting. No longer are media audiences defined by broad demographics: segmentation by lifestyle and attitude enables an informed advertiser to reach exactly the right audience with greater efficiency. Given that even big brands have relatively small bases of important regular users,[1] accurately targeted advertising can be used to sustain a regular 'dialogue' with its core consumers. Response mechanisms are used (eg telephone number, website address) to nurture the relationship by making it two-way. A recent survey concluded that 21 per cent of all TV advertisements (and 40 per cent of all satellite TV advertisements) carried a response mechanism – ten years ago this figure

---

[1] 'Pareto effect' estimates that 80 per cent of a brand's sales can be attributed to 20 per cent of its consumers.

was less than one per cent. On the day this article was written, an informal survey of the national newspapers found that 78 per cent of all display advertising contained an invitation for the reader to respond. Two-way advertising is here to stay.

The power of the retailer

The third, well-documented factor is retailer power. Increasingly large proportions of sales in most consumer sectors are channelled through a declining number of retailers. Their influence over brand owners becomes stronger every year. Brands that can build ongoing, direct relationships with their consumers can exert a greater control over their own destiny. Intelligent brand owners use this direct relationship to learn more about their consumers and, hence, re-address retailers' advantages in this respect. Many companies have taken this to its logical conclusion by launching brands that are available only direct to consumers: financial services is a prime example here.

Best practice – clear and simple

So how does this relationship-building trend manifest itself in advertising: what guidelines are there for best practice? Lessons can be drawn from understanding relationships between individuals in real life.

Be honest

Attempts to flatter or deceive will be seen through. Consumers, and the advertising regulatory bodies, are aware of ploys that are used to hype claims and are dismissive of those who perpetrate them. Relationships flourish on the basis of trust.

Reward the consumer

This need not be financially based, but it can be rooted in intelligent, practical information. Consumers are increasingly interested in seeing behind the brand, finding out about the company, its attitudes and its people. To be given 'insider information' signals to the consumer that they are respected (and valued) by the company. For instance, Sony maintain a website which informs its hardware owners of the latest software often before it is available in this country.

Invite response

If the relationship is two-way, consumers will feel more committed and involved with the brand. Response can range from stimulating fresh thoughts to provoking action to ask questions and find out more. Since 1994, the British Heart Foundation charity has built a relationship with the public, informing them about the problem of heart disease. Advertising carries a phone number which has drawn high levels of enquiries – remarkably so, given that the campaign runs principally on large poster hoardings on major roads!

Amaze and surprise

Relationships flourish when the unexpected happens rather than the routine and predictable. One should not rely simply on the creative idea to be amazing. The strategy and message of the communication should strive to surprise and challenge consumers: it should look to the future rather than be over-reliant on consumer research and, so, reflect only the present. Sales of Boddingtons have grown quickly, exploiting the previously un-ale like quality of creaminess, while many consumers' relationship with Haagen Daz's ice cream was initiated by advertising the deadly sin of lust.

The relationship should evolve over time as both the brand and consumers' attitudes change; relationships that are static wither. The heart of Nike's relationship with its consumers has always been sport. However, over the years, via a spectrum of advertising, the relationship has evolved by embracing the humour and 'show business' of sport, its power, its grace and athleticism, its inherent competitiveness and the social issues that surround it. This has resulted in Nike becoming an extremely rich and strong brand which can provoke massive response and passion from its audience: testimony to a deep relationship that consumers have developed with it.

Advertising's growing realisation of its ability to initiate and develop consumer relationships will give it a fresh and important role over the next decade. In moving along this path advertising should remember the words of Oscar Wilde and not simply 'amuse … or shock' but 'feed people'.

35

Institute of Practitioners in Advertising 1996 Advertising Effectiveness Awards

Janet Hull
Director of Advertising Effectiveness and Judge, IPA

The Institute of Practitioners in Advertising (IPA) 1996 Advertising Effectiveness Awards were run in association with *Marketing* magazine and presented on 12 November, 1996. They are highly regarded because they are the only competition to reflect advertising's contribution to business success.

The major awards are detailed below. Specific case histories will be included in *Advertising Works 9*, published by NTC in spring 1997. It may be ordered from the IPA, 44 Belgrave Square, London SW1X 8QS, telephone 0171 235 7020, fax 0171 245 6079.

Grand Prix   BT/Abbott Mead Vickers

BT wanted to grow its residential market. An advertising campaign – using Bob Hoskins – was devised to break down the barriers to calling. Every 100 TVRs (TV rating points) in any given month produced an eventual monthly return of 1.79 per cent. The sales uplift is calculated to be £297 million of advertising-generated income.

Category 1 (for products which are new or have no significant advertising history)

Gold Award   Orange/WCRS

Orange was last into the highly competitive cellular phone market. Its positioning was a 'wirefree' future. The advertising generated 61,000 connections or £128 million additional revenue (four times payback).

Silver Award   Daewoo/Duckworth Finn Grubb Waters

Daewoo's UK launch was the fourth Korean entry in an oversupplied market. Its models were also unexceptional. The advertising strategy centred on there being no dealers, a hitherto unheard-of approach. Its sales target was to attain a 1 per cent market share within 3 years. In the first year Daewoo sold 18,005 cars, giving the brand a 0.92 per cent market share, the most successful car launch ever. Brand awareness is at 89 per cent; 71 per cent of buyers said it was the advertising that prompted them to visit a showroom. An advertising budget of £22 million generated £109 million revenue.

Silver Award   Felix/BMP DDB Needham

In the 1980s Felix cat food was a minor player in a market dominated by Whiskas. It came in few flavours and had no distinct identity. The relaunch budget was £250,000 (what Whiskas spent every eight days). Since then, Felix has been transformed through its advertising campaign. Its share has quadrupled. Its user base has tripled. The £17 million spent on advertising between 1989 and 1995 has generated an increase in sales of £108 million.

Bronze Award   BBC Education-Literacy/Bartle Bogle Hegarty

The aim of the advertising was to persuade illiterate parents to apply for a learning pack using 'emotional' techniques. The BBC target for enquiries was 40,000. 321,049 were achieved, 78 per cent of respondents claiming that the advertisements had motivated them to reply. In total, 127,000 parents took direct action to address their literacy problems. (It has been calculated that each individual with poor literacy costs industry £2450 per year, in total £4.828 billion per annum.)

Bronze Award   Frizzell/BMP DDB Needham

Frizzell Insurance used selective targeting to make a difference. As a result of its advertising campaign – September 1994 to December 1995 – brand awareness rose by 200 per cent and the income generated was equivalent to a return on investment of 24.9 per cent per annum.

Bronze Award   Reebok/Lowe Howard Spink

Reebok accounted for 1 in 3 of all sports shoes sold, except in the football market where it was 1 in 20. Reebok's advertising campaign concentrated on gaining football credibility using celebrity endorsement. Total ad investment was £2 million. Volume sales increased by 282 per cent (vs competitive growth of 73 per cent). Share improved from 5 to 10 per cent. Rank positioning improved from seventh to fourth position and trade sales turned around with an uplift of 174 per cent. Incremental profit calculated to the end of the decade is £8 million.

Category 2 (for new campaigns for previously advertised brands which resulted in significant short-term effects on sales or behaviour)

Gold Award   BT/Abbott Mead Vickers

See Grand Prix listing above.

Silver Award   Safeway/Lowe Howard Spink

As a food store, Safeway appealed mostly to single people. Safeway's advertising campaign, using toddlers Harry and Molly, was designed to attract mothers and young children to a more 'caring and family orientated' store. Spontaneous awareness increased sixfold. Like-for-like sales increased by an average of 7 per cent and basket size by 12 per cent. Pretax profits rose by 7 per cent.

Silver Award   Walkers/BMP

BMP's advertising for Walkers crisps, an already successful brand, stimulated a 22.5 per cent growth in the first year with its use of Gary Lineker.

Bronze Award   Automobile Association/HHCL & Partners

In 1992, AA member sales had been declining for three years. In 1993 it began advertising itself as the 'Fourth emergency service' Since then, new-member sales have increased by 24 per cent. Annual retention is also back in growth, with the AA keeping an estimated 140,000 members a year.

Bronze Award   BT/BDDH

BT faced competitive threats for its share of the business market. To relay its core values, its advertising centred on the first-ever business drama. Recall was 33 per cent above target, 56 per cent of the business audience felt that BT could help them get more out of their working day and 60 per cent felt they could turn to BT for advice. This in turn led to 51,448 enquiries which translated into 16,977 sales leads, 79 per cent above target.

Bronze Award   Murphy's/BBH

The survival of Murphy's as a brand was in question in 1993. Guinness was the king of stout with 80 per cent share and 90 per cent distribution. As a result of an 'Irish' advertising campaign, Murphy's saw an uplift of 97 per cent on volume sales. This represents 131,542 additional barrels nationally.

Category 3 (for advertising campaigns which have benefited a business by maintaining or strengthening a brand over a longer period)

Charles Channon (Gold) Award   Barclaycard/BMP DDB Needham

Barclaycard's advertising helped it to reverse a declining share trend and with a continuous presence stimulated an average turnover of 3 per cent per year. (Total credit card turnover in the UK is £30 billion per annum.)

Silver Award   Gold Blend/McCann-Erickson

This is now a £91 million brand thanks to its 'soap opera' advertising which has grown the brand's volume by 60 per cent, at a time when other markets were static or declining. This is valued at £60 million a year in incremental sales at an advertising cost of £5 million a year.

Silver Award   Philadelphia/J Walter Thompson

Philadelphia cream cheese was seen as a luxury/special occasion purchase. As a result of its advertising campaign it is purchased once a year by one-quarter of households. It has also maintained its dominant 50+ per cent market share and kept its price premiums of 20+ per cent.

Silver Award   Stella Artois/Lowe Howard Spink

Stella's position as number one in the premium lager market was under threat during the recession with its 'reassuringly expensive' theme becoming more inappropriate as time passed. £14.2 million has been spent on the new theme, 'the lager of supreme quality and worth', which yielded a return of investment of £6 million. The incremental profit due to this new advertising campaign was in excess of £70 million.

Bronze Award   Renault Clio/Publicis

The Clio was launched in 1991 to compete with cars like the Ford Fiesta and Vauxhall Nova. As a result of its continued advertising campaign its market share has nearly doubled since launch.

Bronze Award   I Can't Believe It's Not Butter/McCann-Erickson

Through the eyes of 'cow world', this is now a recognised brand. Penetration has grown from 15 to 21 per cent, and volume is up 26 per cent.

36

Tying up the Strapline

Timothy R V Foster
The Slogo Register

I have for a long time felt that it would a useful resource to have a database of advertising slogans – something to check when you're ready to pitch, for example, just to make sure your line wasn't just used by the client's arch rival. So I built one. I call it The Slogo Register™ (the slogan by the logo). It has over 10,000 lines and is growing every day. Now I offer search services to the advertising and marketing industries.*

This chapter contains some thoughts that have arisen in building this research. It is only when you start putting large groups of slogos together *en masse* that you begin to see the real depths of humour (or horror) in them, or just the real depths.

There are the puns, some being quite nifty: 'Barbados. Goodness. Gracious'; 'The appliance of science' (Zanussi); 'Everything you hear is true' (Pioneer); 'Running water for you' (Thames Water); 'Keep our wits about you' (*The Times*); 'Taste. Not waist' (Weight Watchers frozen meals); 'Won't make a pom tiddly' (Swan Light); 'Changing oil' (Shell Oil). But, of course, where there are puns there are groaners – gotta get that brand in there somehow: 'A little Lextra care' (Lex Vehicle Leasing); 'It 'asda be Asda'; 'Say good Bisodol to indigestion'; 'Visa's Delta blow to cheques'; 'So Farley's, so good'; 'Good mornings follow a good Nytol'; 'Be smart, BT' or 'I think, therefore IBM', for example.

Then there are the abject apologies, based, no doubt, on guilt: 'We're getting there' (British Rail); 'Working to be your choice' (Continental Air-

* The Slogo Register can be reached on 0181–763–2225, or by e-mail on <fostair@atlas.co.uk>.

lines); 'After all, if smoking isn't a pleasure, why bother?' (Newport Cigarettes) or the horrible: 'Slam in the lamb' – surely a convincing reason to become a vegetarian?

Some target their competition very specifically: 'Why go for the copper when you can go for the gold?' (Kodak Batteries vs Duracell); or 'We have no serious competition' (Melrose Films vs Video Arts, the maker of humorous training films); or 'More than just a number' (Wrangler Jeans vs. Levi 501s). Some suggest rejoinders based on reality – for example: 'We have to earn our wings every day' *because we can't afford to own them overnight* (Eastern Airlines, now bankrupt); or just demand a slogo to be added to the slogo: 'We offer you more, we charge you less' *or vice versa* (Ryness).

Some slogos are so specific, what else can be said? 'Manufacturers and distributors of quality narrow woven-edged fabrics since 1923' (Bally Ribbon Mills); or 'The name in rack and pinion elevators' (Alimak). Some are meaningless: 'A company called TRW' (for a company called TRW, I guess), 'We're Exxon' (Exxon? Who are they, *Valdez?*), 'That's Lite Tuff!' (what's a Lite Tuff?).

Some try to be helpful: 'Having the right sign can be cheaper than a fine' (Safety Sign Systems), and some demand the response *'so what?'* or something like that: 'A woman-owned company' (Geneva Gage Inc); 'The only wool company run by a woman. And it shows' (Sirdar), or even 'RAM is a woman-owned small disadvantaged business' (RAM Enterprises).

Is this what they call a command economy?

Don't be vague. Ask for Haig.	Haig Scotch Whisky
Don't chance it. Chubb it.	Chubb
Don't dream it. Drive it.	Jaguar
Don't get a complex. Get a complex that helps.	Gliss
Don't get a complex, get Amplex.	Amplex
Don't get into a rut, get into Reed temping.	Reed
Don't get mad, get Malibu.	Malibu
Don't get skin problems, get Skin Solutions.	Wilkinson Sword
Don't get vexed. Ask Teletext.	Teletext
Don't imitate, innovate.	Hugo Boss
Don't just book it, Thomas Cook it.	Thomas Cook
Don't just buy them. Wear them.	Durex
Don't just get across. Cruise across.	P&O European Ferries
Don't just set the table, set the mood.	Towle
Don't just sleep on it – live in it!	Royal Auping
Don't just style your hair … Finesse your style.	Finesse
Don't knacker it, cracker it.	Jacobs Cream Crackers
Don't miss the boat. Insist on Bisto.	Bisto

Don't play, compete.	Hi Tec Shoes
Don't rough it. Live life in comfort.	Comfort
Don't say brown, say Hovis.	Hovis
Don't say French, say Noilly Prat.	Noilly Prat
Don't say vinegar, say Sarson's.	Sarson's
Don't settle for less – just do I.T.	Forbes UK
Don't worry. Be happy.	AXA Equity & Law

Here are a few more clarifications:

It's not just a car … it's your freedom.	General Motors
It's not just a castle, it's a kingdom.	Sam Lord's Castle
It's not just the business, it's the lifestyle.	Hull
It's not just an aircraft. It's a Beechcraft.	Beechcraft
It's not just styling, it's your hair.	Pantene

Or how about the world's favourite generic slogo?

American Express	The natural choice
Bovril Instant	The natural choice
British Gas	The natural choice
Budget Rent-a-Car	The natural choice
City of Croydon	The natural choice
Cullens Grocers	The natural choice
Danepak Bacon	The natural choice
Emmental Cheese	The natural choice
European Heritage Tiles	The natural choice
Hanson Brick	The natural choice
ITT Sheraton Hotels	The natural choice
Millets Sports	The natural choice
Mobil Gas	The natural choice
Poland	The natural choice
Pulsar Watches	The natural choice
Scotch Beef	The natural choice

Then again, here's another key brand differentiation, inspired, no doubt by Tina Turner: 'simply the best'. The Slogo Register lists 20 of these, ranging from Abercrombie & Kent (travel) to the Woolacombe Bay Hotel.

By the way, how do you achieve excellence? Take your pick:

Excellence through experience.	Team Aer Lingus
Excellence through knowledge.	Management Research Group
Excellence through performance.	Dillon/Quality Plus, Inc
Excellence through total quality.	Ames Rubber Corp

Well, enough for now. Someone wants to check a line.

37

Touching the Customer – Direct Marketing

David Robottom
Director of Development, British Direct Marketing Association

The title is a classic oxymoron: direct marketing never actually touches the customer, that's the very point. Direct marketing uses paper, telephony and electronic means to touch the customer. It uses individual data on the customer to make direct contact, to achieve quantifiable marketing objectives.

Direct marketing has existed for many decades, initially on the premise of convenience and credit. The three stages of evolution – paper, telephone and electronic – have accelerated the direct marketing business to a UK expenditure of £5.2 billion, generating in excess of £20 billion turnover. This represents approximately 3 per cent of UK gross domestic product (GDP).

Despite these impressive figures, direct marketing is something of a poor relation to the US model, where the industry spends $135 billion, generating $1.1 trillion of turnover and employing 19 million people. A sign of things to come, some would argue.

There are probably five key factors which explain why direct marketing is growing: the growth of the sophisticated consumer, customer control, consumer trust and confidence, polarisation within society and proliferation of media. These can be grouped into the consumer and media. Let us first examine media and their proliferation.

In an excellent book by Peppers and Rogers, *The One to One Future*, the authors examine the classic economies of scale and contrast them with economies of scope. In essence, economies of scale drive mass marketing to compete for share of market; economies of scope drive the battle for share of customer, one at a time.

The explosion of media is not restricted to multichannel TV; radio and publishing offer a wide array of outlets focused on specific groups. But the most dramatic change is the proliferation in new electronic media, with interactive environments, driven by the convergence of information and communications technologies, giving the consumer immediate direct access to more organisations than ever before.

Coupled with this is the enhanced database marketing made available by this convergence. These advances are a product of the development of optical fibres, improved microelectronic performance, vastly reduced cost, speed of software and application development, the ability to communicate worldwide and the development of digital technology. Computer intelligence is built into transmission networks, allowing the blend of different technologies. This can lead to new products and services never before considered.

Companies introduced telecoms systems into their customer-service operations, initially on the premise of reduced manpower and therefore reduced costs. But convergence gives options never before dreamed of and will force companies to readdress their customer-service function as a profit centre not a cost centre.

Convergence is not a pipedream; there are many examples of companies linking their telephony systems with their database systems. The obvious examples are in the financial sector, with the move initiated by costly salesforces and branch networks to create 'direct' products. But it can be argued that the catalogue industry has been developing and implementing this idea for many decades.

The link between telephony and information systems allows customer-services staff to identify the caller through CLI (caller line identification), and access the customer records through their database, all *before* the call is answered.

The growth and anticipated growth of the Internet make it the epitome of 'direct', but in cyberspace. Already you can visit Web sites on the WWW (World Wide Web), input your details and access information on products and services never before accessed. But the real beauty lies in your next visit. You access the Web site, immediately you are recognised and the products and services are tailored *specifically* to you; not to C1 C2 aged 16–35, but to you as an individual.

But surely the Internet has barriers to entry, the cost of PCs, modems etc? For many consumers this is true, at the moment. But already, the whole issue of universal access to the Internet is being explored and developed through outlets such as libraries, council offices and schools. In addition, technology is accelerating at such a rate that we should not presuppose that the infrastructure required at present will be needed in ten years' time, five years' time or even next year. The technology exists for mobile phone users to access the Internet through their phone and place orders, browse or pass on information. The development of TV digital technology implies that the PC could become redundant in the home. For that matter, it is increasingly likely that keyboards will end up on the scrapheap of redundant products. The development of voice recognition through digital technologies will lead to consumers literally to talking to their TV set.

Imagine five years hence (a conservative estimate): you come home from work and find that your washing machine is broken down, or you need this product urgently. You have no time to go round showrooms, order the product, wait for delivery and installation, or to panic!

You tell the TV set to switch itself on and ask for information on washing machines. You are presented with a Web page showing various suppliers. You ask for information on Zanussi. The screen changes to show film of a family demonstrating the latest Zanussi washing machine. But you know from bitter experience that there are some delicate fabrics that washing machines just ruin. You tell the TV that you want to see the result of washing silk shirts. The screen shows silk shirts being washed, with a guarantee from the manufacturer. You decide you wish to buy the Zanussi product. You tell the TV you want to buy the product on screen and you will pay using your Access card. The TV accepts the payment, as all your credit card details are logged on your TV, protected. The screen gives you option of accepting delivery and installation tonight *or* having delivery and installation while you are out at work, tomorrow. This is actioned by the secure key arrangement which you have with your Internet security company. All communications and transactions are actioned for you. The whole process from realisation of the problem to panic to order lasts 90 seconds.

Consumers

In this globalisation through technology, where do consumers fit? They are, after all, the key. This brings us to the second important factor explaining why direct marketing is growing – the consumer.

Consumers are undoubtedly becoming more and more sophisticated. They want more relevant, focused ways of dealing with organisations that give them added value in their lives. Consumers will look for new sources; communication and interaction technologies will provide them. Consumers want not just to *feel* in control but to *be* in control. This can be achieved by freephone and customer-care lines. Organisations need to generate consumer trust and confidence. We live in uncertain times. Those organisations that respond to customers, alleviating their fears, will undoubtedly generate their trust and confidence. They will become their advocates.

The final area related to consumers is the nature of the society in which we live. Society is changing. We have groups and subgroups. Society is breaking into smaller and smaller groups with differing needs and circumstances. The one-to-one future espoused by Peppers and Rogers is not a theoretical concept, it is a reality.

Organisations cannot rely on mass media, they are no longer relevant. Technological and societal developments make them untenable. Companies must realise that they can no longer communicate to homogeneous masses. They must organise their business around the needs of the customer. In a one-to-one future, the consumer holds the database of companies, through electronic technological developments. They can access, globally, whom they want, when they want. Those companies who recognise this will succeed. But they must also change.

The classic marketing department organised into brand managers who have responsibility for a brand, with market-share objectives, can no longer be considered. The key is the share of the consumer, *not* the share of the market.

We only have to consider those companies which have realised the opportunity and commercial reality of direct marketing, such as Heinz, Marks and Spencer, HSBC, Sainsbury's. All these are traditionally not direct-marketing companies, yet now they embrace the reality of direct marketing and the future through one-to-one communication.

Sainsbury's and many other food retailers saw this in the early 90s, with the development of their loyalty cards. But that is only the visible element to the consumer. Behind it is the use of technology, barcode scanning to track purchases, advanced scanning to recognise individual consumers as they purchase. Very soon, consumers will buy their groceries at a food outlet, will be offered special incentives/discounts as they pick products from the shelf (through a scanner within the shopping trolley) and be personally addressed by the checkout assistant as they load their groceries. This is only the start: technology will reap even more benefits for food retailers and their consumers.

Within this technological revolution, as important as the industrial revolution but on a larger, global scale, is the area of customer service alluded to earlier.

Companies must realise that customer service is a profit centre not a cost centre. The customer-service dialogue must be enhanced, measured and reappraised on an ongoing basis. Historically customer-complaint handling was measured on keeping complaints to a minimum. This must be reappraised. Any complaints should be actively encouraged and fed back into maximising customer satisfaction and brand loyalty. If a customer does not complain and ceases to purchase your product and services, what do they do? They damage your product, they communicate their dissatisfaction to their friends and colleagues. Without the encouragement of complaints you do not know why the consumer stopped purchasing *or* the damage they are inflicting on your brand.

There is a further twist to this. With the development of the Internet we now have people on the Net with common interests, who form themselves into groups and give each other advice and information. They see themselves as a key reference point for decisions, yet they have in all likelihood never met. It's word of mouth through cyberspace. If you believe, and you should, that word of mouth can both damage and promote your brand, imagine the possibilities on a global scale.

Peppers and Rogers perhaps summed up the one-to-one future best when they said, 'the only software genuinely worth having is the customer relationship, based on mutual advantage and trust. Individual, differentiable customer relationships will be the ultimate software of businesses in the one-to-one future.'

Technology is developing faster than most of us can cope with. The harsh reality is that many advanced technologies could become obsolete very soon. The constants are the consumers: you must react to them, meet their needs, inspire trust and confidence, and develop and enhance the customer relationship. This can best be achieved by utilising direct-marketing approaches.

38

The Role of Conferences and Events in Corporate Communications

Richard Birtchnell
Director of Special Projects,
2Cs Communications Ltd

Popular notions of our time, like the cashless society and the paperless office, have been conceived and much heralded on the assumption that escalating technology will make traditional forms of information exchange obsolete. But they are as yet unfulfilled concepts; more cash is in circulation than ever before and paper resources need careful husbandry.

Such mythology is widely expressed about the role of conferences in business, and it is not difficult to see why. After all, our PCs are quite capable of linking each other across hemispheres and markets simply by access to a telephone socket. Within seconds, given the right kit on the desk, we can be communicating and interacting, singly or in groups, in a visual environment through video conferencing – or should we now refer to it as 'desktop television'? Discrete TV networks, intranets, the ubiquitous Internet and the humble e-mail now span the globe. New media employed by business now generate a level of communications traffic such that radical forecasters predict we will all be working from home in the future. For some, undoubtedly this is true. Technology has liberated them. But where does this put the conference if even a corporate office is hard to justify?

The cynic could argue, with some reason, that the isolating experience of working alone is itself a stimulus to the conference trade, for lonely home-bound executives want to get out and meet each other from time to time, for sanity, self esteem, peer bonding and good old-fashioned networking.

The realist, however, recognises more fundamental and dynamic forces are about. It is simply this: there is no substitute for face-to-face communication, and there never will be. Alternatives are virtual or next best. This is implicit in the claims of the videoconferencing marketer: 'Just like they're in the room with you!'

There is much to be welcomed of such virtuality, particularly when used at real meetings as an electronic insert or to complement the interaction. But today the bottom line is that, despite wider access to broadcast technology, the conference and exhibition industry is enjoying an all-time high, after a downturn in the late 1980s, which was caused simply by prevailing economics.

Increasing supply

We are currently witnessing a global expansion of meeting facilities. In many countries, governments, airlines and hotels work together to attract inbound delegates – after all, they are good for the economy and may well return with their families as tourists. In *Meetings and Incentive Travel* magazine (January, 1997), the London Convention Bureau's Rebecca Byrne was reported to say that London needs 19,000 new hotel beds and a new convention centre for the turn of the century.

Less exotic but closer to home in Britain, one city after another is coming 'onstream' with purpose-built convention centres and exhibition halls, together with attendant improvements in local infrastructure. Seaside towns have long been familiar hosts for political and union conferences; whereas cities like Birmingham, Harrogate and Edinburgh can boast space as good, if not better than elsewhere in Europe. Manchester is the latest to announce a new 3,500 delegate convention centre ready for the millenium.

The meetings organiser has never had such a wide choice of venue – which is all very well, but if supply is increasing, can we assume so is demand?

Increasing demand

Emphatically, yes is the answer. Evidence of market growth abounds. Hotels big and small are reporting longer-term bookings and healthy increases in numbers. Unfortunately, the knock-on effect is reflected in their prices. Exhibition arenas are fully booked, in some cases, well into the next century. Incidentally, Britain hosts over 700 trade shows a year which attract 10 million visitors, one million of whom come from abroad. The British Tourist Authority reported a 30 per cent increase in conference activity in 1995.

The 'educative' conference and seminar market is enjoying growth too, with an accelerating need for professionals to keep up to date with accounting standards, business practice, legislation (a fair amount being 'Euro-driven') and constant advances in science, medicine and technology.

Presentation standards are rising, assisted by technology, but also because audiences expect more professionalism from their presenters. Thus, new 'executive coaching' and 'presentation skills' services are expanding.

Specialist group travel agencies abound, along with destination-management companies, venue finders and ground handlers. New publications and trade association for conference organisers have sprung up in the last five years. All this recent activity is no accident, but a planned response to demand.

In competitive corporate life, getting the message across has never been so important. If you want to inform, motivate, change the culture, or just entertain, you will succeed best in a live environment. 'Corporate evangelism' some would call it. No wonder that new product launches, motivational sales conferences, city presentations and shareholder meetings are regular fixtures.

It is always best to persuade in person. Oratory is the tool, as history demonstrates, from the wild-west huckster with his miracle cure to Abe Lincoln, Martin Luther King, Churchill, Hitler and Mandela, who moved entire nations.

Remember these models at your next conference. Face-to-face. Nothing else comes close.

39

Integrated Marketing – A Case History

Cheryl Freeman
Maritime Region Marketing Director,
Andersen Consulting

When Andersen Consulting first became an independent entity in 1989, marketing efforts understandably centred on awareness and image building. As our business has grown (at a phenomenal rate) we have refined this and developed our own integrated-marketing approach. Integrated marketing helps us grow our business by building image, developing markets and creating relationships in a highly connected, synergistic, efficient fashion.

Our integrated-marketing framework has three components: image development, market development and business development. Each component represents a process in marketing as it moves from a macro level of global strategy down to a micro level of individual opportunities and engagements and then back again in a continued rotation. Our comprehensive approach to integrated marketing also carries the concept to its logical conclusion, emphasising that each of the components should not be implemented in isolation but should achieve synergy by leveraging each other.

Integration implies, for example, that image initiatives and client-development efforts are part of one seamless process focused on moving the target audience from one point in the relationship to the next, with the ultimate goal of a long-term partnership. To achieve this we strive to ensure that:

- Consistent messages are maintained across all our marketing vehicles so that they reinforce each other;
- Andersen Consulting client-relationship partners are an integral part of everything we do. Integrated marketing aims to leverage the regular contact clients have with our partners and ensure they receive the same message from our marketing efforts;
- As a global organisation, we speak with one voice. We manage our brand globally and all our communications – written, visual and verbal – represent the same cohesive organisation.

Integrated marketing works when, at the moment of decision, a desired client chooses Andersen Consulting. In a long-term business relationship, that moment arrives more than once and each of the elements of image development, market development and business development work together synergistically and play a part.

Image development

Image development lays the groundwork for the partnerships we establish with our clients; it also plays a role in reinforcing those relationships. As we build our image, we develop awareness of, and communicate a distinct personality for, Andersen Consulting in the marketplace, which in turn contributes to our global brand.

Our brand is established through all aspects of integrated marketing, but image development is the most visible contributor. We use several tools throughout the image-development process, including research, identity, graphics, events, media and industry-analyst relations and advertising. Each element contributes to our brand in a unique way, and all communicate a consistent message and tone.

Advertising in the consulting-services category has changed radically in recent years. Andersen Consulting was the first management consultancy to advertise and has now been copied by competitors. Since 1989, the number of consulting firms that are advertising has grown enormously; there are now more than 20 firms advertising in the US alone.

We introduced global campaigns for the first time in 1995, which reflect our own brand values as a global firm. Our clients are also increasingly global in their approach. Consistent advertising throughout the world ensures that, wherever they are, they receive the same seamless brand message from Andersen Consulting.

Market development

We use research extensively to help refine our understanding of client needs and industry trends. Based on this, focused offerings and solutions are developed that we believe will achieve a desired business result for a client. These market offerings might be industry-specific or they might address a common need across multiple industry segments.

Our marketing professionals work with our consulting staff to develop marketing messages that can help to clearly communicate our market offerings. In particular, we focus on expressing the offering and the value it delivers in terms that are relevant to the client's specific situation.

One of the tools we use that is extremely valuable in this process is our Business Integration Centre. These centres enable us to bring clients to a location that is dedicated to a particular industry or process and show them our offerings at work. Business Integration Centres provide a forum in which our partners can demonstrate their perspective on, say, a particular industry, and clients can gain direct experience of the next generation of ideas in action.

Business development

Business development leverages Andersen Consulting's brand and offerings to help develop relationships with clients into mutually beneficial long-term partnerships.

A particular client may have many needs; we focus only, however, on those areas of a client's business where we believe we can really provide business value. Part of the business-development process, therefore, is working with the client to identify those opportunities we should pursue together.

Increasingly, clients are looking to outsource certain of their business processes. Andersen Consulting has a substantial Business Process Management (BPM) practice that meets this need. Our business-development teams play a pivotal role in shaping these BPM arrangements.

Business development can seem to be the culmination of the integrated-marketing process. In fact, business development may begin the cycle which continues time and again with our clients. Recognising and realising the potential synergy of having the three elements of our Integrated Marketing model working together as part of one seamless strategy is key to the success of Andersen Consulting.

40

Communications and Customer Care – A Case History

Chris Forrest
Planning Director
and
Rachel Walker
Account Planner,
Duckworth Finn Grubb Waters

The extraordinary success of Daewoo's launch into the UK car market has attracted much praise, being voted the Marketing Society's 1996 Durables Brand of the Year, *Campaign*'s 1995 Advertiser of the Year and winning a Silver Award in the 1996 Advertising Effectiveness Awards of the Institute of Practitioners in Advertising.

The advertising from Duckworth Finn Grubb Waters made a defining contribution to the whole Daewoo offering, and developed a campaign whose effectiveness was crucial to Daewoo's rapid success.

The market

Daewoo's UK launch was the fourth Korean entry into an already over-supplied market. Its models were unexceptional in the UK market and

Daewoo had set an extraordinarily ambitious sales target of 1 per cent market share within three years.

Extremely challenging sales targets call for radical solutions. Further investigation indicated that there were unmet needs of a fundamental kind in the marketplace which represented a big brand opportunity.

It is car owners' collective experience that the process of buying and owning a private car is far from ideal. A huge opportunity was identified for Daewoo to address these unmet needs and become the most customer-focused and friendly car company in the UK. Daewoo could set a new agenda by selling car ownership as a service rather than cars as products.

Daewoo's response to the agency's recommended brand positioning was to dispense with dealers altogether.

The need to build a brand

To meet the unmet needs in the market, Daewoo needed to be a brand, building long-term customer relationships. Advertising needed to overcome three potential barriers to this relationship:

- *Ignorance:* The brand building needed to start early. We had a daunting target. We would also have far slower distribution build than with a conventional (dealer-franchised) launch, so people would need to be more motivated than usual to find a Daewoo outlet. Daewoo's corporate credentials were communicated six months before any cars arrived;
- *Scepticism:* People in the UK distrust car companies. We needed to convince them of our sincerity. We used advertising as consumer research through a customer dialogue. This enabled us to:
  - seek ideas;
  - be seen to ask;
  - build a database;
- *Apathy:* To encourage people to get involved with Daewoo's research we developed a promotion offering cars free for a year's test drive to 200 advertising responders.

By operational launch in April 1995, Daewoo had developed an impressive brand offer, but it required simplification to help people assimilate the offer. We organised the brand offer into four core brand values and labelled them: Direct, Hassle Free, Peace of Mind, Courtesy. Each of these became the subject of its own TV commercial, and more than one ad was shown in each break to maximise the opportunity for the audience to see all of the ads.

We needed a differentiated advertising approach to overcome motorists' cynicism about promises of customer focus. Daewoo advertising is deliberately different. It avoids the typical car clichés and is down to earth and unpretentious.

Daewoo sold 18,005 cars in the first year, giving the brand 0.92 per cent market share and making it the most successful car-marque launch in the UK since records began. What could account for this result?

Advertising has achieved its objectives and built a strong brand:

- Ignorance has been overcome; brand awareness is at 89 per cent. People feel that Daewoo is different and customer focused;
- Scepticism has been overcome; people feel they can trust Daewoo;
- Apathy has been overcome; many people have visited Daewoo showrooms and increasing numbers would consider Daewoo when they next come to buy a car.

Only advertising could have overcome these barriers. We find the following:

- Brand measures move in line with adspend;
- Daewoo's Awareness Index of 12 in post-advertising tracking is far higher than all other car brands on our study, showing its efficiency;
- Advertising was motivating; 71 per cent of Daewoo buyers say it was the advertising that prompted them to visit a Daewoo showroom.

Nothing other than brand strength could account for the rapid success:

- Daewoos were not irresistibly cheap in the UK. Prices started at 37 per cent more than the cheapest upper-medium-sector model, and 92 per cent more than the cheapest lower-medium-sector model;
- The offer with the cars is very generous but advertising needed to tell people about the offer in the first place. Moreover, advertising needed to create a strong brand to reassure people that Daewoo was a committed, differentiated long-term player, so that the offer would be believed and have value;
- Distribution was unexceptional.

Therefore advertising established the brand. The strength of the brand is responsible for the sales achievement. Advertising performed the dominant role in Daewoo's exceptional sales result.

41

Communications Through Business Partners – A Case History

Shaun Orpen
Director of Marketing Services,
Microsoft Ltd

Microsoft Corporation was established in 1975 by Bill Gates and Paul Allen. It was founded in the belief that better software and smaller hardware could move the computer from the backroom of large companies into the mainstream of everyday life. Microsoft believed that with the right software, the computer could become a tool that would make people more productive and provide them with new sources of information and entertainment in their homes, school and work.

Microsoft Ltd was founded in the UK in 1982 and was the first subsidiary set up in Europe by Microsoft Corporation for the sale, marketing and support of its products and services.

Marketing overview

When Microsoft first began marketing its products back in the late 1980s it was to technical customers who understood the need for software and were even ready to make a choice. This was a select community, so our marketing focus was narrowly focused. But as the allure of the personal computer grew, Microsoft found that product features were no longer the key messages customers wanted to hear; we had to start marketing benefits.

The Microsoft name was fast becoming a worldwide recognised brand; we were competing against companies such as Nike and Nintendo, rather than just Novell or IBM. However, we found that the further 'mass market' our products became, the less easy it was to stay close to our customers. We concluded that our brand must be used to communicate more clearly with the customer and become something they could immediately identify with.

It was clear that we needed a consistent message to be communicated to our millions of customers. We did this with a global marketing push designed to show that all Microsoft products and services are unified to bring customers access to a whole new world of thinking and communicating. Microsoft's technology is designed to help them achieve their objectives and this sentiment was encapsulated in our strap line launched in November 1994: 'Where Do You Want To Go Today?'

But consistent 'one-to-many' communication with a customer is not enough in today's business environment. To achieve the highest levels of customer satisfaction, companies must engage their customers in a 'personalised' dialogue. Microsoft Ltd now has a much more 'customised' relationship – building profiles of its customers as individuals and ensuring that the messages they are sent are targeted, sequential and relevant. We must form personalised relationships with customers based on our knowledge of them as an individual and show them how our message is relevant to them. The success of this venture is dependent on two factors: effective customer database management and effective customer satisfaction.

But how do you achieve this if your marketing communication and customer satisfaction are dependent on third parties? Microsoft has a very strong third-party business model to ensure that we remain focused on our core business of developing software. As a result, a high percentage of our external communications is channelled through independent companies with their own brands and identities. Added to this, the majority of our products are sold through independent vendors and resellers, again with their own identity and brand values. If our message is to be clear we must ensure that our brand and reputation are also maintained and embodied in these external companies.

Invisible partners

As the leading PC software vendor in the world, with over 100 million customers, Microsoft receives a large number of telephone calls asking for product information, product and sales support and a host of other requests. In the interest of customer service and business efficiency, a majority of these calls are outsourced to third-party companies that specialise in providing these services, but as far as the customer is concerned, they are talking directly to Microsoft.

This provides us with a significant marketing challenge. For the customer, their experience with Microsoft Connection or Microsoft Solution-Provider Hotline, for example, must match their expectation of what the Microsoft brand stands for. The customer expects anything with the Microsoft name to be efficient, easy to deal with and user friendly. Ensuring this is difficult. It is only possible if the companies who handle our customer telephone enquiries also encompass the brand values of Microsoft and provide the level of service our customers expect. It is our job to ensure that this happens.

From our point of view, Teledata, the company that manages the Microsoft Connection line and Microsoft Solution-Provider Hotline, is an 'external employee' of Microsoft. Microsoft runs training courses to provide product and company information, allowing the telephone support people to answer customer enquiries. The training and communication are also designed to give these 'external employees' the feeling of being a part of Microsoft, allowing them to absorb the culture and the brand values of the company.

The close integration and relationship between Microsoft and its invisible partners act to reinforce the brand values and strengthen our reputation to our customers.

Visible partners

Microsoft sells its products through the indirect channel – independent companies that sell our products and implement the solution for the customer. The channel therefore is incredibly strategic for Microsoft and as such is a central audience for our marketing activity. It is also a very well-defined audience – we know exactly who is there.

It is vital that the people selling our products in this channel are communicating the same messages about Microsoft. Hence we invest a significant percentage of marketing budget into communicating effectively with the channel. A wide range of tactics is used to educate and inform this audience, ranging from specifically targeted direct mailings and account-management relationships to private Internet and intranet sites and one-to-many seminars and roadshows.

Much of Microsoft's marketing to the channel is about information dissemination. It is very important that we ensure that this audience has enough information to position the product as Microsoft intended. It also allows the wider, above-the-line marketing activity to map into the messages being given by the channel.

A second tier of visual partners is composed of the marketing consultancies retained by Microsoft to devise and carry out specific marketing tasks. For example, Microsoft's above-the-line advertising strategy is realised by Euro RSCG WNEK Gosper, its public and media relations strategy by Text 100.

These companies must communicate the same overall messages as Microsoft. Information dissemination is obviously vital, but so is a sense of ownership and identity. Microsoft views its external consultancies as a part of the overall marketing team and gives them the same access to information and brings them in at the earliest stage in the decision making. Our working relationship with these strategic organisations is not one based on the traditional approach of giving the brief then waiting for the proposal – these partners help us develop our strategy. By working with third parties in this way, Microsoft not only benefits from greater efficiency and cost-effectiveness in its marketing, but as we work with some of the leaders in their field, they help us achieve our goal of innovating not only in software but in our marketing.

The right partnership is not enough. In an industry that changes daily, having the correct communications infrastructure with your third parties is vital. Communication tools such as electronic mail (e-mail) allow us to communicate almost instantaneously with our partners and allows them to reply, feedback and act in significantly shorter timescales. The e-mail communications between partners mean that they are as up to date as internal Microsoft employees on important issues, ensuring that there is no information gap between ourselves and our representatives.

Through a partnership based on trust, information sharing and joint strategy development, Microsoft's consultancies have embraced our brand values and work hard to ensure that they are maintained and reinforced in all external communication.

Microsoft has spent a significant amount of time, energy and resources on marketing our brand. This brand is designed to evangelise the benefits gained from giving individuals at work, school or home easy access to information through the personal computer. All our communication must reflect this ease of access. The brand is generally well understood by our customers and is designed to act as a guarantee that any interaction with Microsoft, its products or partners will be fast, efficient and user friendly.

Through training, communication and information, we work hard to ensure that our partners are embracing our brand values, acting to promote the company and strengthen our reputation with the customer. By consulting with partners in strategic marketing decisions and making them feel that they are part of an external workforce, Microsoft believes that it maintains a very cost-effective business model, ensures a consistent story is told and that customers receive industry-leading service from companies that, like Microsoft, are at the forefront of their industries. However, we know that a business which is dependent on third parties for communicating its brand has extra challenges. Making sure that our marketing really lives up to the promise of our brand is a constant challenge.

Part 8

Opinion Communications

42

Managing Perceptions to Achieve Business Goals at a Time of Radical Change

Professor Alan Watson, CBE
Chairman, Burson-Marsteller Europe

As we approach the millennium, businesses are re-examining their goals. The reason is not a desire for neatness as one leaves the old century to enter the new. It is an acknowledgement that the pace of change is quickening and that, while capitalism may have won the Cold War, it has still to win the peace. Business has to prove its social as well as its economic value in the new century. Goals need to be redefined. Expectations need to be reassessed. Thus companies are thinking anew about themselves and the world in which they will operate and they are having to consider how both their goals and their performance are likely to be perceived by others.

In short, history did not end with the fall of the Wall in Berlin in 1989 and the subsequent collapse of European communism. In fact, quite the opposite occurred. In Jacques Delors's well known phrase, 'history accelerated' and not only for the politicians. For business leaders in every field the challenge is to understand the nature of success in a rapidly altering environment.

Some of the pressures for change are clear. We are living through an extraordinary technological revolution. Its evident expression is the change in information technology, but even here, the effects are only beginning to show. The long-awaited convergence of telecommunications and computerisation is now happening. The arrival of digitalisation, the burgeoning expansion of the Internet and the potential of successor technologies – all these are harbingers of a new commercial, economic and social environment. National markets of all kinds are now open to international competition. Regionalisation and globalisation are shaping new political and commercial communities. These changes create both new dimensions of competition and also new expectations of corporate behaviour. Fresh regulatory frameworks impose new rules and the 'licence to operate', so vital to the future of any business, has to be re-examined on almost a continuous basis.

If this was not enough, companies must also face a new media environment shaping and determining the way in which they are perceived and evaluated. Transnational television and the advent of 24-hour news channels will put companies under intensified focus. The newsrooms of channels such as CNN, Sky and BBC World will give significant portions of time to business- and consumer-related coverage. Issues such as the environment and the safety of products and systems will be paramount. The manufacturers of food and pharmaceuticals, the providers of transport by land, sea, air and telephony, the sellers of services from hoteliers to supermarkets, banks to insurance companies, will all come under unprecedented scrutiny.

Which companies will be spotlighted? Inevitably, those that operate within the network's transnational television footprints, namely multinational companies. These need not be enormous conglomerates: the transnational niche company has arrived along with the globalisation of world trade. It too is fair game for the unblinking 24-hour television eye.

The crucial news criterion is that of relevance. A company's products, services or behaviour must be perceived by the viewers to be self-evidently important to them. This can stem from the strategic nature of the product or service, for example energy, computing or avionics; or from the daily relevance of products and services. This means inevitably that all companies selling toiletries, chemicals, medical products and above all, food, must expect to be scrutinised.

It has been said that the politics of today and tomorrow are not about the creation and distribution of wealth but about the creation and distribution of public attention. This is now well understood by the political classes. The twenty-first century may be non-ideological, but it will have its own powerful imperatives. What matters is what interests the public, because it is those issues that will win or lose votes. Focus groups will identify and map the political terrain and politicians will adopt positions accordingly. These will be bewilderingly new and unrelated to the traditional left/right divide. President Clinton is an arch exponent of the new politics and, to this point, its most conspicuous. Others are sure to follow, as evidenced by the Labour Party's concentration on the Clinton campaigning formula.

In this new battleground, single-issue campaign organisations will play a new and enhanced role. Campaign organisations have understood the nature of the media revolution, which is visual and investigative, transnational and consumer oriented. Chris Green, the campaign director at Greenpeace, said at the end of 1995 that companies above all will be the targets of such campaigning. They are, in his words, 'The iron-clad battleships of commerce, slow to manoeuvre and vulnerable.' What is more, from the campaigners' perspective, they are the organisations most responsible for environmental damage and most able to do something about it. Thus Chris Green has argued that while one hundred governments negotiated to repair the damage to the ozone layer, twelve companies manufactured the gases that did the damage. Future single-issue campaigns will target companies according to media criteria, providing exactly the pictures and events which focus attention. Greenpeace and its campaign groups are masters of the distribution of public attention.

So, what does all this mean for business goals and the ways in which companies are perceived? The most obvious and most important outcome is that business goals cannot ignore the new political emphasis on the distribution and focus of public opinion. Put more bluntly – business goals will become unachievable if public opinion removes, restricts or radically alters the freedom to operate. The regulators and the politicians will respond to public attention. Public opinion, however formed, ultimately determines the licence to operate. Businesses, therefore, can no longer ignore the task of managing the way they are seen. Active management of reputation has become a strategic need.

The second imperative for companies is to understand the nature of their audiences and their disparate make-up. These are changing and two developments in particular stand out.

First, companies are confronted with rising expectations on the part of society, which itself is now local, regional, national and supranational. Thus in parts of the developing world a company may find itself virtually a government in local areas where the state has collapsed. Equally, companies have to deal with the traditional nation-state increasingly concerned with its loss of sovereignty. In the European Union companies must take account of a regulatory framework that spans the continent. At all these different levels there are rising and changing expectations. With the shrinking of the nation-state's role as a provider of security and of employment, stakeholders in the broadest sense look to business for both. This may be unfair; it may be unrealistic; but the expectation is there.

Thus companies need to manage the way in which their contribution to

No two people see the same thing the same way. That's what makes life fun. And business hard.

How people see your product, your company or your positions on issues affects their actions. It's simply not enough to have the right product or do the right thing – you must also be seen that way.

Which is why we believe it's crucial to understand not only what people perceive, but also how those perceptions are shaped.

With this knowledge, we design communications to help manage the perceptions that lead to your desired business results. To learn more, contact Annabel James, (0171) 831 6262. Website: www.bm.com

Burson·Marsteller

Managing Perceptions · Creating Results · Worldwide

International Executive Development Programmes

Second edition

Consultant Editor: Philip Sadler

"... this guide will be a valuable source of reference in an area which is central to the success of any global business." SIR MICHAEL PERRY, CHAIRMAN UNILEVER PLC

The second edition of this important international directory is the ideal resource to address the problem of executive development. The directory covers: management development programmes, open learning programmes, in-house company training programmes and a special section on executive MBAs. It includes:

* profiles of training organisations
* an extensive listing of over 3,000 organisations
* a series of practical articles written by leading management experts, business academics and industrialists.

£75.00 Paperback ISBN 0 7494 2257 2 400 pages A4 May 1997

Ethics in Organisations

David Murray

The question of ethics in business has become a major concern for many organisations in recent years. Avoiding the theoretical stance too often adopted by writers on the topic, David Murray shows how managers can approach the dilemmas they face in an uncomfortably complex world. Looking at both top-level policy and the day-to-day concerns of people throughout a company, this book shows how everyone can make a real difference within an organisation.

David Murray is an independent consultant concentrating on the field of business and professional ethics. In recent years he has worked extensively in the post-communist economies of Central and Eastern Europe.

£13.99 Paperback ISBN 0 7494 1592 4 160 pages April 1997

The Corporate Healthcare Handbook

Consultant Editor: Helen Kogan

In order to comply with government and EU legislation, organisations of all sizes are committing themselves to 'best practice' in corporate healthcare.

Published in association with The Industrial Society, this new book aims to be a comprehensive guide for all organisations who have made this commitment. It provides authoritative and practical assistance on all aspects of health in the workplace, and guidelines on implementing strategies for good corporate healthcare. With illustrated case studies providing greater insight, this accessible handbook is a 'must' for all healthcare managers.

Topics covered include:
* cost/benefit analysis
* risk assessment
* health and safety issues
* health promotion
* work organisation

With a membership of over 10,000 organisations, and a 77-year track record, The Industrial Society has unparalleled knowledge of what constitutes 'best practice' in the management of people and how to achieve it.

£20.00 • Paperback • ISBN 0 7494 2154 1 • 320 pages Published April 1997 • Order no: KT154

prosperity and to jobs is perceived. It is no longer enough to explain the rationale for downsizing or even for rightsizing. It is more important to explain how companies see the future of work and their contribution to it. If companies do not want employment obligations they cannot meet, then they must have a view about the future of employment. What is to be the role of part-time work? What is the contribution of project contracts? The moral high ground is there to be taken, but too few companies have moved to occupy it. Capitalism in the post-communist age must make sense about jobs as we live through the most radical technological revolution since the one that transformed Europe and America in the nineteenth century.

Second, companies are confronted with the clash between stakeholder and shareholder expectations. Shareholder pressure grows remorselessly in a global marketplace. Short-term returns are demanded and expectations are ever higher. Financial analysts become ever more rigorous and unforgiving. Company executives are distracted by the endless pressure to meet the expectations of institutional and other investors. Privatisation is multiplying the numbers of businesses subject to these pressures. As state ownership recedes across the globe, shareholder power grows apace. If this limits the ability of companies to respond to their other stakeholders, to their customers, employees and society itself, then indeed capitalism will place corporations firmly between the proverbial rock and a hard place!

Confronted with difficulties of this order, companies will need to abandon their traditional view of communications. The effort required to manage stakeholder perceptions and corporate reputations positively rules out the 'bolt-on' methodologies of much of public relations. 'Well, let's decide what to do and announce it afterwards' is an approach of perilous vulnerability. Actions need to be evaluated in terms of their impact on perceptions from the planning stage onwards and implementation must be in line with the very best communication practices. Anything less is irresponsible. Negative perceptions can wipe millions off the share price within hours.

It is not simply a matter of spending more time on communications and behaving more professionally. It is also a matter of major rethinking, reorientation and retraining. Companies are used to communicating rationally. Only in their advertising do they appeal to the emotional dimension. Yet, as we have seen, the media are now emotional – picture driven and consumer driven. This requires a new form of corporate communication. It is not enough to appeal to the mind alone. The appeal must be to the whole person. Shell believed that the best engineering solution and scientifically the most responsible action was to sink the Brent Spar oil platform in the middle of the North Sea. Theirs was a rational position. The argument was not and Shell lost it. Similar examples abound and more occur with every month that goes by. Companies used to excluding the emotional component from a public argument suddenly appear vulnerable and their advocacy inadequate. What are needed therefore, are professionalism, persistence and a new imagination about the emotional and visual dimensions of communication.

How do companies go about this?

Perception management

Burson-Marsteller is the largest communications consultancy in the world. It operates in all key markets and numbers among its clients a vast array of multinational and transnational businesses – large, medium and small. It has developed a methodology called perception management to guide and assist businesses in meeting the challenges thus far described.

With our clients, the starting point is the acceptance that every product, every service, every company and every organisation is vulnerable to how audiences perceive them. These perceptions can be an asset or a liability and the difference between the two can mean success or failure – even extinction.

Understanding the true mindset of target audiences or stakeholders is the starting point of any attempt to manage perceptions. Professional research and analysis of these audiences is the beginning of knowledge. Such analysis carried out in a new and uniquely rigorous fashion identifies which perceptions will give a particular company or organisation a positive benefit with a particular audience, and equally which will detract and damage. The gap between desired perception and actual perception is mercilessly exposed.

Such research uncovers the in-depth reasons for audiences liking or disliking what a company offers and represents. It measures the company's level of influence, and above all, it focuses on the factors – messages or actions – that will alter perception. Identifying such factors is a hugely important step. The purpose is not simply to know what people think and feel about a company, a city, an organisation or a cause. The objective is to pinpoint what will make people change their minds!

No traditional marketing budget can shift a product unless it understands and focuses on the right levers of perception. If these are not seen or understood, high levels of expenditure are wasted. They may alter secondary perceptions but do not move the ones that matter most. Thus a motor company can spend a fortune trying to persuade audiences that it is a good public citizen and environmentally friendly, when the perception that matters most is that it doesn't make very good cars!

Equally, the view that publicity is, in itself, a good thing can be extremely foolish. What matters is strategic exposure which moves perceptions. Equally, the hope that the best publicity is none at all and that a low profile is always preferable ignores the nature of today's media and, above all, the power of investigative journalism. The dynamic of such journalism, coupled with the media's appetite for pictures and events and the ability of single-issue groups to generate both, is awesome. A well-planned protest outside a company's office can destroy invisibility with the speed of fog lifting from an airport.

Companies need to know who they are, what values they espouse, what benefits they bring to stakeholders and to shareholders. Above all, they need to know how to communicate these so that they appeal to the perceptions of emotion as well as mind.

In case this raises the spectre of vastly expensive consultancy, the next stage of perception management should bring relief. Perception management strategies must be based on a company's real business needs. The objective is not communications *per se*. Perception management supports the business bottom line directly, because it improves those company images that themselves have a direct impact on business performance and profitability. Perception management is a carefully evaluated business tool, not a communications gimmick.

Having identified the company's perceptual assets, the next stage is the development of targeted communication programmes. Communication initiatives need to be set in a firm timeframe and their results measured against the business goals set. What will matter is not exposure itself but the impact of exposure. What will count is not a 'good feel' about the company but the actual and measurable change in perceptions of it.

Thus, perception management is performance driven and value driven. It requires the full support and involvement of management and of all employees. Everyone owns the company's perceptual assets.

Business goals, corporate values and the management of perceptions are all interlocked and interdependent. The companies that will succeed in the new millennium will be those able to understand the art and science involved. The next millennium's winners will be those companies adding value, delivering products and services of competitive quality, investing time and resource in the effective communication of who they are, what they do and where they are going, to all the audiences that matter. These audiences are the jury. Their verdict will be decisive. Their perceptions of a company and its products will prove that company's viability.

43

A Common-sense Guide to Treating the Shareholder as a Customer*

Pamela A Jameson
Principal, Jameson Investor Relations Inc

Today, successful corporations pride themselves on being customer focused – in carefully identifying their target customers, analysing their wants and needs, and meeting them in terms of product design and service. A corporation that is customer driven generally believes that, to achieve business goals, it is necessary to have a strong marketing function which continually evaluates the company's success in satisfying the customer.

Increasingly, investor relations is viewed as a marketing function with communications and financial responsibilities. Hence investor relations needs to assume marketing responsibilities. These include knowing and understanding the shareholder base and ensuring that the company's message and published material address the information needs of investors and are presented appropriately.

* This a shorter version of an article that originally appeared in the *Journal of Communication Management*, Vol 1, No 2, 1996.

Creating the message

Investor relations does not have a tangible product to market to its customers. Instead, it markets information and data to promote and explain the investment opportunities provided by the company. How these are viewed varies with the investor and the portfolio.

Historically, management's challenge was to create a strategy for growing the business and then implementing it. Today, its responsibilities extend to keeping shareholders informed of the strategy and of progress being made. Without a well-constructed message, it is hard to ensure that management's strategies and plans for creating shareholder wealth are communicated to investors in ways that ensure that they are understood and the company is properly valued.

Frequently, management is reluctant to discuss its strategies, believing that competitors will benefit. But the probability is that any such information is already known by the competition. They can surmise significant detail about growth strategies simply by assessing the company's capital expenditures as well as its relations with customers, employees, suppliers and vendors.

Management should show how shareholders will benefit when constructing their message. It needs to present the company's current position and growth potential fairly and honestly. And it needs to give the insights required for the type of analysis and valuation work completed by professional investors specialising in the industry. The information should also be presented in a format that is user friendly to the shareholder-customer base.

A useful starting point is to consider the knowledge base of the average investor compared with the complexity of the industry. For example, a message directed to all shareholders needs to contain the level of detail required to satisfy an analyst with professional experience in a technical field. The average shareholder will not have the industry background to assess the company's business strategy and future prospects satisfactorily if too much focus is placed on technical aspects of the business.

As a generalisation, the concerned corporation will construct its investor relations message and present data on both the industry and the company to provide important insights to the average shareholder rather than the industry expert.

Company-specific factors

A major concern in preparing the message for the shareholder-customer is to ensure that the company's strengths are well articulated. Industry fundamentals are important for an understanding of the company's dynamics, but the company and its fundamentals are clearly the primary focus of the financial communications programme.

When crafting the message, the focus should be on what the company is and not on what management would like it to be, if it is to develop credibility with shareholders.

The following are key elements to include in the message for shareholders:

- management's strategy for the company;
- company's position within the industry;
- realistic assessment of the company's strengths;
- competitive challenges;
- capital spending plans;
- capital structure of the company compared with the traditional structure;
- management;
- financial targets and measures of success;
- dividend policy.

Formatting the message

Credibility is of primary importance to managers and their companies. This extends throughout – from relationships with vendors and customers to their shareholders and the financial community. With the financial community, credibility largely reflects the ability of management to meet expectations. Therefore, the message to communicate current conditions and plans for delivering shareholder value should include updates and revisions as conditions warrant. When key elements of the message, such as business and earnings expectations, change significantly or materially, these must be broadly and quickly disseminated.

An important consideration for message development is not only what information investors want and need for their analysis, but also the standards set by competitive companies. Generally, a simple benchmark for formatting and disclosure can be established by comparing and analysing the shareholder documents for a group of peer companies.

A formalised disclosure policy is also key to communicating effectively with shareholders and treating them as customers. Basically, management can view disclosure in two ways: 'Why not disclose that?' or 'Why should that be disclosed?'

Research by the University of Michigan's Mark Lang and Russell Lundholm shows that more complete disclosure of financial information results in better stock performance. However, it cannot be proved that better disclosure actually lowers the volatility of a company's stock price.

Shareholders, particularly institutional investors, want as much information as possible about operations and management's plans. However, most investors also understand a company's need to limit disclosure of proprietary information.

Prior to deciding to release specific information, it is worth considering whether management would be willing to release the information consistently, in good times and bad, to all investors. If not, then it should not be provided at any time, to any investor. The company's credibility suffers when disclosure differentiation exists – either with inconsistent disclosure of data or inconsistent disclosure to different investors. This is not to say that the same depth of detail needs to be provided to small individual investors as to very large institutional investors, who conduct sophisticated analysis. However, there should be no material differences in the information released to institutional and individual investors.

The benefits of treating the shareholder as the customer

The actual benefits that accrue to a company are difficult to measure. The problem is multidimensional, in that to date there have been no ways to measure how effective such communications programmes are.

Essentially, however, it appears that a company that treats shareholders as valued customers lowers the risk to its stock price and, in many cases, to the careers of senior management. Intuitively, two primary reasons exist for treating the shareholder as a customer, both of which are fundamental and connect directly with why most companies today have formalised investor relations programmes.

One major benefit is obvious when business fails to meet expectations or an event occurs over which the company has no control. When a proactive programme has been in place – with shareholders identified and communications tailored to address their needs – management has a ready-made forum for rationalising or explaining its position. While there are many alternative venues for communicating with shareholders, an existing programme that has generated goodwill and built management credibility by providing information tailored to meet investors' needs allows the company to get its story out directly without the filter of either the brokerage-house analysts or the media.

The second benefit is that management will be more aware of, and understand better, investor interests and concerns. These, which vary and change over time, are frequently important both for structuring the company's message and alerting management to significant business and competitive issues.

Stocks that appear to be undervalued compared to their peers and the market may open up investors' questions. These may include industry factors, financial strategies, competitive positioning or management. Corporations are generally aware when their stock price is not being valued at the same level as companies in their competitive universe. However, management is frequently unaware of investors' concerns and the methods of valuation most often used. Without this knowledge and understanding, the company may not be able to alter its message to provide an explanation or rationalisation of the factors causing the disparity in valuation.

While treating shareholders as valued customers and providing information that meets their needs are important at all times, these seem less apparent when stock markets are going up or when earnings momentum is strong. However, the full benefits that can be derived in treating the shareholder as a customer will best be achieved if the plans are made and the programmes put into place during good times. Then, when the market turns soft, the company will be in a position to benefit from its understanding of its shareholder base. And, at this time, the importance of knowing its customers well will pay off.

44

Grassroots Communications

Mohammed Mirza
BNFL Corporate Communications Unit,
University of Salford

How convenient it would be for organisations if they could just go about their daily business without having continuously to worry about the repercussions of their actions. In the fast-paced and information-hungry world we live in today, even small business manoeuvres are carefully reviewed by multidimensional constituents.

It took four years of meticulous scrutiny, examination and discussion before government approval was granted for the first British North Sea oil platform to be dumped at sea. All of this came to no avail as Greenpeace succeeded in its demolition campaign to mobilise public opinion against Shell and the UK government. Greenpeace succeeded in its actions through clinical precision in its communications strategy and execution.

So how can communications strategies help or hinder an airport's plans to build another terminal, the government's plans to bulldoze its way through green pastures to build a motorway link, or an oil company's attempts to dispose of its oil platform in the middle of the North Atlantic?

Communication professionals are beginning to recognise a fundamental change in how people receive and process information. New technological innovations have made communications faster while at the same time creating new audiences for communication products who are more eager to express their attitudes and beliefs through their actions and not just words (hence the term 'political consumer'). These electronic technologies have made us image sensitive and therefore, arguably, words no longer play the sole critical role in communications that they once did. What many fail to appreciate is that communication, just like any other organisational activity or asset, has not only to be managed, but more importantly for it to reap reward, it has to be managed effectively. As we approach the new millennium, the fostering of effective and powerful communication remains embedded in a few basic principles.

Be precise

There are two immediate reasons that communicators should concentrate on precision of meaning. First, people are now less imaginative and draw less on their own imagination; second, unlike advertising, which plays and evokes on the target audience's imagination, when attempting to communicate serious information nothing should be left to the individual's imagination, as this can lead to a variety of interpretations and misunderstandings.

In addition, you must emphasise what is most important for the target audience (set the priorities). When you attempt to emphasise everything, you will fail to emphasise anything. What you mean to say is really of no consequence, it is the message which is actually being interpreted by recipients which matters, and of paramount importance is how your message is interpreted and acted on.

Be true

Make sure that what you say is true, then make it convincing and believable. Openness and honesty do not necessarily mean telling everybody absolutely everything. However, deceit, dishonesty and false fronts are recipes for disaster from which a company may never recover.

Target your efforts

Even large organisations have constraints on resources and time, which make it almost impossible to concentrate on all of the company's publics all of the time. Quite often substantial time, money and energy are wasted on people and groups who are simply lost causes. These people will not be persuaded no matter what is said or done. Another group which is often the target of considerable resources is made up of those who are definitely on your side anyway. Through mapping, both primary and secondary audiences of the company can be identified, after which initial attention should be focused on 'fence-sitters' who are more prone to persuasion. At any given time on any given issue, the stance that a company's publics take may vary from active or passive to latent. Naturally, the company's energy and resources should be directed towards those publics most active at the time.

Build coalitions

When faced with overwhelming public opinion and opposing organisations, as in the case of Shell UK, coalitions built on common interests should be fostered. The UK government had continued vigorously and publicly to demonstrate its backing of Shell's decision. Imagine the government's surprise when Shell finally announced its climb down without first communicating this decision to its most valuable champion.

Avoid making assumptions

Informing media people and responding to their needs does not necessarily equate to informing the public and responding to *their* needs. You can not assume that just because something is said during a press briefing or in a press statement that it will reach the public. Therefore, organisations should also go directly to the public. The media have a thirst for, and concentrate on, the more dramatic 'news' stories, which are not always in the best interest of your organisation. Good communications should take steps to ensure that what the media report is correct as well as being the information the company wants to get across.

Take action

Action speaks louder than words, so when you are communicating, do so in conjunction with some action. If you say you are going to look into something, hold a public meeting or do something else, then stick to it, and more importantly communicate the action you have taken.

Rules of thumb

For each of these principles, there are some rules of thumb to ensure that your company's messages have the best chance of zeroing in on targets and achieving the results you want. Resistance and prejudice to communications exist in all of us. Most people are sceptical of the messages they receive from organisations and government. Communicators must recognise that most people reject a large proportion of the messages they receive and only absorb a small percentage of communications directed at them. To inform, persuade, convince and teach people who are 'overmessaged' and oversold, a communicator's task is to break through the communications clutter by greatly oversimplifying and repeating the message again and again, until it begins to sink in. At all times remain consistent.

Communication is an ongoing process. It is happening all the time and nothing can be done to stop it. Bad news travels faster than good news. On a wider scale, this is usually a result of the lack of interest shown by the media who view good news as no news. To combat this, businesses must move faster to communicate bad news and work harder to get the good news across. Phocion may have been justified for saying some 2300 years ago that 'the good have no need of an advocate'. Today, however, communications technology has rendered obsolete that noble thought.

Effective communication is based on strategy, which in turn is itself reliant on effective and timely communication. Before you can solve any problems, you have to be able to communicate, and break down the barriers of communication. All this takes work, and work is what grassroots communications is all about. It may be a long, slow process, but when it works it lasts. The greatest problem in communications, George Bernard Shaw once commented, 'is the illusion that it has been accomplished'.

45

Issues Management as the Foundation for Public Affairs Success

Gloria Walker, ABC, MIPR
*Public Affairs Manager, Lucas Industries,
and President, UK Chapter, International
Association of Business Communicators
(IABC)*

In my company, issues management takes up the majority of time spent on public affairs programmes. Although it is integrated with our government relations activities, issues management is the foundation on which other public affairs activities are built.

From the time it came into being some two decades ago, issues management has evolved into a systematic process that helps an organisation identify, assess and deal with threats and opportunities in the external environment. In a world characterised by constant change, every private and public-sector operation needs a distinct system which provides a wake-up call and an early warning by pointing to emerging social, political and economic trends and issues.

The targets

Issues management programmes are usually targeted at elected representatives and appointed officials at all levels of government, as well as pressure groups and industry coalitions. It is also important to inform internal audiences about the company's position on particular issues. As well as being involved in the programmes, managers and employees meet with customers, suppliers and other stakeholders on a regular basis. It is necessary for internal spokespeople to carry a consistent message to these influential audiences.

The four stages of an issue

Many people believe that issues management is only important in a time of crisis. An effective issues-management programme can help organisations invest their resources most effectively by recognising that an issue often has different stages.

- A *potential* issue consists of trends or ideas which are not yet in the public domain, even though some experts or publics may be aware of them. These issues can be identified through green papers, media reports and government or industry studies. It is important to monitor the activities of target audiences in government to identify potential issues;
- During the *emerging* issue stage, one or more publics are trying to push an issue forward to legitimise it and build support. As yet, the potential impact is unknown and it may be possible to take steps to stop the issue from growing;
- A *current* issue is enduring and intensive. The full potential impact is now apparent. Governments may be coming under pressure to introduce constraints to change the behaviour of the organisation or industry. Be aware, however, that a current issue may have a long lifespan. Our work on industrial design rights, a current issue, has continued for three years and will probably be on our agenda for several years more;
- A *crisis* issue has reached the point where constraints or a backlash could cause real damage. Although the organisation's options have decreased, it must set a policy in response to the crisis. It is at this time that lobbying most often comes into use to show support for an organisation's position and to exert maximum pressure on government to enact or endorse it. Management of a crisis issue will involve other departments within an organisation, so it is important that crisis planning includes all aspects of a potential problem.

Public acceptance

Due to the exponential growth in the potential number of stakeholders on any given issue, organisations now have an additional bottom line – public acceptance. People today don't have the same respect for authority and enterprise that existed when issues management first developed. A large number of people no longer care about an organisation's products and services. They are concerned about equal opportunity, wealth distribution, health protection and environmental impact. To avoid being legislated or regulated out of existence, producers of goods and services know that they have to build bridges between themselves and today's movers of public opinion.

The need for networks

No single issues-management professional can know everything about an organisation's activities. A network is needed to identify potential issues and to develop strategies for change. By working with people from a wide range of internal areas, a campaign can be designed to make the best case for the organisation's position. You can also identify those individuals who should become involved in the implementation of the campaign itself. This involvement builds support for the issues-management programme, which makes it more effective in representing the organisation to external audiences.

Results

Through effective implementation of the issues-management process, an organisation can shape government policy on issues that affect it, rather than just adapting to policy changes that have already been made. Such opinion-forming programmes can only be effective if issues are managed and influenced from the earliest opportunity. The earlier an organisation becomes involved in an issue, the more options there are for accelerating development of events which might present opportunities, redirecting possible threats and developing recommendations for internal change which allow the organisation to adapt to a changing world.

We are involved in a number of European issues which could have an impact on our businesses: air quality and vehicle emissions, aerospace policy, industrial design rights, funding, environment and tax, and competition, to name a few. Our early involvement has enabled us to influence the development of policy during the discussion stages without undertaking costly lobbying activities.

For example, before the EU emissions standards for 1996 were accepted, we had identified issues which we felt should be changed in the next round of reductions set for the year 2000. With the support of our advisers, we identified the appropriate EC officials and invited them to a briefing at one of our sites in the UK. Senior management and technical personnel discussed the issues in detail and established a working relationship with the officials. Our views were accepted and these issues further investigated with other interested parties, resulting in changes to the proposed regulations.

Building credibility

This one briefing achieved not only our short-term objectives, but positioned the company as a source of information for the Commission on a range of vehicle emissions issues, thus enabling us to continue to be involved in the development of emissions policy.

Our work on EU industrial design rights is another example of a low-key approach yielding important results. Several years ago a green paper was prepared on this issue, which indicated that it could have an adverse effect on our business. We continued to monitor progress and began to set out our strategy if draft legislation emerged, which it did in 1993. The proposed legislation meant that anyone could register a design for any purpose and secure the sole right to use of that design for a period of 25 years. This design protection included such diverse items as shoes, pottery, wallpaper, clothing, textiles and automotive parts like door panels, brake shoes and spark plugs. We believed that this legislation as drafted had serious implications, so we outlined an issues-management programme to change it.

An internal team was assembled which included specialists from the relevant divisions and departments. We carefully scrutinised the proposals, identifying those articles which we believed should be changed. After clarifying our position internally, the team met with EC officials for an initial exchange of views.

In my view, this initial exchange is one of the most important steps in a successful issues-management programme. It sets out the starting position and those areas which are negotiable. In the case of design rights, both parties were on clearly opposite sides of the issue. This initial exchange also formed the basis of a working relationship which has continued throughout the programme and has yielded valuable insight into the workings of the Commission.

The importance of knowing who's who and what's what

While working with the Commission, we also knew that we would have to determine a strategy for approaching the European Parliament and its Legal Affairs Committee which would review the proposals. Most of our contact with the committee was through written briefs and personal briefings for targeted members, particularly those from the UK. We believed that events were proceeding smoothly until some internal EC problems came to light. Work on the proposed regulation was halted and the focus shifted to the proposed directive which would set out the general provisions on the legislation. After two years of work, we had to re-evaluate our position, revise our strategies and identify additional individuals to brief. These included several industry associations which were promoting various changes to the legislation, some that we supported and some we did not.

After reviewing all the available information, both formal documents and informal intelligence, we agreed that the best way forward was to secure an amendment to Article 1 of the Directive which would change the definition of design to 'outwardly visible' during the use of the product, thus eliminating those parts which are not subject to appearance criteria. Our amendment, tabled by Christine Oddy, Member of the European Parliament and a member of the Legal Affairs Committee, was accepted by the full Parliament and has been incorporated into the revised text of the Directive.

Successful issues management also demands the ability to recognise when the best approach is to take no action whatsoever, while closely monitoring and consistently assessing developments. This is the approach we are now taking to the design rights issue. We achieved our objective but continue to maintain dialogue with the Commission and to monitor events.

46

Environmental Communications

Ray Palin
Director, Energy from Waste Association

Few companies enjoy the luxury of being in total control of their environmental profile. But most people would argue that business has a social responsibility, and that this extends to the protection of the environment.

As Anita Roddick, founder of The Body Shop, has written: 'Business leaders have a choice: they can build a PR wall ... or they can listen and respond ... Will they choose more smokescreens and inertia or will they listen and act? Consumers will be watching.'

How much businesses should do, how much consumers expect and how fast change is coming are not easy to forecast and depend a great deal on circumstances. What is right for one company in one sector may be disastrous in another situation.

Many companies publish statements of environmental policy. These are often framed in glossy brochures duly printed on environmentally friendly paper, but cut little ice with consumers who expect nothing less and campaigners who ask a great deal more. Such manifestos express good intentions – but as pieces of communication, they are not very effective.

Increasingly, there is a welcome trend towards monitoring and reporting back progress on key measures of environmental performance, in place of statements of intent. Vulnerabilities and performance are assessed, often with independent help, benchmarks established and future achievement against plan frankly reported on – warts and all. Immediately, communication becomes more effective, because it is two-way and because it is rooted not just in communications *per se* (the familiar green paint) but in actual change.

As long ago as the mid-1980s companies such as IBM instituted assessments of environmental performance and published key goals in environmental protection, energy conservation and waste minimisation. As a retailer, Sainsbury's has probably done as much as most companies in the field of social responsibility. Yet, probably owing to the constraints of the supermarket sector, it only produced its first environmental audit of products and trading practices in 1996.

Such programmes can be extended to include supplier performance and what has been called 'corporate environmentalism' – the creation of a culture where employees at every level are more conscious of the effect of company activities on the environment.

The problem is that environmental agendas are by definition different from business agendas. Furthermore, they are constantly shifting and can indeed often be contradictory. One has only to look through the headlines over time to see inconsistencies. An example is the diesel engine. Once so popular that conversion to diesel fleets was proudly reported on among environmentally conscious companies, the diesel engine has now become the villain of our High Streets and is reportedly the largest single contributor to PM 10s (particulate emissions below 10 micrometer in diameter).

Another in my own field is the apparent conflict between the need for more generation from renewable energy sources to combat the increasingly well-documented threat of global warming and NIMBY ('not in my back yard') opposition to the development of energy-from-waste power stations, without which targets for the replacement of fossil fuel generation are unlikely to be met and vast potential resources will go unused.

Such inconsistencies make it very difficult for business, with its extended planning cycles and relatively slow policy and communications implementation procedures. The agenda is of course also largely formed without business participation. It is thus doubly difficult for corporate communications departments to keep programmes on track, relevant and topical. Lack of preparedness – even isolation – is the biggest danger, and one which must be constantly countered by research, renewal and strategy reappraisal.

Media activity closely complements that of campaigners, whose very existence requires editors to publish scare stories – and not to dwell too much on the lack of evidence for them or, if true, the trade-offs that lie behind them. However, as Richard D North, author of *Life on a Modern Planet*, observed at the Energy from Waste Association national conference in 1996, the situation is gradually improving. The public and some journalists have realised that the issues are complicated and too important to vulgarise.

Thus when the BBC and others suddenly wondered why they had used so much campaigners' footage during the Brent Spar episode, the principle that journalism's job is to be sceptical and independent was re-established.

In a world where concern for the environment, its sanctity and supremacy form one of the strongest moral driving forces of the day, when scientific experts are no longer trusted and where in the minds of some activists and their supporters no expense or technical difficulty is too great to limit or prevent the achievement of a particular outcome which they have decided is desirable, politics take over from science and emotion replaces logic.

The key is to realise that facts alone will never win the argument. The emotional aspects of environmental communications are just too strong.

The tools that work best in this difficult arena are those most calculated to build trust. Those that are ineffective include self-serving recitals of 'facts', a failure to recognise the fundamental attitudes of the target audiences and over-reliance on the media, the most fickle and least controllable of channels.

Perhaps the need for research and more research is the most important result of some recent high-profile experiences. Personal briefings, open dialogue, community involvement and coalition building, although costly in management time, are more likely to be successful. To an ever-increasing extent, these activities represent essential investment in positioning and communications programming.

The environmental crisis – about which so much has been written – brings home the lesson quickly and often painfully for those involved. Timescales are telescoped, pressures mount and the organisation freezes. Without well-honed crisis-management procedures, the damage is uncontrolled and the opportunities provided by the sudden spotlight of interest go uncaptured. Good preparedness involves a regularly updated crisis manual, top management involvement, the mobilisation of specialist media teams and a wide range of direct communications tools aimed at key publics to bypass the media. Everyday environmental communications involves similar principles, but at an easier pace.

Trust can be built over time, in the ways mentioned. But it can be lost in a few hours. There can be no automatic assumption that borders, custom and practice or the attitude of regulators will contain an issue – or even that a hard-won green image will be respected or even understood in a fast-developing new situation. Dynamic communication is key and should guide the development of every environmental communication strategy if it is to succeed. The descriptor 'dynamic' here means a willingness to react to changing circumstances, the flexibility to marshal a range of activities –

including senior management and allied organisations – at short notice and mount or change campaigns in terms of weight, message and target audience within days, even hours. In other words, a well-developed rapid-reaction capability, driven by a close monitoring, research and issues-management capability akin to that employed by the campaigners themselves, or by a modern political party.

There is no certain path to green virtue. Superior communications and even good deeds are not enough, as we see daily – although they are certainly necessary. The only rule is that there are no rules; little in the politics of the environment is given or permanent.

The one thing that is certain is that the groundswell cannot be ignored. Each business must be aware, remain in touch and respond actively.

There has been little room in a brief essay such as this to cover in more detail the nuts and bolts of environmental communications – auditing, target selection, tone of voice, channels of communication and message selection.

If you have to ask, you're probably getting it wrong.

47

PR Service in the 21st Century

Jackie Elliot
*Chairman, Public Relations Consultants
Association, and Chief Executive,
Manning, Selvage & Lee Ltd*

As the new century approaches, public relations practitioners, whose own profession has only been developed in recent times, are facing a breathtaking array of new services, media outlets and required competencies.

The creation and spread of information technology, and the breadth of all forms of direct and indirect communication that it has delivered, plays straight to the skills and discipline of public relations practice. The variety of our work, its creativity and flexibility, make it the ideal catalyst for effective new media communication. And as the industry and its clients seek evaluation methodologies and benchmarks, the new data-based media and ease of quantitative analysis will increasingly provide the solution to measurement and performance dilemmas.

A number of the new services which will enhance our standards of professional practice are already available, but they are unpackaged and poorly marketed to mainstream practitioners and are still too much the prerogative of the media nerd.

Globalisation of programmes has led to most consultants needing to work in several languages and yet translation software capability does not yet match that of the many on-line media outlets. At the same time, one of the fundamental tools of our trade – the media list – is still bogged down in country-by-country parameters. The World Wide Web is showing all of us how to talk on a genuinely transnational basis – other media, and the rest of us who are *nyet* net-savvy, must follow.

Staying in the area of media relations, as the volume of electronic publishing increases so will the need for educated monitoring services. We simply will not have the time to scan the enormous amount of information pertaining to our clients and the issues and opportunities they face in the global marketplace. Information gathering, analysis and evaluation will be a key service for all public relations practitioners in the coming years – and those services able to add experiential intelligence to the process will be the winners.

The old-fashioned benefits of personal contact will diminish as the editorial staff of on-line or web-based publications, wherever they are in the world, become the targets of messages and news put out by consultants a couple of continents away.

Paul Holmes, publisher of the US's influential *Reputation Management*, points out that the Internet is a medium that sits best with the communications skills that public relations presents. It is a medium that is educative rather than didactic in the way of traditional advertising practice. It demands more subtle audience interaction than heavy sell and already its nature tends towards editorial, commentary and debate, whether on a commercial site or with a single-issue pressure group.

Public relations practice has long been the only real means of developing strategies to reach all the constituencies that are involved with, affected and targeted by, a commercial organisation. The new breakdown in media barriers will increase the value of this all-encompassing role and it will be a foolish CEO who seeks to give one message to his investors, another to his customers and yet a third to his employees – as has sometimes been the case. In the boardroom of successful organisations in the twenty-first century, the corporate communications chief will guide policy to a much greater extent than his or her mid-twentieth century predecessor. In those days, this role was primarily concerned with the dissemination of information ... of influence, but of influence after the event.

Soon, fortunately, much more attention will be paid to broad communications counsel. The impact of corporate behaviour on the success of product, service or share price will require this, as will the need for advocacy across a wide range of stakeholders' constituencies. No amount of 'spin' can turn a sow's ear into a silk purse. So tones of voice will become more productive and less patronising than before.

To give that counsel, the public relations practitioner will move from what has often been a media-focused background, to that of law, psychology, social policy and business studies. Simple marketing communications will become a better integrated function of the marketing department, which in turn will report to the corporate communications executive – even now possibly the only corporate officer to have a whole company health check as part of his or her responsibilities.

48

The Institute of Public Relations 1996 Sword of Excellence Awards

Jeremy Weinberg
Press and Marketing Officer, Institute of Public Relations

The Institute of Public Relations conducts its Sword of Excellence Awards programme each year to find, recognise and publicise the best in public relations practice in the UK. As well as the obvious benefits to the winners, the programme provides a rich source of case-study material for students, academics and practitioners. The winning cases highlighted here are described in detail in a booklet available from the IPR for £15. The comments below are based on those of the judges.

1996 Sword of Excellence Winner: Divorce: A Fair Deal for Families (Public Affairs)/Fishburn Hedges

This was a £60,000 political and media campaign on behalf of The Solicitors Family Law Association (SFLA), representing 3600 family lawyers. The Family Law Bill sought to change the grounds for divorce to include a minimum waiting period of a year, including various information and mediation procedures and a lesser role for lawyers.

SFLA's main concerns were:

- to promote the case for legal advice before, during and after mediation;
- to ensure that there would be a genuinely free choice between negotiation through lawyers and mediation.

The programme contained all the elements of a well-rounded public affairs project. Objectives were fully met; all target audiences reached; research was used intelligently; qualitative media coverage was achieved. At no point was the government antagonised. 'Briefing of the client, and communication with its members, were exemplary,' said the IPR's judge.

Runner-up: Public Awareness Campaign – Extortionate Credit (Low Budget Programmes)/Carlisle City Council

From a desk in a small office in Carlisle came one of the most socially-responsible national initiatives of the year. Carlisle City Council used a range of public relations techniques to highlight the national problem of loan-sharking, and achieved real and significant improvement in the financial hardship experienced by a particularly deprived group of citizens. On a budget of little over £600 the campaign reached six million people, won the support of 14 other councils and two national agencies, and pinpointed usury in modern-day Britain, where the poorest suffer under the burden of interest rates in excess of 1000 per cent APR. The campaign drew all-party support including over 100 signatures for an early day motion in the Commons. The issue has been taken up by the Minister for Consumer Affairs.

Category Winner – City, Financial & Investor Relations: New Year's Resolutions '96 for Independent Financial Advice Promotion/Lansons Communications

This was an example of good populist public relations. The campaign 'New Year's Resolutions' generated substantial press coverage, both at national and local level, and cleverly utilised the national obsession with making New Year's resolutions. It also coincided with the quietest time of the year for most independent financial advisers and fitted neatly into the other initiatives being run during the rest of the year. The campaign had some good measurement indicators, including usage of the IFA promotion hotline and take-up of the *Daily Mail* IFA Promotion Financial Planning Log Book. There was also a very satisfied client, which is in itself an important indicator.

Category Winner – Internal Communication: United Friendly: Rebranding from the Inside Out/Fishburn Hedges

The objective was to communicate the rationale for the acquisition of a financial planning company from American Express; enthuse the employees from both companies, uniting them behind one brand; and to motivate the sales force. The campaign was fully researched, well planned and implemented using attractive materials and with a personal and participative approach. Evaluation was built into the programme and logistics addressed. The nature of the programme and objectives generated an appropriate cost/benefit ratio.

Category Winner – Consumer Public Relations: Compaq – Bringing Cyberspace Down to Earth/The RED Consultancy

This campaign was strong and supportive of Compaq's commercial objective to increase market share in the home PC market. A strong research base led to an imaginative programme which achieved the objectives of breaking into the consumer media, demystifying computer jargon and achieving the desired increase in market share.

Category Winner – Industry & Commerce: The KPMG Leadership Programme/KPMG

A highly targeted, carefully considered public relations programme designed to achieve two main objectives which would have a considerable impact on the business. It demonstrated the importance of understanding customer perceptions in creating an effective PR programme.

A combination of good research, thorough planning, attention to detail during implementation, professional measurement of results and a close working partnership with senior management within the client company produced an excellent result.

Furthermore, it is a skilful example of using personality to raise profit – most especially in terms of the managing partner.

Community Relations: The Esso Living Tree Campaign/Scope: Communications

The campaign achieved opinion-former recognition of corporate concern for key environmental issues, built lasting partnerships, increased awareness of Esso's involvement and resulted in the planting of over one million trees. Good research and evaluation complemented well-produced and targeted literature using a strong corporate identity created to promote the campaign. The tangible results of the campaign are a real benefit to the environment as well as the enhancement of corporate image. Measurement of opinion-former awareness and media coverage confirmed the impact of the programme.

Not for Profit Organisations: 150th Birthday of Thomas Barnardo/Barnardo's

Research played a major part in shaping a succinct and effective campaign. The use of surveys to generate media interest is well proven and, in this case, helped to sustain activity right through, from briefing volunteers to the climax. All the material worked hard and the entry presentation was first class.

Special Programmes: Guardian Insurance World Transplant Games/Staniforth Public Relations

The task was to achieve regional and national publicity for the World Transplant Games held in Manchester in order to raise the profile of transplantation as a medical success story and to encourage more people to join the NHS donor register. Worthiness alone would not guarantee coverage and a well-researched plan was devised and implemented which achieved its objectives and subsequently has been adopted as a template by the World Transplant Games Federation and organisers of the next Games in Australia.

Part 9

Crisis Communications

49

When Will They Ever Learn?

John Clare
Managing Director, Lion's Den
Communications Management

Memorandum

To: Corporate Affairs Director
From: AJ Nalist
Re: Tactics that don't work in a crisis.

Having watched you and your fellow directors make a hash of things in the public prints (not to mention TV, radio and for all I know the Internet, World Wide Web and at conferences in fancy hotels all over the world) here are my observations on things you do that don't help in a crisis:

- PR as sticking plaster does not work.
- Smoke and mirrors don't fool anyone.
- Blaming the media is not a good idea.
- Sweeping things under the carpet doesn't hide them.

PR as sticking plaster

If you are, say, the director of a shipping line and your biggest ship is named after the current monarch, don't set out across the Atlantic with a shipload of passengers when the loos don't work, there's no heating and the bedrooms aren't finished. For a start, the passengers (I know they're unreasonable) might take the view they've paid good money for the trip of a lifetime and are being short-changed. With modern communications technology, they might just ring their friends back home to complain, one of whom might tell a journalist who won't take your side if you've sent the ship to a foreign dockyard for a refit while British dock workers stand idle. I know it's unreasonable, but if you do own the flagship of the British merchant fleet, the media will expect higher standards than if you're running the ferry across the Mersey (though that itself always makes a good headline, so don't take risks even if that is your line).

PR people think this is tragically accurate – too little, too late. Reporters find this type of thing hilariously funny. Sometimes, when they've finished a hard day's reporting on a crisis, they gather over a drink and swap stories of their favourite corporate cock-ups. They say things like, 'How did they ever expect to get away with it?' and 'When will they ever learn?'

Smoke and mirrors

Many journalists are simple people, so they ask simple questions. If, for example, you are running a monopolistic gas corporation which has been privatised in the teeth of fierce opposition from politicians, unions, consumers and the public, don't give the boss a whopping great pay rise at the same time as you're announcing the closure of showrooms, because journalists will put the two things together and ask, 'How can you justify this?' If your answer is along the lines of having to pay the going rate for the job in a competitive environment, economic trends, supply and demand, and refers to profit ratios, share options and complex bonus arrangements made ages ago, they will scratch their heads and say, 'Silly me, I thought it was because you were cashing in on the record profits, and his pension would be pegged to his final salary, so he won't have to worry about things like the cold weather allowance in his old age.' I know they're unreasonable, but that's how they are.

If journalists are simple, other people who don't agree with you are very clever. You should watch out, for example, if you hear the union have hired a pig and given it a name similar to the boss's, and are bringing it along to the AGM with a trough. (Equally, beware if people dress up as fat cats on the steps outside your HQ.) They know how to attract journalists and get their pictures in the papers with reporters on their side – maybe you should recruit one of them?

Blaming the media

Let's say you're a high-profile, soccer-loving, self-publicising politician who will remain nameless, and you have a secret – you're having an affair with an actress. If the media find out, they won't accept that it's their fault, so it's no use blaming them – especially if you happen to be the minister in charge of looking into privacy laws and you have a talent for saying things which attract attention, like 'The press are drinking in the last chance saloon.' You may find reporters looking puzzled and saying things like, 'We didn't kidnap him, frogmarch him round to a bedsit, dress him in a Chelsea kit and tuck him up in bed with her.'

Here's another tip – if you do go down this road, and decide to sue a national newspaper for claiming, say, that you've taken money for asking questions in Parliament, make sure there are no documents in existence that could destroy your case and prove embarrassing, because journalists are very good at finding these things – in fact they regard it as an enjoyable part of the job, and usually rise to the challenge. If a number of your chums have already been caught out up to no good, reporters start writing words like 'sleaze' (which is another good headline word).

Sweeping under the carpet

This is related to the above, but fails just as spectacularly. Let's say you're the first company to announce details of your bid to run part of the railway system – the jewel in the Government's latest privatisation crown – and know that an internal inquiry will unmask a serious fraud. You try and bluff it out, but journalists regard bluff-busting as part of their job. So again, you end up with egg on your face.

It's the same if you and your wife stay at a posh French hotel, and can't remember exactly who paid the bill – was it a prominent businessman, or did your wife pay? It's easy for these things to slip your mind, but journalists will find out if they want to, and again your picture will be in the papers for the wrong reasons.

Recommendation

You can probably spot a trend in these stories, and even think of other examples which fit the pattern. It seems to me you are making life easy for journalists by doing many of these things in the first place. Several pieces of advice spring to mind, but they all come down to the same thing because, as the Bible put it, 'Be sure your sins will find you out'. Maybe you should take Abraham Lincoln's advice to heart, and agree that you can't fool all of the people all of the time. My friends in the business of crisis management put it succinctly: 'We're used to making silk purses out of sows' ears, but we do at least need a sow's ear. We're not magicians, we can't make things disappear, nor can we unsay things that have been said. We are, in effect, jugglers, not conjurers.'

50

Preparedness Planning and Simulation

Mike Seymour
Managing Director Issues & Crisis Management, Burson-Marsteller/Europe

Corporate management, faced with a serious issue or emergency in the public domain, is immediately challenged by an exceptional and demanding set of management problems. Once the situation reaches crisis proportions the agenda begins to be driven from outside the company. Suddenly the three most common characteristics of any crisis begin to take effect:

- *Surprise* – the timing will never be convenient, usually at a weekend or in the middle of the night, when key players will be unavailable;
- *Increased noise* – the clamour, particularly from the media, will cause dissonance and increase tensions within the situation, while facts are replaced by distortion, rumour and speculation;
- *Lack of accurate information* – while there will be no shortage of allegations and accusations in the public domain, key decision makers will discover that vital information will be unobtainable.

These characteristics and their consequent effects on management lie at the nub of the problems that will face senior managers, as they struggle with increasingly complex situations, which carry both short- and long-term implications for the organisation.

Contingency and preparedness planning

In any market, laws and regulations lay down detailed requirements for operational and emergency procedures. Furthermore, risk assessors and insurers will seek to impose contingency parameters that reduce the possible effects of identified physical and criminal threats to the organisation. However, preparedness plans need to integrate the wider management functions which will be required in managing a crisis:

- defining and solving the problem;
- controlling internal and external communications;
- managing the rest of the business.

Thus the scope of crisis preparedness is wider than normal contingency planning, encompassing a larger range of management and communications functions and resources. In order to prepare a business organisation to anticipate and handle crises, a logical process is required for risk assessment and plan development. Here is a step-by-step approach to preparedness planning, which has been successfully developed for use with a wide range of industries and business sectors in markets across the world.

Step 1 – Assessing risks and threats

The first step in preparedness planning seeks to define the worst-case scenarios that an organisation could face. Since these situations will be played out under the glare of public and media scrutiny, it is necessary to conduct the assessment, taking an objective external view of the business.

It has been found that in order to gain an objective viewpoint, the process of assessing risks and threats involves a co-ordinated programme of information gathering through:

- discussion with key management at corporate and middle manager levels;
- site visits and operational tours;
- review of existing plans and procedures;
- examination of internal and external systems.

Assessment is best undertaken by a multidisciplinary team, augmented by external support, to ensure objective review and analysis, drawing on the experience of other companies where possible.

At the conclusion of this first stage, the assessment team should produce a report for senior management which includes:

- a list of risks and threats to the business ranked by level of risk and probability;

- recommendations on how current plans, procedures and systems can be improved;
- a proposed programme for further preparedness planning and crisis training;
- assessment of the management and financial resources needed to execute each recommendation.

Step 2 – Crisis plan development

Once top management has agreed the programme for further work, plan development can commence. Procedures, systems and facilities for crisis management need to be designed with the following objectives:

- To equip management to monitor and pick up early warning signals of any impending issue or incident with the potential to have negative impacts on the business;
- To alert key management and speed timely accurate information to crisis managers, to permit rapid situation analysis and decision making;
- To assist corporate management in quickly convening the optimum strategic team, supported by the most appropriate internal and external technical and specialist expertise. To facilitate tightly co-ordinated management of operational and integrated communications activity.

Composition of crisis plans

When a crisis hits, timelines crumble as external groups and individuals pressurise management for information, opinions and decisions. Media deadlines quickly begin to shape the corporate schedule of events. Under these circumstances managers do not have time to read long and complex procedures and instructions. Plans and systems need to be succinct, with the emphasis on guidance for decision making. Check that systems will ensure critical analysis or planning steps are not omitted.

Good preparedness plans comprise easy-to-access checklists and guidelines, supported by contact information. Communications materials can be prepared in advance in outline formats, thus permitting rapid updating as situations escalate.

Once preparedness plans have been completed in draft, the principles need to be cleared by those top managers most likely to comprise the crisis-management teams. At this stage inclusion of their experience and expertise will ensure the relevance and effectiveness of the final plans, procedures and systems.

If crisis-management manuals are to cover all possible risk or threat scenarios, it will be necessary to include procedures for handling confidential or sensitive situations. These confidentiality constraints will demand that crisis manuals are prepared, distributed, held and used under secure conditions.

During the planning process it will be necessary to define the facilities and support that crisis teams will require. Normal telephone, fax and secretarial arrangements will be insufficient when corporate management is handling a series of complex problems in the middle of a blitz of calls, faxes and meetings. At the same time security, catering and sleeping arrangements may have to be considered. Finally, plans should be made for handling a serious incident when normal offices or buildings have had to be evacuated or abandoned due to threats or damage.

Testing and validation through simulation

The process of preparing an organisation fully to anticipate and react to crises will take several months and requires active support and participation by management at all levels. However good the assessment and plan-development phases, senior management cannot be fully confident that procedures and systems will operate satisfactorily without testing and validating their plans.

Experience of working alongside corporate management in crisis shows that only realistic simulation techniques can successfully test and validate crisis-management plans. The techniques and sophistication of simulation can vary according to the level of experience of the crisis managers and the scenarios that could face them. However, all simulation modules involve the presentation of problems to crisis managers, against scenarios which become steadily more complex as timelines are rapidly reduced.

Crisis situations can be fed in through telephone calls, faxes, messages and role-played meetings and interviews with customers, consumers, regulators, politicians, local authorities, emergency services, local residents, community leaders and the press represented by journalists plus TV or radio reporters and newscasts. Simulation training and exercises should be planned and run to test teams and stress procedures and systems in order to identify and highlight deficiencies and problems. Individuals should not be made to feel threatened and each session should aim to offer a learning experience for all participants. The balance between realistic pressure and teaching lessons through hands-on experience should be achieved through a combination of tight co-ordination within the facilitation and exercise-control teams who run the simulation. The same control teams, who should be experienced crisis managers or counsellors, should analyse and discuss their observations of the information handling, decision-making and communication actions of the players. Follow-up reports should recommend the next planning and training steps to augment and improve plans and build team capabilities.

At the conclusion of a successful simulation exercise, senior management will be confident that their organisation is alert and ready to handle crisis situations with speed and assurance. Only then are business organisations truly ready to face issues and incidents of crisis proportions.

Preparedness planning – a corporate necessity

Any business organisation could be faced by a crisis at any time. The risks, pressures and challenges of handling these serious issues and incidents under the glare of public and media scrutiny demand detailed assessment, preparation and validation. Preparedness planning and testing through simulation of crisis situations are essential steps to ensure that any company is truly ready. Such precautions are now seen to be an integral element of corporate responsibility.

51

Surviving Corporate Disaster – A Case History

Peter Hill
Head of Corporate Communications,
Lloyd's of London*

From Bangkok to Baltimore, it would be rare indeed to find a taxi driver who had not heard of Lloyd's of London. True, those who know the word Lloyd's may not be familiar with what it is, what it does and its more recent near demise, but they recognise the name. It is a name synonymous with insurance, and yes, with ships, specifically the insurance of their hulls and cargoes, but much, much more besides.

For more than 300 years, Lloyd's has been at the heart of the London insurance market, that centre of world insurance expertise which continues to oil the wheels of commerce and industry, providing insurance and reinsurance cover for a bewildering array of risks, from restaurants in Alaska to nuclear power stations and from the vocal chords of opera singers to the mundane four-door family saloon.

Structure

Lloyd's is distinctive. It is, however, a marketplace not a company and,

* The views expressed in this article are those of the author.

until 1994, its capital was provided solely by wealthy individuals who traded on the basis of unlimited liability. For generations, this unique marketplace flourished as it had done down the centuries – give or take the odd setback when the market produced a loss; after all, insurance is a risk business – and it seemed set to sail on effortlessly.

Trouble looms

But in 1988 the first signs emerged of something going awry. Not too much of a problem perhaps; after all, other insurers faced up to the cyclical downturn compounded by too much capacity chasing rates downwards and an unprecedented run of natural and industrial catastrophes. Between 1988 and 1992, Lloyd's syndicates which constitute the marketplace had racked up losses aggregating more than £8 billion. Lloyd's investors, known universally as Names, reeled and reacted. Unlimited liability became a reality. Worse still, many found that their losses stemmed from the reinsurance of American insurance companies which had provided insurance cover to companies engaged in processing asbestos.

The vagaries of the American justice system produced judgements which fell ultimately on Lloyd's current members, even though the policies being claimed on may well have been purchased decades earlier.

Crisis

The crisis at Lloyd's was complex both in its origins and in its resolution: this was not a product recall nor a single disaster of Bhopal proportions capable of resolution or containment by well-tried and tested communication-response mechanisms. Here was a situation, set to last for years, where there was a severe danger that clients of the market would pull their business out; where investors became bitter, angry and litigious and simply refused to pay; where a jewel in the City's crown threatened to become a canker with implications far beyond the confines of the Square Mile.

The foundations for averting catastrophe were laid in the implementation of radical reforms recommended by a taskforce which reported in 1992 (an underwriting year for which Lloyd's recorded a loss of £1193 million) and there were sound indications of profits – significant profits – for 1993 and beyond. But could the time gap be bridged, would clients be persuaded that the market would be able to accept their business and, most importantly, continue to meet their valid claims? The prospects were reasonable, but the investors – the Names – were angry.

Ill-organised at first, disparate, but at all times vocal action groups (to number more than 60 eventually) geared up for legal action against the agents who represented their interests at Lloyd's. Lawyers rubbed their hands and the clerks of the Commercial Court wore fevered brows at the prospect of Lloyd's-related litigation clogging their courtrooms through to and beyond the millennium.

In 1993, Lloyd's published its first ever business plan, introduced corporate members' trading on a limited liability basis and made an attempt – unsuccessfully – to reach a settlement with its investors.

Towards a rebuild

It was beyond doubt that to avert disaster, any further settlement offer would have to achieve two objectives: first, it would need to be based on consensus and support from the action groups and their members worldwide; second, it would need to provide every member with 'finality', an end to their exposure to and liability for the ruinous losses arising from asbestosis, pollution and health-hazard claims. It was a monumental challenge and involved one of the largest financial reconstructions ever undertaken.

Finality would be provided by a new company, Equitas, which would enable all members to reinsure their liabilities for 1992 and earlier years. But Lloyd's also needed to ensure that finality was provided at a price which was affordable, while at the same time emphasising that no one who wished to accept the settlement offer would be denied it through lack of financial means.

The reconstruction and renewal proposals (R&R) were outlined in May 1995 with a settlement package valued initially at £2800 million. A year later the offer was raised to £3100 million and in July 1996 the package had a value of £3200 million.

The need for communication

To build consensus, communication with investors worldwide through meetings, seminars and a steady flow of written information, allied to an effective media campaign and backed up by tracking research, became a priority. At the heart of 'R&R' was the need to ensure that the membership understood clearly the consequences for themselves as individuals of the offer being made to them. Pro-forma indicative statements were issued in March 1996, followed in June by updated figures before final statements were issued in late July 1996.

The breakthrough came in June 1996 when Lloyd's reported a profit for the 1993 account of £1084 million and projected profits of a similar order for the following two years. In the following month, members voted overwhelmingly in support of making a refundable special contribution of £440 million towards the funding of the plan. Tracking showed a rising level of support for acceptance, although tolerance levels at the deluge of documentation being unleashed on members were reaching breaking point.

By early August, it appeared from every indicator available that the lifting of conditions for the authorisation of Equitas was a mere formality and that the reconstruction would be achieved. There was one potentially devastating event to unfold. A group of American members brought an action in a Virginia court and, on the Friday before the August Bank Holiday weekend, the judge found in their favour. Four days later a panel of three appeal court judges overturned the potentially fatal judgment in an expedited hearing.

R&R was set to go forward, acceptances of the settlement offer were over 90 per cent and on 4 September the funding of Equitas was approved. Lloyd's famous Lutine Bell was rung an unprecedented three times to commemorate the achievement.

This had been a marathon which had begun five years earlier when the first losses had emerged and went on to confirm the old adage that things usually get worse before they get better. So what can be learned from the prolonged agony of the reconstruction? There are many factors to be considered beyond the essential qualities of patience, persistence and above all a commitment to securing a single objective – in Lloyd's case, its own survival.

Clearly, the prospect of a return to profitability provided the financial bedrock to make the theory of the reconstruction a reality and communication was a key component, with both chairman and chief executive officer actively involved – not simply in evolution of strategy, but also in its implementation. There really is no substitute for the senior officers to be seen (and heard) espousing the cause and fielding often hostile questions in a confident and convincing manner.

It is a commonplace these days to draw the analogy between the techniques used by the military and their deployment on the commercial battlefield. Strategy, tactics and campaign are words which translate easily from one context to the other. Make no mistake, the securing of Lloyd's reconstruction involved a prolonged campaign carefully planned – especially over the final eight months – with particular attention paid to the awesome logistics of printing, packing and distributing more than 100 tonnes of printed material (with a series of postal workers' strikes thrown in for good measure). As they say in military circles: 'If the logistics are OK, the tactics will look after themselves.'

It was also important to ensure that this huge exercise in communication, the shaping of messages (not necessarily soundbites) and briefing of press and media needed to be controlled. For many years Lloyd's had been the focus of media attention; after all, capital (in the shape of its traditional members) has a very human face. But were the messages getting through? Intelligence is vital and, in this campaign, tracking research among members and evaluation of media coverage played a vitally important role and on more than one occasion prompted a revision of tactics. Research among members showed beyond any doubt that the flow of information provided to them was appreciated but it also showed a rising level of support for the reconstruction package. Similarly evaluation of close on 11,000 press and media references both in the UK and North America showed a rising trend in favourability.

So where were the weaknesses in the campaign? In retrospect, it is clear that Lloyd's members in the United States posed a bigger threat than anticipated at the outset. A hard core of members there waged a vigorous and virulent campaign of vilification which was designed to provide them with the leverage to secure better terms. This potential threat was identified at the end of 1994, but pressure of events and, at the time, seemingly more important issues obscured the danger they posed: a case of the 'enemy's' strength being underestimated.

The tolling of the Lutine Bell on 4 September marked the success of the reconstruction, but it also served to remind everyone how extremely close Lloyd's had come to disaster.

52

Crisis on the Net*

Alan Coon
Editor, Interactive PR News

It must be shocking to see your company blatantly attacked in front of what seems like the whole world. But the Net is, after all, the great equaliser, putting the average citizen back in mass media. And a lot of companies are feeling the heat:

- A disgruntled Kmart ex-employee put up a Kmart Sucks Web site to belittle management incompetence;
- Several Web sites have gone up to oppose giant retailer Wal-Mart's plans for new stores in several communities;
- McDonald's was lambasted on the McSpotlight site. This featured the UK McLibel trial, a David vs. Goliath affair that has become a notorious public-relations disaster for the food chain.

Corporate interests call these 'rogue' Web sites. The opposition sees its mission as more noble, eg McSpotlight says, 'McDonald's spends over $1.8 billion a year broadcasting their glossy image to the whole world – this is a small space for alternatives to be heard.'

Then there are the newsgroups, which have instilled fear in many companies ever since Intel's famous 1994 Pentium processor debacle, which flared in newsgroup discussions and spewed over into traditional media. Intel's processor had one highly arcane glitch that would affect few users during their lifetimes, yet the masses were demanding replacements. There also are rogue newsgroups, such as <alt.destroy.microsoft>.

* © *Interactive PR News*, used with permission.

Investor-relations threat

Not to scare anyone, but far more serious threats to corporate and product brand equity may lie ahead. Environmental groups and other tough-playing advocacy groups are far more sophisticated than most of their corporate counterparts in the use of the Net for issues management. They continue to hone their on-line skills, and new Net technologies will continue to provide sharper weapons. At the same time, new consumer eyeballs continue to come on-line at a brisk pace.

Also, companies will be increasingly threatened on the investor-relations front, according to Steve Goodman, a partner with Poppe Tyson Public Relations. 'The kind of crisis you're going to see more and more of on-line is where companies are feeling the impact of on-line efforts against their stocks or securities,' he said. Goodman currently has a client who believes newsgroup activity is dragging down its stock by railing against an important new product. When under attack, many companies resort to one of two polar strategies: flex corporate legal muscle, or just do nothing at all. Both strategies risk major problems, not to mention opportunity costs, and Net-savvy public relations professionals counsel a middle-ground approach in most situations.

Don't sic the lawyers

On the legal front, trademarks must be protected and infringements resolved, otherwise you could lose your ability to enforce your rights in future cases. But it's an entirely different matter when you bring in the lawyers to intimidate the Web site owner into backing down under the threat of mounting legal fees, no matter how legally protected they feel they may be.

Cliff Purkiser, on-line relations manager for Intel, called this 'a bad communications strategy' because it is more likely to encourage the opposing Web site and give it more visibility and credibility. 'There's certainly a large portion of people on the Net who are libertarians and would be glad to help publicise the case of David and Goliath,' he said. 'That's news.'

Indeed, the Internet community is awfully touchy these days when it comes to free-speech issues. And even if you have a legitimate legal beef, while you might win in the court of law, you could lose in the court of public opinion.

Charles Lukaszwski, managing partner of eWorks!, which operates the eWatch on-line monitoring service, pointed out that the recipients of these nasty cease-and-desist letters can, and in fact often do, post them verbatim on their Web sites, embarrassing the plaintiff. Lukaszwski uses real-world analogies to explain his solutions to virtual problems, and he has one for

the legal-intimidation strategy: 'A guy behind a counter, hearing somebody who's buying a Big Mac slamming the food, and jumping over the
counter and beating the customer up – you wouldn't tolerate that in the
real world.'

So what does happen in the real world when substantial pages of air
time are given in traditional media to attack a company or its products or
values? What would a Mobil or Philip Morris do? 'They would go out and
buy double-page ads in *The Wall Street Journal* and get a consistent place
where they express their point of view,' Lukaszwski said. 'I would argue
strongly that the rules are precisely the same in this medium.'

Fight fire with fire

Lukaszwski may well be the world's most seasoned veteran in on-line
issues management, having worked with well over 50 clients on different
on-line visibility crises during the past year and a half, eg, Mrs Fields
Cookies, which showed up on an OJ Simpson boycott page two days after
the acquittal, with the accusation that Mrs Fields provided free cookies to
Simpson's victory party, and ended up on the TV news show 'Hard Copy'
and other mainstream news media shows.

'With every single passing month I am more and more convinced that
the right way to handle these situations is to fight fire with fire,'
Lukaszwski said. 'If fire is somebody putting up a Web site and expressing
a point of view, your fire is the same thing in reverse.' In every case he's
been involved in where a company has gone on-line with its point of view,
the issue has gone quietly away, he said. Lukaszwski advises companies to
seek to exchange links with an adversary.

When the funding practices of client Save the Children were attacked in
a *Penthouse* article, resulting in a *20/20* (documentary programme) piece on
TV, eWatch put up a response Web site and negotiated links with *Penthouse's* site and the author's own Web site. It was one of the first examples
of using the Web to tell both sides of a story. 'Essentially, the issue went
away,' he said. 'It was completely effective. And we've done this any
number of times. It literally just shuts things down.'

Silent majority

'Putting a link to somebody's site does not amount to an admission of
guilt,' he said. 'It enables some communication, which is really the bottom
line. You can't defend these things on-line, period. There's no Supreme
Court of cyberspace.'

The Web site that fights you is one thing; newsgroups are quite another.
Newsgroup discussions can be neither isolated nor controlled, and their
amorphous and unpredictable nature makes companies hesitant to

respond when under attack. While it's tempting to want to do nothing in the face of negative newsgroup discussions, Intel's Purkiser noted that a newsgroup's reach and influence may be too large to ignore.

'You're not really writing for the ten people who are participating in the discussion,' Purkiser said. 'You're writing for the thousands, or potential reporters who don't participate but read it anyhow.' Purkiser calls this audience 'the silent majority' and said that they tend to be more reasonable, more 'normal'.

'Unlike other media, the assumption is that the person who stopped responding first conceded that the other side is correct,' he said. Poppe Tyson's Goodman makes the point that not all newsgroups are alike, and if one is particularly difficult, others may be more receptive. 'Just because there's a newsgroup saying horrendous things about you doesn't mean there aren't newsgroups full of potential supporters,' he said. 'So rather than jump into a hostile group, build support in other newsgroups.'

When you do respond, what you say and how you say it is critical, because newsgroups are not moderated, ie, there's no editor to ensure your communication is appropriate.

How to get flamed

Lukaszwski said that a 'standard corporate legalese-type response' or simple position statement is 'guaranteed' to get flamed (be the subject of a huge barrage of negative e-mail and comment via newsgroups on the Internet). He said corporate responses should provide something that is concrete and helpful, because newsgroup participants are looking for answers to questions, solutions to problems.

The Intel Pentium processor case is a perfect illustration. Intel customers wanted answers, and only when the answers were not forthcoming did the problem build. The Intel case underscores the need to apply conventional public relations practices to the Internet: implement a sound crisis preparedness plan to try and avert the need to implement crisis management. With newsgroups, this means being vigilant about monitoring, and being prepared to respond. 'We tell our crisis and on-line clients that the key is to have an ongoing stream of communications prior to a crisis,' Goodman said. His advice is to identify important newsgroups from a product or brand perspective, begin to monitor them and, ideally, participate in them.

Purkiser said that for a company like Intel, participating in newsgroups is 'critical,' as both 'an insurance policy' and to take advantage of opportunities. 'It's nice to be able to monitor the buzz about your new products; then you can alter your traditional PR message to help fine-tune that,' he said. Intel uses newsgroups to quickly enroll high-quality beta testers for its products. Intel now has a formal process for monitoring and a formal process for responding, Purkiser said. It even has a contingency plan should another crisis arise.

Intel's success

And it works. Purkiser offered a successful case study where Intel prevented a potential flare-up over a problem with a third-party chip used on Intel's RZ1000 motherboards. A discussion of the problem started off in an OS/2 (IBM's operating system) newsgroup, and Purkiser personally jumped in to say Intel was aware of the questions and investigating the problem. He explained specific action steps Intel was taking, eg, working with software vendors. And he requested the assistance of newsgroup participants to report any problems with other operating systems. Inside the company, Intel had engineers drop what they were doing until they figured out every situation where there could be a problem.

Purkiser kept the newsgroup up to date, posting information on Intel's Web site, until the problem was resolved to everyone's satisfaction. Intel provided users with software patches that worked around the hardware problem, an infinitely less expensive solution to replacing motherboards. 'The story hit the local paper and then it got picked up by the AP and two days later there was "The New Intel Seems To Be Dealing With This One A Lot Better" type of story,' Purkiser said. 'It got slightly less coverage, but the newsgroups were happy with it. I think we did a pretty good job of handling that one,' he added.

Part 10
Dealing with Government

53

Government Communications – A Broader Perspective

Edward Bickham
*Managing Director, Public Affairs and
Corporate Policy, Hill and Knowlton (UK)*

In the past, working in the government affairs function of many companies was like being posted to the far-flung limits of an Empire to man the ramparts – largely reactive, and relatively quiet, punctuated by occasional assaults by the savages (for which read politicians) on the Empire's (company's) interests. In the last few years, most firms have got smarter.

Most companies whose scale or fields of operation leave them vulnerable to adverse regulatory developments, now rightly demand rather more of their government affairs function. In future years, they may need to expect even more, irrespective of who wins the approaching General Election. This is because of the growing need for government affairs to have an increasing interface with both the corporate communications and strategic planning functions.

Whether or not one accepts the vocabulary of stakeholding, there is little doubt that the demand for companies to be seen to be more widely accountable is increasingly promulgated politically and, predictably, in the media. A whole range of audiences, from investors through pressure groups to activist consumers, want an explanation of how the business is being run and what are its values and ethics. These demands increasingly affect the time, attention and priorities of senior management. It provides a strong opportunity for the government affairs function to step into the limelight as the custodian of the corporate public policy agenda.

Moreover, companies can turn this interest in corporate input to the policy agenda to advantage. Companies such as The Body Shop and to a lesser extent Virgin have built their corporate brands in part through using the policy agenda to define their values and ethics. Less trendily, B&Q has managed to achieve clear differentiation from other retailers through their proactive policy of employing older workers (which also happens to make good commercial sense, since people seem to prefer to buy their DIY goods from greybeards rather than pimply youths). In the process of promoting the policy, B&Q has also been picked out by government as an example of best practice and the column inches of media coverage have followed.

Aside from the potential corporate reputation spin-offs from companies complementing their corporate profile through the use of policy issues, they can also generate significant goodwill from being seen as net contributors to policy discussions. This need not – and indeed should not – require a company constantly to be grinding its own axe. Nevertheless, a company can build a store of political capital if it is seen to take a view beyond its narrow self-interests and provides objective information or informed perspectives to political discussion, especially if it involves complex or technologically based topics. In the financial services area, for example, Prudential has pursued an impressive programme of stimulating and inserting itself into high-level discussions of key issues such as welfare reform and financial services regulation. It may in the process have been able to promote specific ideas for reform. But even if it has not, it has, in the process, gained profile, credit and influence with many politicians looking for a guide through a notoriously complex sector.

Such opportunities are also there for technology companies, since the political world is not well stocked with people with an instinctive bent for technology or an up-to-date awareness of its potentialities. Technology increasingly impinges policy making, whether it be through digital developments in relation to broadcasting policy; the implications of the Internet; the increasing number of IT applications in furthering government policy objectives; the potential growth of teleworking; or the introduction of identity and smart cash cards. Politicians, many senior officials and certainly most political journalists are by nature generalists and are usually more than willing to listen and learn from companies who have interesting views or detailed knowledge of initiatives being pursued abroad. Even if one assumes (probably wrongly) that Ministers and officials know all there is to know, it is always worth targeting Opposition spokespeople and their advisers and Select Committee members for presentations or with well-presented information.

It is easy to underestimate the paucity of resources with which Opposition spokespeople, and parliamentarians in general, have to try to do their jobs. Moreover, with the reduction in Civil Service numbers and the hiving off of sources of expertise to agencies, government officials are far more likely to welcome well-informed contributions from outsiders than was often the case a decade ago. It is fair to say that this is even more true of the European Commission, where at least some officials are well aware of the dangers of seeking to develop policies in Brussels which are too far removed from the industries which they will affect.

I mentioned earlier the importance of companies integrating the work of the government affairs and, where one exists, the strategy development functions. Where industries operate in an environment vulnerable to regulatory change, they need to escape from the 'victim' syndrome. It is common to come across firms which express disdain for politicians and the political process, and deny any locus for seeking to suggest where the public interest may lie, yet when they are faced with an immediate legislative or regulatory threat, they will spend large sums trying to block it – usually from some way behind the game.

In my experience, both of public affairs consultancy and in Whitehall, firms can benefit from a more regular engagement in the political process. A sensible manufacturing or services company will seek to anticipate what its customers are likely to want, say five years hence, and drive its product development accordingly. Conversely, few companies seek to read where relevant regulatory developments are likely to go over a similar period. Those who seek successfully to read the regulatory runes – through looking at developments in North America and continental Europe, analysing political pressures and looking at ideas circulating among influential academics and thinktanks – may be able to use it as a source of competitive advantage. Furthermore, investing a little in influencing embryonic ideas may prove far more cost-effective than seeking to divert proposals once political machismo has been engaged.

I have concentrated on looking at the wider strategic and communications dimensions of government affairs. But it will be equally important over the coming period to ensure that legitimate lobbying and influencing of government and of the political process do not become tainted with the high-profile abuses which so enthralled the headline writers in 1996. Politicians often find themselves harried and run ragged by the media and a myriad of pressure groups. It is vital that the interests of industry and the productive economy do not become stifled in the post-Nolan age – but engagement in the political process needs to be done professionally, transparently and consistently if it is to succeed.

54

Government Relations: Lobbying

Nicholas Comfort
Political and Media Consultant, Politics International

Few aspects of public life are changing as fast as the lobbying business. Month by month it is becoming more focused; it is apparent that as lobbying comes of age, clients are better able to judge the quality of service they receive. While much of the most effective work is, by its nature, conducted behind the scenes, lobbyists can no longer portray their craft as a mystic art and hope to get away with it.

One important change is that lobbying has become predominantly issue-oriented. There is an increasing realisation that while contacts in key positions are important, there is far more to giving a client exposure in political circles than inviting the usual suspects to lunch, and that what really counts is how the case is made when a specific point of importance arises. There are still practitioners who conduct the bulk of their business around the dinner table, and they have some successes. But what matters most to the client is not the ability to exchange pleasantries with a minister over the hors d'oeuvres, but the knowledge that if some problem or opportunity arises, that minister and his or her officials will be open to a thoroughly professional briefing reflecting the client's point of view. A lobbyist's basic craft involves intervention with the powers that be on a particular issue – an item of legislation, a draft regulation, a contract in the offing – and the deployment of the most effective arguments to secure a result. Such intervention needs to be thoroughly researched, tightly focused to hold the attention of the politician or official being lobbied and, above all, sincere and credible.

The realisation that lobbying is an effective and proper part of the process of public decision-making is spreading in government, too. Civil servants as well as politicians now recognise that when a major issue is being debated – not to mention some apparently smaller question which turns out to have unforeseen repercussions – they will hear the nuances of the argument for those affected at a meeting arranged through the lobbyist.

Many companies, trade associations and the like have now dealt with lobbyists for long enough to know when they are getting value for money. The days when a consultancy could keep making a convincing pitch to get its contract renewed without ever delivering the goods are firmly in the past. Equally, many clients have enough experience of the business to be realistic in their expectations, and understand that not every initiative will be crowned with instant, total success. They are also more ready to appreciate that quiet activity may bring better results than razzmatazz, even if the flute seems a less satisfying instrument than the tuba. Against this background, respect between lobbyists and clients is growing ... though none of us has any cause for complacency given the growing strength, variety and professionalism of the competition.

Lobbying or PR?

There is also a growing appreciation of the difference between lobbying and public relations. Most companies and organisations that engage a lobbyist already have an in-house PR department or an outside agency, but there is no need for conflict. Most lobbying consultancies have no desire to get involved in a firm's day-to-day PR or indeed its marketing; those are separate skills requiring a different range of knowledge and contacts. Conversely most PR practitioners have enough on their plate without venturing into the alien world of government. Some in-house or external PR presences do try to block the appointment of a lobbying firm to protect their turf, even though this leaves an important job undone, and there are clients who call their lobbyist in desperation saying: 'Our PR department is useless. Can you get us on News At Ten?' But such cases are few. Moreover, close contact between PR and lobbying practitioners is increasingly encouraged to ensure the two operations dovetail with each other.

The Nolan Inquiry

Of course the conduct of lobbying cannot be guided solely by the demands of clients, not that these need be in any way unethical. Revelations of parliamentary sleaze and, in particular, the links between some MPs and lobbying and PR organisations, have rightly caused public concern. This led to John Major – in the face of considerable resistance from his own benches – setting up the Nolan Inquiry, and in turn to the House revamping its own ethical and disciplinary codes.

No one should underestimate the importance of Nolan, or the service he has done to the ethos of lobbying. By setting firm standards of conduct for MPs, he has curtailed the burgeoning practice of them selling their services as consultants instead of representing their constituents, and forced them to ask themselves if they want to be in the Commons or not. More importantly to us, he has, by forcing MPs to be ethical, removed from lobbying a largely unjustified stigma; he has created a climate in which we can prove we achieve results for our clients through professionalism and the ethical deployment of a case (without paying off people who are supposed to be on the other side of the fence). By banishing the murky practices of a few, Nolan has endowed the practice of lobbying with a transparency warmly welcomed by the vast majority.

Pre-election challenges

The imminence of a general election has set three extra challenges for anyone seeking to catch the ear of government. First, there is a tendency for Whitehall to coast in the run-up to an election, with decisions left unmade unless ministers see political kudos in them. A good deal of lobbyists' time in recent months has been spent ensuring that government departments keep their eye on the ball: that contracts due for letting are let, that long-awaited decisions which translate into new opportunities for a client (or indeed votes) are not shelved. Inertia is the most potent force in Whitehall and, frequently, the lobbyist's task is not to ensure the decision-making process comes down in favour of the client but make sure the decision is taken at all.

The second pre-election challenge stems from the chance that an issue impacting on a client may become a 'political football'. There is obvious mileage in persuading a party to make promises that would be to the client's advantage, and dissuading it from commitments that would do them harm. Yet often there is also the need to keep a particular issue out of the political arena, so that any decision taken after the election will be made on the same basis as previously, regardless of whoever is in power.

Second to needless delay, nothing frustrates a client more than lack of continuity – and that need not stem from a change of government.

The final challenge concerns the need to maintain links with both the present rulers of the country and those who aspire to succeed them. All lobbying firms have lines open to both major parties, and some have committed members of each on-board who have worked at party headquarters or in the leader's office. Most politicians do not mind that the largest firms can field both a 'government' team and a 'shadow' team. Yet just as much can be achieved with government or the opposition by consultants whose experience is grounded firmly in one party or indeed in none, provided their work is perceived as diligent and effective. In the end, it is how good you are that counts for most.

55

Dealing with Europe – the Role of National Governments in the EU Legislative Arena

John Duhig
GPC Market Access, Europe

European and national politics increasingly affect all spheres of business activity. Understanding and influencing the European Union (EU) agenda is crucial in order to minimise political risk in strategic planning and decision making and to maximise commercial opportunities for companies and businesses in the UK. The impact of political and regulatory decisions may be direct or indirect, positive or negative, short or long term, but in every case there is some commercial, financial or administrative consequence.

With the evolution of the EU and the increase in the power of its institutions, the detailed formulation and implementation of policy have become ever more complex. The various stakeholders will, accordingly, need to become more sophisticated in communicating with the decision makers, whether in London or Brussels.

Increasingly influential stakeholders within the national and European legislative arenas are the environmental and consumer pressure-group lobbies. Their role in the legislative procedure has increased dramatically in recent years, providing a direct and powerful link between the citizen and the European institutions. The European Environmental Bureau, the umbrella organisation which represents the interests of more than 130 environmental non-governmental organisations (NGOs) to the European institutions, presents a memorandum to the rotating presidency of the EU Council of Ministers twice annually, outlining areas in a broad range of European policy sectors which it believes must be progressed by the presidency. The concerns of these particular stakeholders are taken seriously by the decision makers – many NGOs have privileged access to the European institutions; the European Commission has separate directorates dealing exclusively with consumer affairs and environment policy.

The mid-1990s witnessed the apogee of the so-called environmental second wave in Europe. The leading environmental NGOs, secure in the knowledge of the key role which they play within the European legislative process, are adopting a more conciliatory approach to erstwhile industry and other foes. In September 1996, the first ever Greenpeace Business Conference was held in London. Peter Melchett, Greenpeace UK's executive director, in describing his organisation's new strategy of 'solutions enforcement', highlighted the need for more co-operation with companies because it is there that the capacity for change rests. The focus in environmental developments in coming years for UK business interests will be to grow more sophisticated antennae to pick up the warning signals of potential conflicts ahead.

In the late 1980s, Greenpeace concluded that it needed to shift away from drawing attention to problems as environmental impacts towards drawing attention to problems in the shape of solutions which are not being implemented. One of the key lessons of the Brent Spar episode in 1995 was that companies were mistaken in their belief that to ensure broader approval for environmentally controversial decisions it was only necessary to deal with government policy makers and regulatory authorities.

The clear message is that businesses would be unwise to rely as heavily as they have done in the past on governments to help them succeed in defending the status quo. The controversy over Brent Spar has emphasised the difference between policy and politics, a distinction which will become ever more relevant. It has become increasingly important for business interests to be more aware of the issues which concern NGO and consumer groups and factor these considerations into the future strategic planning and development of its industry.

Dealing with the European institutions remains a complex procedure. Dealing with Europe also involves liaising closely with the national government – in this case the UK – because, ultimately, it is within the EU Council of Ministers that decisions on proposed legislation are taken. Therefore communicating effectively with the decision makers, both

Market Access

Europe's Leading Public Affairs Consultancy

GPC Market Access Europe
Julia Harrison
Managing Director
Rue d'Arlon 50
1000 Brussels

Tel +32 2 230 05 45
Fax +32 2 230 57 06
100670.752 @ CompuServe.com

Market Access
Michael Craven
Managing Director
7 The Sanctuary
London SW1P 3JS

Tel +44 171 799 1500
Fax +44 171 222 5872
Compuserve 100306,2271
Internet : PJRMACCESS @
EASYNET.CO.UK

London • Brussels • Edinburgh • Paris • Bonn • The Hague • Canada

national and European, as proposals for legislation are drafted is crucial for all UK businesses.

In environmental matters, UK laws and regulations are determined by European legislation. EC directives, implemented as UK law through the Environment Protection Act 1990 and the Environment Act 1995, are having a growing impact on businesses in the UK. In addition, agreements reached on an EU-wide basis as a result of the Rio Earth Summit in 1992 play a strong role at local government level in the UK through the Local Agenda 21 programmes. It is also worth noting that the chairman and one of the vice-chairmen of the European Parliament Environment, Public Health and Consumer Affairs Committee are British MEPs.

The need to be aware of the key regulatory issues as well as the prevailing economic and political trends within Europe is of vital importance to ensure that the competitiveness of EU industry continues to develop. Those industries which have forged links with the national and European institutions can often achieve such competitive advantage in their field, which in turn allows them to communicate their relevant priorities to the opinion formers. Increasingly, industry groups across Europe are realising this and are aiming to be the primary interlocutors for their business interests and those who legislate at the national as well as the European level.

National governments are very much at the heart of the EU decision-making process and policy issues of strategic national importance such as defence, taxation and EU institutional issues, require unanimous voting within the Council of Ministers. Individual governments can exercise their right of veto should they oppose any proposals which they believe would profoundly affect their national interests and thereby are the crucial link for businesses with the European legislative machinery. The issue of securing co-financing from EU funding programmes provides a good example to highlight the important role of national governments in the process. Receiving financial assistance from the Commission programmes can often be complicated. There are many official and other criteria which need to be adhered to before a submission is accepted which require more specialist knowledge than is contained in the application literature. The fact, for example, that there are opportunities to present a draft of a proposal to relevant Commission officials is not specified. The additional advantage of undertaking this course of action is that the Commission can offer guidance and advice on the best ways of presenting a proposal.

In the case of EU co-financing of infrastructure projects, an applicant seeking funding must also approach the national government for support. The Commission will accept submissions, but gaining the support of the relevant ministry within the national government is often what counts. In this instance, an applicant needs to lobby both the Commission in Brussels to gain support for the proposed project and also the relevant ministry within the member state. The latter is the key player, responsible for prioritising a project which will ultimately be presented as the member state's final list for proposals for funding to the Commission.

National and EU-level decisions are increasingly part of a complex whole rather than separate processes. As the EU regulatory environment becomes more labyrinthine, with many more stakeholders involved in the issues, regular and effective communication with the legislators in London, as well as in Brussels, will increasingly become a necessity for UK businesses and companies in order to retain industrial competitiveness within the European Single Market and beyond, as we approach the twenty-first century.

Part 11

Global Communications

56

Global Communications

Lord Chadlington
Chairman, Shandwick International

Drive into town from almost any airport in the world and you will be confronted with the same brand names. MasterCard, Digital, TNT Express Worldwide, and a range of others which have become household words across the world, confront you at the airport and on shops and hoardings along the roads.

I mention these partly because they are instantly recognisable from Delhi to Denver, and partly because they are all Shandwick International clients. They are now co-ordinating the same message in 22 countries and in every key market in the world.

The new age of global communications, which has been predicted for many years, has now arrived. And together with our international clients, we have been on the cutting edge of global PR – turning it into a powerful force which can profoundly affect the reputation of clients and accelerate their success. This has meant working with forces which have been affecting communications everywhere in the 1990s. These forces are:

- globalisation;
- technology;
- reputation;
- effectiveness;
- practitioner skills.

ONE

NAME

MAKES

WAVES

WORLDWIDE

With 132 offices in 45
countries worldwide,
Shandwick can ensure
your voice is heard
throughout the
international arena.
Our heritage of local
market understanding,
combined with our global
scope and approach,
builds brands and
manages reputations –
worldwide.

UK
Colin Trusler
Managing Director - UK
Shandwick plc
18 Dering Street
LONDON W1R 9AF
UK

Tel: + 44 171 355 1908
Fax: + 44 171 499 1757

Continental Europe
Volker Stoltz
Managing Director
Continental Europe
Shandwick Continental
Europe
Bismarckstrasse 13
D-5313 BONN
GERMANY

Tel: + 49 228-91-4430
Fax: + 49 228-91-44328

Americas
Larry Kaplan
Regional Director
Shandwick North America
666 Third Avenue
NEW YORK NY 10017
USA

Tel: + 1 212 309 0609
Fax: + 1 212 983 6426

Asia Pacific
Michael Murphy
Managing Director
Asia Region
Shandwick Hong Kong
18/F Dina House
Ruttonjee Centre
11 Duddell Street
HONG KONG

Tel: + 852 (2845)-1008
Fax: + 852 (2845)-9809

Shandwick

GLOBAL
REPUTATION
MANAGEMENT

Globalisation

Regions, countries, corporations and citizens are increasingly interconnected. But this is not in a way which makes everything the same: increasing globalisation is also powering an opposite force which makes people value what is local and traditional. That means that communication now has to combine a global strategy with extraordinary sensitivity to its local impact – which is why our approach at Shandwick is to 'think global and act local'.

Technology

The coming of the Internet is the first social transformation – integrating advertising, marketing and communications – in which PR can play a lead. It allows organisations to communicate directly to individuals in a way which was never possible before, and receive messages back. It brings with it enormous opportunities in a new kind of interactive communication.

Reputation

Chief executives are increasingly looking at their corporate reputation as something which can be managed, just as sceptical consumers want to look behind the brands to the corporations that support them.

Effectiveness

International companies increasingly see their communication as an investment, to make sure that the different aspects are supporting each other and producing the returns they want. Audiences will see their advertisements, read about them and hear about them from friends all at the same time. That is why other global communications companies are in the business of tracking the total effect of communications, so that it is more efficient, in money terms, and more effective.

Practitioner skills

The skills required of PR practitioners now go way beyond the good written communications which used to be their stock in trade. The most successful now possess a range of business skills, including counselling techniques, an understanding of effective departmental structures and systems, technological knowhow and a focus on results.

These five trends mean that integrated global communication is an increasingly important, but increasingly complex, aspect of running a large organisation. The perils are increasing too: paradoxically, the more information which becomes available, the lower the quality of that information. The result is that prejudices increase rather than decrease, and there are now a growing number of controversial views about a growing number of issues around the world.

That is why PR people who deal with public opinion are increasingly busy, especially if they are doing so across international borders. The idea of managing reputation is becoming particularly important, even though the term is only just entering the management lexicon. Managers know that, whether they are sending consistent messages to customers, employees, shareholders or media outlets all over the world, they can make the difference between success and failure.

The wrong strategy can be disastrous: reputation seems to be much easier to damage than it is to build. IBM provides a vivid example of this, as it tries to rebuild its once-unquestioned reputation for quality, service and technology which it managed to dissipate in a very short time. But if you get your reputation right, it can lead to increased sales, a bolstered stock price, better employee morale, lower staff turnover, defence in times of crisis and the ability to influence people's thinking around the world. When Russia and China welcomed McDonald's, they did so because their reputation – not their cooking – was able to pave the way. Character wins out in the end.

So what does reputation consist of? Marketing and advertising can attract customers to your brands, products and services, and can also make customers more loyal. But it is your reputation – the sense of who you are – that turns customers into loyal advocates. Brands are what your corporation does. Reputation is what your corporation is: it is the world's ongoing evaluation of the total sum of your brands, services, citizenship and what people are saying about you.

If you fail to bring your brand messages and your reputation into line, it can create a kind of 'drag' in the market. If you can tune them together, they will support each other – creating a kind of 'reputation velocity' which magnifies your impact and sales.

Propaganda and simple 'image' are no longer enough for the world's increasingly sophisticated consumers. They can tell what is real; PR agencies can help organisations communicate what they are already doing well. And using reputation management, they can also help turn investors, customers and employees into enthusiastic advocates. In fact, PR seems to be the discipline which is particularly well suited to the business of building loyalty and advocacy.

While we saw that the era of global reputation was on its way as long ago as the mid-1980s, we underestimated how quickly it would arrive. As one CEO of a major company told me recently: 'You didn't realise deeply enough that only reorganised and restructured corporations can communicate globally.' Often it has been crises which have driven these reorganisations.

When a crisis hits them, companies will usually battle to apply creative new solutions to fit the changing situation. As a result, the crisis may seem like a blessing in disguise. The companies which take the risks may succeed or fail; the ones which just stand still always lose.

As a result of these changes inside and outside corporations, they are now becoming virtual networks of minds – linking the communications between them and their various audiences. Chairpersons or CEOs have the authority to implement a global plan, but only those on the ground can understand their local community enough to communicate effectively there. That's why plan 'ownership' at every level of an organisation is probably the single overriding factor which decides whether they will succeed or not.

Just as the Internet has created a world of instant interactive messages, corporations have to recreate that 'feedback-ownership loop' within themselves.

Leading corporations now think and conduct their communications on a worldwide basis, and by the end of the 1990s only a handful of the world's top 500 will fail to communicate globally. That is why, as we head towards 2000 and beyond, managing global reputation has become the most vital PR skill of all.

57

How Can You Possibly Think Global, Act Local?

Michael Robertson
Assistant Vice President, ABB Corporate Communications, Zurich, Switzerland

Being truly global and local

With the globalisation of trade, precipitated by a focus on the strongly growing emerging markets of Asia Pacific and the new opportunities arising from the opening up of Central and Eastern Europe, companies are scrambling to position themselves as global players. But 'global' can have various interpretations. On the one hand, there are international companies which are based really in only one country, where most of the added value of their production is performed, and which sell their products through global sales outlets. On the other, there are those which believe in putting down deep roots in the many global markets in which they operate, joining with local partners in joint ventures to produce products by adding value in the countries in which they sell.

Such a company in this second, truly global category is ABB (ABB Asea Brown Boveri), an international electrical engineering group, which has relentlessly pursued this policy since it was created in 1988 out of the merger of two 100-year-old engineering competitors – ASEA AB of Sweden and BBC Brown Boveri of Switzerland. Today the group comprises 1000 companies in 140 countries, employing 217,000 people. But 30,000 of these are located in manufacturing operations in Central and

Eastern Europe, established since the Iron Curtain collapsed in 1989. A further 26,000 are located in Asia, where most are in new joint ventures established since the early 1990s, with 14,000 in India and China alone. This same decentralisation is evident in the rest of the world, where ABB has 70,000 employees in the European Union countries, 32,000 in the Americas and 10,000 in Africa and the Middle East.

So the phrase 'think global, act local' represents the group's fundamental idea of strong local companies working together across borders to gain economies of scale in many areas. Local companies use the Group's total resources in research, product development, low-cost manufacturing, distribution supply, information technology, benchmarking, business experience, access to capital markets and international financing. Yet in each country the group's operations are local and flexible. This multidomestic organisation enables knowhow to be transferred across borders easily and, being close to the customer everywhere, ensures a swift response to market conditions and new opportunities to meet the special needs of local customers. Moreover, combined experience and know-how gained in local markets can be used to deliver greater value to customers groupwide.

Communications within the matrix

To make this global/local strategy work in an optimum way, the ABB Group structure is based on a matrix, where everyone reports and communicates along two dimensions. For example, the unit which manufactures motors in Finland reports geographically via the country manager in Finland to the group executive committee member responsible for ABB's activities in Europe. But the unit also reports via the global business area manager for motors (who happens to be based in Switzerland) to another executive committee member responsible for the global industry segment. In this way, local strengths to serve local markets are developed through the geographic dimension, while global leverage (research, technology transfer, market allocation, product development and investment) is provided through the global business area dimension.

In order to recreate small company dynamism, the large group organisation is broken down into 5000 profit centres and 1000 legal entities. Having real balance sheets and bottom-line responsibility at the local level encourages managers to focus on what customers want.

This same decentralisation is also evident when it comes to communications. For a global group organised in this way, effective communication to external and internal audiences must also be decentralised, tuned to the culture, language and environment of the country in which the targeted audience resides. Therefore, ABB has established a network of communication managers based in all the main countries, each reporting along the matrix structure to their country manager and also liaising with the very small number of communications staff in group headquarters, Switzerland. Simple ground rules lay down the framework within which communications are to be handled worldwide. But basically, each country is encouraged, and has full responsibility, to conduct a comprehensive communications programme, including external and internal announcements, covering all matters relevant to ABB activities in their country, without reference to the headquarters. In addition, they receive global announcements from the group headquarters which they are then free to translate and distribute within their country. They are also free to modify most of these announcements to add a local angle, if relevant.

But as part of the ground rules, country communications managers have an overriding obligation to inform headquarters in advance of any matters which:

- are very important;
- are very interesting;
- could influence ABB share prices;
- could also affect group activities in other countries (cross-border).

As regards matters which could influence the group's share price, these are defined to include:

- major orders, ie for a company such as ABB, above US$100 million;
- acquisitions, divestitures, joint ventures, cooperation agreements;
- major investments – new or modernised factories;
- major new product or technology development;
- major changes – personnel, factories, offices, management;
- all crises – no matter how small.

But to maintain a well-coordinated public relations image on a global scale in such a decentralised structure, the last of the ground rules requiring the notification of cross-border matters is indispensable. Without such global coordination, good news for one ABB entity – say, ABB Thailand on acquiring a complete new factory transferred from Denmark – can be bad news to another – ABB Denmark on giving up this factory. Therefore, the following comment could not be more applicable to preserving professional communications worthy of a truly global player: 'Think global before you act local'.

Top-down decentralisation

Responsibility for communications is decentralised downwards from the top of the group along the two dimensions of the matrix according to competence. In the group executive committee we are fortunate to have some of the best communicators, who are supported by the group corporate communications staff.

The three regional executive committee members, located in their respective regions, also each have a regional communications manager, as do all the major countries within each region. Furthermore, some of the larger manufacturing companies within the countries also justify having their own communications manager, the smaller ones relying on the services of the country communications managers.

The three segment executive committee members are supported by communications staff, as are the 36 business areas that report to them.

The aim is to have competent communicators at each of these levels within the group.

This global network of over 200 communication specialists (although not all have only communications as their function) are linked together through the group's internal private corporate network, based on Lotus *Notes*, which can also communicate over the Internet and X.400. Having a sense of urgency and speed of action are job requirements which are instilled into the group's culture. Networking together then becomes all important in order to direct and control global communications in a proactive way, rather than resorting to a reactive approach and being a hostage to events.

The communication managers are the facilitators, but it is normally the executive managers at the various levels already mentioned, down to the level of company president, who are the oracles of all communications.

Internal and external communications

Communications can be divided into two general categories – internal communications, targeted at all employees of the organisation; and external communications, directed at important audiences outside the organisation, such as customers, the investment community and the general public.

For each category there is a wide range of communication tools at one's disposal. Internal communications can utilise noticeboard bulletins, announcement broadcasts by fax and e-mail, house-magazines, employee-oriented versions of annual reports, regular video bulletins and, most important of all, regular face-to-face presentations.

For external communications the range is even wider, such as corporate literature, brochures, company profiles, annual reports, facts and figures, corporate videos, newsletters, presentations, exhibitions, conferences, corporate advertising, together with media services comprising press releases, press conferences and interviews. Here, top management can play a very constructive role by taking a proactive approach in giving interviews to selected media, speaking at international business conferences and at institutional and government forums, in order to raise the public profile of the company and its activities, and to demonstrate the contribution it can make to the benefit of society at large.

Making communications pay

Within many organisations, the cost of communications, although subject to normal budgeting scrutiny, is nevertheless handled as an overhead. This approach runs an inherent risk of unnecessary waste, caused by overproduction of products and services and the hoarding within the company of corporate brochures, overheads, videos, annual reports, etc, simply because they are 'free', quite irrespective of whether the item is really needed or not.

Such waste can be drastically reduced by drawing up an internal itemised price list for all such products and services and then charging the various company departments for what they use. This leads to an immediate consideration of 'need to have' rather than 'nice to have'. If one department wants to pamper its customers by sending out 5000 annual reports, whereas another department focuses on only 500 recipients, it is only fair that the costs of the document are distributed according to consumption.

This principle can be taken a step further by spinning off the communication function into a profit centre, or even into a separate company, which is given the mandate of at least covering its costs by charging its internal customers for its services. The number of items which cannot be charged for in this way, such as corporate advertising, media relations etc, are thereby reduced to a minimum and, for example, can be covered in a levy applied to all parts of the group, calculated, say, according to the sales turnover of each department, division or company. If necessary, certain strategic items which must be widely utilised within the group can always be provided free to ensure unrestricted circulation.

This approach quickly shows on which items to concentrate and where savings can be made by discontinuing low-demand products or services.

Monitoring effectiveness

In many other business activities, successful performance becomes quickly apparent, for example by the trend of sales and profit figures. In communications, much can be produced and transmitted without apparent feedback of whether it is hitting and positively influencing its target audiences. Therefore, it is all the more important to install a regular evaluation process to check the effectiveness and performance of all group communications to all audience categories.

Starting with internal communications, where the checks can be performed by in-house resources, a simple questionnaire can be distributed within the group. Respondents can be asked to rank in importance and usefulness the various communication products – management newsletters, corporate brochures, overhead presentations, videos, posters, announcements, guidelines etc. Suggested improvements and proposals for new products can be invited.

For external communications, a comprehensive 'image and awareness' survey should be repeated at regular intervals to benchmark the image of the group and people's awareness of it against a selection of the group's main competitors. Such a survey would be carried out by an external agency and would comprise several thousand interviews in target countries with representative categories of all major audiences – clients, media, academia, politicians, the general public etc. Questions need to be carefully formulated to ensure unbiased responses and can be tailored to draw out information on the group's strengths and weaknesses.

In the case of media relations, monitoring and analysis of press clippings and other media coverage provide simple feedback of how the communications output is received. In addition, a separate independent survey can be commissioned at regular intervals to obtain the judgement of the important media in all major countries about the group's performance in serving their needs. Again, to be really instructive, the survey should benchmark its results against selected competitors, showing where particular effort is needed to overtake their superior positions.

In conclusion

Maintaining good communications is so vital for a company, in particular for a global player, that the company's objectives and proper handling of this function need to be set from the top down. The company should lay down the principle to supply rapid and accurate information to its internal and external audiences openly, factually and honestly. The external goal should be to develop good relations with customers, the investment community and other audiences, and also to present the status and core activities of the company to the general public. The internal goal should be quickly and consistently to communicate the company's objectives and status, thereby encouraging open discussion and a free exchange of ideas among employees at all levels. Employees should receive important information concerning the group and their own company on a first-priority basis. Even if stock-exchange or other regulations make this difficult, the objective is to reach employees directly and not via the media.

To end with a salutary reminder; communication in an organisation is like the lubricant in a gearbox. By the time you realise that you do not have enough, it is too late.

58

A Review of Global Communications

Peter Hehir
President, International Consultants
Organisation, and Chairman,
Countrywide Communications Group Ltd

Who do you trust these days? Think hard. Yes, the more you do, the more difficult it is to produce a decent list. It wasn't always as bleak; in the 'old days', you trusted your bank manager, your doctor, your solicitor, your headmaster ... and the Queen. Maybe the government, big business, the 'serious' press. 'The great, the good' was not such a cynical expression, more an acknowledgement that the establishment created a certain order that could be relied upon.

Not now. It's not just our business leaders who are distrusted 'fat cats', not just our politicians who are scorned, and not just our social order that is in disarray. The age of deference, as we might call it, is dead and not just in the UK but in vast parts of the 'civilised' world.

It is against this background of the opening up of society (ironically, by media which themselves become more powerful while more cynical and untrustworthy) that corporate communications is floundering. While corporate governance or ethics are more widely discussed than ever, standards in public life are perceived to be falling. Rather than seeing the exposure of company competition as a sign of a vigorous regulatory system (first Barings and then Morgan Grenfell) the press and public seem to believe the City is not what it was.

Rather than seeing Shell's retreat over Brent Spar as an encouraging victory for environmentalists (well German ones, anyway) it has been seen as big business trampling on our sensitivities and then gracelessly backing down.

Yet business is more sensitive to public opinion than ever before. Openness has brought with it a heightened sense of responsibility among business leaders. They care – they *have* to care – about the opinions of all their shareholders, and how their opinions are formed. The death of deference means that communication with employees has to be constant, fast and truthful. Whistleblowing by disgruntled employees may be more associated with the civil service; but especially with e-mail and the Internet, companies will soon discover the potential for their plans, particularly the unpopular ones, to be broadcast to the world. The threat of disclosure and a media ready to carry the message has never been stronger, so any company aiming to buck this trend is in for trouble. Open internal communications mean that business leaders have to take more time and trouble to ensure their policies and the progress of their plans are fully explained in ways their people can understand – no longer just the house tabloid newspaper but also business television, thorough cascade briefings and face-to-face appearances.

All the company's other audiences need similarly thorough attention; generally, they are getting it, but achieving a real understanding of what may result from corporate discussions has never been more difficult. Business leaders get some media training, promote their PR people to directors of communication – but seldom have the understanding of the outside world to allow communications professionals to sit alongside them in the boardroom to give advice when it is most critically necessary – before the decision is reached. Maybe by definition, leading a great company can cut you off from the rest of the world. No amount of market research can tell you what the world is really thinking. No focus group can tell a politician what people really believe. It's an almost impossible dilemma: how to commit the time to understanding your 'audiences', though the even bigger problem is to get business leaders to understand the issue in the first place.

The PR industry has not done that job well. Although the international public relations industry has doubled in the past decade (there are 500 registered consultancies in Europe alone), most are working at the coal face, not the board room. True, there are more communications specialists in the board room, but the handful of consultants who are used at the policy-setting stage is woefully small. The norm is to call them in when the issue starts to overheat or to use them to promote products, policies or events that are long off the board's agenda.

Undertaking international PR campaigns can potentially bring many additional and specific problems for client/consultancy relationships: culture; language; time zones and currency. This results in the need for extremely refined planning and co-ordination of the entire programme. The increasing trend is for consultancies to work with the client to develop its international programme centrally, but to deliver it locally in order to ensure it is implemented by those who know their own market and culture. It's easy to underestimate the complexities of local delivery, especially if you are based in the States. As a result, one of the potentially most serious issues arises at the beginning of the relationship: the need to adopt 'realistic' (consultancy's word) and 'economic' (client's word) budgets for making the local programme work. Fortunately, the quality and experience of in-house communications or PR directors have increased dramatically in recent years, so they not only have more experience of the costs involved in briefing consultancy offices in several countries but also in the varying techniques most likely to succeed in various national cultures.

59

The Language and Culture Imperative

Alexander Letts
Chairman, The SMI Group

Dear God

I came into the office last week and had the shock of my life. For the past three years I've been, dare I say it, the successful and groundbreaking marketing director of an American multinational's UK operation. We've created new channels of distribution that the industry has seized on as being original and innovative, we've held our price points though value-adds, and we've even tailored some of our products to reflect opportunities exclusive to the UK.

On top of that I've found an ad agency that has produced award-winning, share-gaining creative work. Business in the UK is booming, and people give me much of the credit. My personal stock in the company is such that I was voted, somewhat excruciatingly, 'Most Valuable Employee for the First Quarter'.

Then ... bang, this happens. 'Well done,' they said, 'The CEO has heard about your work,' they said. 'We want to give you a broader canvas to paint on,' they said. It was only then that I saw the train coming down the track, but before I could get my pre-emptive strike into place, it hit me head-on: 'We want you to do the European job. Congratulations on your promotion to Director of Marketing Europe.' And then they were gone.

Of course it was a stitch-up. I'd been a poacher, but too successful for them to rope in. The previous Euro-incumbent could hardly rock my boat when share points were climbing in the UK and falling in other European markets. And anyway his remit was too fuzzy to allow him to exercise any leverage, on me or the others. The Danes and Norwegians were his blue-eyed brethren, but then they couldn't afford a decent agency and were always wetting themselves to have a European ad campaign and some kind of centralised purgatory for all communications.

It didn't take me long to wind up the Germans and French to kick all that tosh into touch. It's the easiest game in town.

Poor old Buzz, doing the Euro job finished him off. No market, no cash, no power, but with a mandate to 'create a unified brand'. So now he's gone, and I'm the new gamekeeper, with all the poachers out there playing the game whose rules I established. Am I washed up, or what?

Yours faithfully

A Lost Sheep

Dear Mr Sheep

Whilst I'm omnipotent, European marketing is the one area that I prefer not to get involved in, as it's absolute hell. Being a caring kind of guy, however, I have forwarded your letter to both of our sister offices in Hemel Hempsted and Hades.

Yours eternally

God

Dear Mr Sheep

We are in receipt of your letter to God dated 29 July 1996 and forwarded to us by the same. I'm truly delighted to hear about the situation in which you find yourself and thought it might be satisfying for me to gloat over a few of the problems facing you. Let's, for a moment, set aside the many broader marketing issues that will cause you pain over the coming months and flag the one that will torture you from day one and ultimately ensure that your career, health and good looks all disappear down the great sewer of life.

It's the most contested, most visible and most political issue that faces you and I'm delighted to let you know that we launched this product in the mid1980s especially to meet the punishment needs of successful well-paid executives such as yourself.

I'm talking, of course, about advertising across Europe. We are proud in Hell to have invented this exquisite form of agony. As well as destroying the lives of the marketing people involved, it has the delightful added benefit of grating horribly on all other parties that come into contact with it. These include ad agencies (the only people whom we in Hades truly admire), and consumers who can't avoid these revolting mutated ad creations. And of course, as the icing on the cake, it ultimately destroys the market share and share price of the companies that pump millions of pounds into their development and broadcast. As for you, can I just quickly let you know how each step of your career will now progress? We find this forecasting service to be helpful to our customers in ensuring maximisation of the frustration and inevitability of their own personal decline. It will start with a promise from head office that you are empowered to run advertising from a central point, and that you are expected to execute against such a strategy forthwith.

The truly neat thing is that there is no mechanism for you actually to do your job. You will appoint an agency on huge fees with offices all over Europe, contrary to the wishes of the individual markets who already have close relationships with their own agencies, and you will develop a brilliant campaign. You love it. But the work will immediately be destroyed by all the local offices, both to your face and behind your back. Remember your own tricks? 'Irrelevant to our market position.' 'It won't work in the French language.' 'You just can't use that imagery in Germany – it ignores sensitivities.' 'Our schedule is already booked up well into the next millennium.' 'Of course, he got lucky in the UK, time and place were right. Now he's out of his depth.' That sort of stuff. You'll rebrief the agency, this time with a warning that if they really are a network, their work will work on a Euro-basis. They shrug and resort to formula advertising. It comes back, Euro-bland. You escalate the power and control issue to head office (now you're really exposed). The countries relent. The work runs. It bombs. Market share dives. You're history. The countries all revert to running their own work through their own agencies with the money they didn't spend behind your campaign because it was 'committed' elsewhere. Either that, or you never escalate the issue to head office and your work never gets to run at all, with the same result. You're out. FAILED. History. Remember your predecessor? Obviously there's no way out for you now, so it only remains for me to say that we very much look forward to working with you over the coming months and to meeting you in person soon. Should you have any queries, please don't hesitate to call me on 0800 HELL, or E-mail me (nick@hell.com).
With beast wishes
Lucifer

Dear Mr Sheep

I hope you don't mind me approaching you, but I read about your damnation in the executive appointments section of the *Financial Times*. Please believe me that while your outlook may seem to you to be utterly bleak, you do have an option which in your particular instance may well offer you a path to salvation. Our company is a spiritual consultancy which has a successful track record in helping poor souls such as yourself to emerge, not only intact, but bathed in glory from the situation in which you find yourself. We have based our thinking around the notion that for certain product categories, pan-European advertising is not only relevant to the consumers but the road to competitive advantage, both in terms of brand development and management control. Your new-technology sector is one such area where the highest common-factor-benefits of the products that you sell are globally consistent. I couldn't say the same of refrigerators or personal hygiene products but there are many other sectors which also reflect this opportunity.

The secret to understanding multi-language, multi-cultural communication is to put yourself in the situation in which the consumers around your markets, and indeed the marketing professionals in those markets, find themselves. They are proud of their language, proud of their culture and just as sophisticated as any consumers anywhere else in the world. In this case, why on earth should they be expected to be empathetic to second-hand advertising created by non-nationals, ignorant of their ways and oblivious to anything but their own local cultural and linguistic requirements? Would you tolerate this? Did you put up with attempts to ram someone else's style down your market's throat? No, of course not. And to top this there is the perfectly understandable not-invented-here syndrome which powers a long unreasonable debate.

You think you're in Hell? Well, Hell is nothing to what these people will go through, suffering your high-handed, arrogant attempt to impose some linguistic and cultural hierarchy as the ads which are crafted for the market in which the agency resides are then passed on as suitable, with a bit of translation, for a dozen other nations. OK, so if you start from this view, you have a chance to solve their problems, and meet each other half way. There will, for sure, never be any way around the 'not-invented-here' syndrome, but it can be mitigated; and I'm not just talking about the copy-writing, but about the whole way you work with these people, who are your colleagues, after all!

The solution lies in a combination of diplomacy, creativity that is devoid of hierarchy, and collaborative working. Let's start with diplomacy. Get a mandate to go with your job. Get the right to own all the advertising budget for all the markets; if you don't get this, don't take the job. Without it you are a marketing eunuch. But once you have the mandate, don't necessarily use it. Be diplomatic in your approach to your country colleagues around Europe and explain your dilemma. You have the mandate, but you admire their capability and local knowledge. You need each other. Their input is crucial to success. They know it and so should you. But they should also be aware of the mandate. It doesn't take a Henry Kissinger to work out some kind of effective treaty here. The chips you can bring to the negotiating table are about creativity and collaboration.

Creativity can now be done in a single place, but still be local. It is done not by using the outdated, slow and expensive model of points of creative presence in every market, but by having all the copywriters in one location. The most famous example of this is a company based in London, who are not an agency, but who work with agencies by allowing them to outsource the international copywriting to one office which re-creates the ads from visual and brief. These are agency copywriters on two-year contracts to a Soho-based operation. They love it and they bring their professional advertising skills and their culture and language with them.

Each ad they do is simply a version, and no more, and it is written to work in the market for which they write. In addition, the writers and the local client have a relationship which encompasses discussing the concept and the copy to ensure local satisfaction. And the speed is amazing. Try changing 10 words in one ad in 12 languages in 10 locations across Europe. Three weeks is the norm; do it centrally and three hours is the norm.

But that still leaves true collaboration. Setting aside the ideal whereby you or your agency would be in every one of your local markets every day, how do you truly work together and harness the skill and knowledge of the markets to ensure their input into the advertising process? Thank the Lord – the Internet! Or more precisely the much hyped, little-understood, World Wide Web. An agency in London has become the first in the world to use the Web to create a virtual network. Not only do they use the central copywriting process described above, but they have closed forums on their Web site where the ads in each language are posted to view or print out as proofs. Each ad has pop-up e-mail response forms which allow the countries to input on the concept and their usage of it. The media planning is there too. Timetables, schedules, costs, news and information. The whole account is run by an agency in cyberspace regardless of fragmented geographies and time differences. So, while the countries may not have their own local agencies, at least they don't face running second-hand work, and having no say in the processes. Everyone is always in the loop; everyone can see, quite transparently what is going on. But you are in control. They make the strategic and tactical input but development is centralised. Costs are lower; speed, creativity, consistency and effect are enhanced. It's all very new I know, and it's all a bit cool and groovy, but it works. International businesses like yours are already working this way. Indeed, instead of damnation they are saying it is a route to salvation, not just of the creative work, the market share and the revenues, but of their own careers too. I do hope that you find this advice helpful.

Yours encouragingly

A Samaritan

Part 12
Media Profiles

60

BBC Television and Radio

Colin Browne
Director of Corporate Affairs, BBC

These are important times for British broadcasting. The pace of change has never been quicker. Analogue technology is giving way to its digital successor; broadcasters are about to move from the constraints of spectrum scarcity into an age of plenty; and the development of digital services will hasten the convergence of broadcasting, computing and telecommunications – creating a new sector of great, and growing, economic importance. It is a sector in which the UK is well placed to prosper. We have the priceless advantage of the English language, which is set to be the Information Age's 'mother tongue'; we have Britain's hard-earned reputation for the quality of its programme-making; and we have a unique opportunity to turn such assets to the country's advantage.

These are also momentous times for the BBC, in particular. 1996 saw the sixtieth anniversary of BBC Television; 1997 will see the BBC's seventy-fifth birthday. And, more generally, the remaining years of the twentieth century will do much to determine the Corporation's fortunes in the twenty-first.

The BBC starts from a position of strength. It is not only Britain's leading public-service broadcaster, but both the biggest educational broadcaster and the largest news-gathering organisation anywhere in the world. Above all, however, the BBC's programmes enjoy an international reputation that is second to none. As we approach the twenty-first century, the BBC is determined that its reputation for quality, creativity and independence – the product of seventy-five years' hard work – should be maintained, and built upon, as it moves from the analogue into the digital age.

The opportunities of the digital age

The BBC has been getting into shape for its digital future. Over the last few years, the Corporation has been transformed by a series of radical reforms. Producer Choice has helped to increase its efficiency. Our Strategy Review has further increased the distinctiveness of its output, and the establishment of BBC Worldwide has made its international and commercial activities more effective and coherent. We believe, however, that further changes are needed if the full potential of digital technology is to be harnessed on behalf of all our viewers and listeners.

The opportunities associated with digital broadcasting are enormous. It will enable higher quality picture and sound, a range of new services, and much more choice for the public. Creative opportunities for broadcasters will be immense. For all these reasons, there is no doubt that, in years to come, broadcasting will be digital. An analogue-only BBC would look as odd in this new environment as an exclusively black-and-white BBC would appear today.

The BBC's digital plans have already been published, and licence fee-payers are set to receive a 'digital dividend'. We have already launched a digital radio service – the world's first – that offers both outstanding sound quality and a wider choice of services. *BBC Now*, for example, offers a continuously updated news, business, sport, weather and travel service, and Radio 5 Live is being supplemented by *News Plus* and *Sports Plus* services, offering additional live news programmes while the main network is covering sport, and vice versa. Parliamentary coverage will also become more comprehensive. Having taken the lead, we now look to manufacturers to develop volume production of digital sets to receive these services.

On television, digital technology will allow us to launch a 24-hour news channel; BBC1 and BBC2 in a widescreen format and with a choice of programming; and an enhanced CEEFAX service – all at no extra charge to licence fee-payers.

Digital technology will also allow us to introduce a number of subscription channels and other services, such as, eventually, 'video-on-demand', which will generate additional income for investment in new programmes and services, for the benefit of the licence fee-payer.

Two challenges

But there are challenges as well as opportunities in the digital age of broadcasting. Two issues have been causing the BBC particular concern. The first is primarily financial; the second concerns the regulatory regime that the Government is putting in place.

Financially, the BBC is facing one of the most difficult and demanding phases in its history. The ever-growing number of channels is increasing the competition for many of the presenters, programme-makers and broadcasting rights that the BBC needs. That, in turn, is increasing the amounts that the BBC has to pay. The cost of sports rights, for example, has increased by around 800 per cent in only ten years. Other costs are also rising, albeit more slowly, but still adding to the pressures on the BBC's budget.

The BBC has had to face these challenges at a time when our main source of income – the licence fee – has been pegged to the rate of inflation. Indeed, the licence fee now costs less, in real terms, than ten years ago – and the World Service's grant-in-aid income has also been squeezed. This has happened at a time when industry revenues generally have been rising. Advertising income continues to grow; revenue from subscription services is rising sharply; and several of the World Service's international competitors are being encouraged to expand – and given the resources to do so. The BBC, on the other hand, has been facing constraints on our income at a time when we need to make a substantial investment in digital technology.

We have been working hard to rise to these financial challenges. We have cut our cost base significantly; reduced the size of our workforce by around a fifth (while increasing our output); and have achieved efficiency savings of around £100 million in each of the last three years. To quote from the independent consultants appointed by the Government to examine our track record over the last three years, the BBC has 'made large efficiency savings, generated new output and improved its market positioning whilst reducing its borrowings'. But, like every other organisation in the UK of the 1990s, we cannot afford to be complacent. Tough new efficiency targets have been set, and a major restructuring is helping to streamline our management, give greater focus to our activities, and generate substantial savings across-the-board.

At the same time as reducing our costs, we are determined to increase our income from commercial sources. Much has already been achieved: in the UK, BBC magazines, videos and books (including Sir John Harvey-Jones' *Troubleshooter*) have been sold by the million; further afield, BBC programmes have been successfully exported around the world – often to the most unlikely destinations. The fictitious prime ministers Jim Hacker and Francis Urquhart, for example, have achieved fame as far away as South Africa, Thailand, and Trinidad & Tobago; German broadcasters have screened *Fawlty Towers*; and the BBC is synonymous worldwide, with drama, documentary, news, and natural history programmes of the highest quality. Indeed, the BBC not only accounts for over 40 per cent of British programme and programme-related products, but is Europe's leading audiovisual exporter by far.

Over the next six to eight years, we plan to treble the contribution that these commercial activities make to our core business. But not even a combination of stretching efficiency and commercial revenue targets will enable the BBC to meet all its rising costs and provide enough funding for a proper digital future. That is why, last autumn, we called for a modest increase, in real terms, in the level of the licence fee, and for the cuts in the World Service's budget to be reconsidered and reversed.

We were delighted when the Government decided to restore £5 million to the World Service's grant-in-aid. At a time of particularly tight control over public spending, this represented a major vote of confidence in the World Service. The Government's decision was widely welcomed – not least by members of Britain's business community. We are grateful for the consistent support that many CBI members have given to the World Service. As well as providing its 140 million listeners with authoritative and impartial news and information – often in countries where it is in short supply – it earns the UK a reputation for honesty, fairness and trustworthiness that helps to smooth the way for exports of British goods and services.

There was some good news on the licence fee. While, in a five-year settlement, the licence fee will end up at the same level as inflation, increases above the RPI in years two and three will generate additional revenue of about £170 million for the BBC. We believe that there is a strong economic case for ensuring that British broadcasting is properly funded. Broadcasting is a proven British success story. It is a major employer and export earner. It enhances the country's international image and reputation. It is part of a sector which is set to grow strongly in the short-, medium- and longer-term. And, crucially, it can enable Britain to capitalise upon the immense economic potential of the English language.

A second factor will also determine the extent to which the BBC – in common with other broadcasters – is able to contribute to the successful development of digital television. It revolves around the control of the 'gateway' that will decide which services reach people's homes, as well as the prominence they are given and the ways in which subscriptions and other payments are made. The value of all the services passing through the gateway will be enormous – and the battle for its control will be one of the great business battles of the next century. The BBC believes that those who have invested in digital infrastructure should receive a fair return on their investment. But no one should be able to abuse control of the gateway to restrict competition or reduce the range of services that is made available to the public. If the full potential of digital technology is to be realised, the regulatory regime needs to be able to encourage diversity and discourage dominance.

But we all need to keep the attractions of new technology in perspective.

The medium is not the message – and the digital revolution will fail to reach its full potential if it is allowed to become a first-class way of delivering second- or third-rate services. The attributes of digital technology need to be combined with the values and virtues that have contributed to the success of British broadcasting in the analogue age. The BBC's primary purpose will continue to be the need to make high-quality programmes that inform, educate and delight our audiences, and extend the choice of viewing and listening available to the licence fee-paying public.

It is always tempting to see some long-past era as 'a golden age'. However, we believe that our recent line-up of programmes compares well with anything that has gone before. *Persuasion*, *Pride and Prejudice* and *The Tenant of Wildfell Hall* have restored our national – and international – reputation for classic drama at its best; in contemporary drama, *Our Friends in the North* attracted similar praise. Series such as *The Death of Yugoslavia*, *People's Century*, *The System* and *The House* demonstrated the BBC's strength in factual programming; our coverage of national events – such as the VE and VJ Day anniversaries – helped to bring all parts of the country together; and Wallace and Gromit's latest adventure added to the list of recent BBC successes at the Academy Awards.

Radio

On radio, the controversy surrounding the transformation of Radio 1 has given way to critical acclaim. The record-breaking 1996 Proms season showed the importance of the BBC in general – and Radio 3, in particular – as a cultural patron. Radio 5 Live continues to attract a young audience – and numerous awards – for its unique blend of news and sport. And the *Today* programme, on Radio 4, sets the nation's agenda in a truly remarkable way.

The BBC has unveiled plans to build upon these achievements. We have published, for the first time, a 'Statement of Promises to Viewers and Listeners', containing 230 firm commitments, to make it more accountable to its licence fee-payers, and improve the service that it is able to offer them. We have issued a new edition of its *Producers' Guidelines*, setting out our editorial values and the standards to which our programme-makers are expected to adhere. And we have launched a major new initiative, Talent 2000, to continue our role as a cultural patron, and discover people with the skills that we will need as we look ahead to the next millennium.

The BBC has faced many challenges in its first seventy-five years. In 1997, as we celebrate our seventy-fifth birthday, we are facing many more.

We do not underestimate the size of the task that lies ahead. But we are better prepared to face the future than at any time in our recent history. We are much leaner and more efficient. We are more accountable and, we hope, more responsive. Our programmes have never been better – and we are making more of them. And we have a clear and coherent strategy to help lead British broadcasting into the new, digital age.

61

ITV: Rising to the Challenge

Barry Cox
Director, ITV Association

1996 was an important year for British broadcasting in general and ITV in particular. We spent a great deal of time thrashing-out the key policy issues which arose during the course of the Broadcasting Bill: the challenge of digital television; changes to the media ownership rules; developments in programme and industry regulation. And while the policy framework was being hammered out in Westminster and Whitehall, the battle for audience share and revenue streams between the major broadcasters in the UK market became still more intense.

But with so many policy issues running in tandem and with the broadcasting industry developing and expanding so quickly, it is all too easy to lose sight of our core objective: to produce and broadcast a diverse range of quality programmes for a British audience.

Bearing this last point in mind, it is perhaps worthwhile focusing on what ITV would consider to be the most important themes of 1996 and how they are likely to develop in 1997 and beyond.

The core business

ITV is in the business of delivering quality, diversity and choice of programming to a mass audience. Our peak-time audience share for the last full year of analysis (1995) was 42.3 per cent (compared to BBC 1's 33.4 per cent, Channel Four's 8.5 per cent and the combined cable and satellite sector's 6.2 per cent) and is a testimony to ITV's continued success in its core business. The audience was delivered on the back of the largest investment in programming by any British channel. Next year we will spend over £600 million on predominantly home-produced original production to be broadcast across the network.

This commitment is underpinned by a £200 million investment in regional programming, delivering to the local audiences of the 15 ITV regions a range of specifically tailored programmes from every genre. Indeed, the federal structure of ITV is unique to Britain and is something which we will be emphasising in the policy arena in 1997.

All this forms part of a 'virtuous circle', whereby ITV attracts large audiences, which in turn maintains a strong advertising revenue stream, which provides the funding for our programme investment, which in turn delivers still higher audiences. To enhance this 'virtuous circle', ITV intends to consolidate the strong marketing of individual ITV companies and the three sales houses, with an expansion of the central marketing function. 'Britain's Most Popular Button' should become even more high profile in the marketing world in 1997.

Arrival of the digital age

The arrival of Digital Satellite Television (DST) in late 1997 and of Digital Terrestrial Television (DTT) soon after will transform the broadcasting environment. The British public will soon have access to at least 500 channels, many broadcasting much sharper, wide-screen pictures, offering interactive services and access to the Internet.

Like the BBC, ITV has had to use 1996 to consider how to rise to the challenge of the digital age. In the technological arena, we are working with manufacturers and retailers on the specifications for new digital television sets and set-top boxes. In the policy arena, we have worked closely with DTI, OFTEL and the Department of National Heritage on the regulatory framework for digital television, particularly ensuring that BSkyB does not exercise monopoly control on the gatekeeper technology that allows other broadcasters to fully utilise digital services. And we are currently examining the possibility of a second service – ITV2 – to utilise the extra capacity made available by the switch from analogue to our new digital multiplex, which we accepted in October 1996 and which we share with Channel Four. 1997 will witness these plans come to fruition.

Broadcasting revenues

At the time of writing, the House of Commons National Heritage Select Committee has started its inquiry into 'The BBC and the Future of Broadcasting'. In our submission to the Committee, ITV points out that the future of broadcasting is dependent on a complex and delicate balance of revenues, derived from the licence fee, advertising and subscription.

If ITV is to maintain the health of its core business and respond to the challenges of digital and an increasingly competitive marketplace, we believe that Parliament and Government should look again at the revenues which it takes from the channel. The licence fees paid by the individual ITV companies to broadcast in a particular region amount to £400 million. This is effectively a supertax which is levied on and above corporation tax.

Combined with the Channel Four funding-formula debate, ITV will be focusing much of its policy work on the revenue issue in 1997 and 1998, not least as licence renegotiation approaches in 1998. We will certainly be working hard for more equitable arrangements in the future.

Regulation: level playing field?

Broadcasting is one of the most heavily regulated industries in the world, with the British broadcasting industry operating within easily the tightest framework of regulation in Europe, and ITV working under more detailed and prescriptive regulation than any other British broadcaster. In short, ITV is probably one of the most strictly regulated businesses on the planet!

Given the power and influence which policy-makers believe rests in the hands of broadcasters, this can be no surprise. And some of the prescriptive regulations laid down in the Independent Television Commission's (ITC) Programme code ensure that programme quality is maintained, which arguably assists ITV.

However, we believe that it is very important for broadcasters to operate on a level playing field of regulation. The fact that they do not – for example on sponsorship, masthead advertising or the 9 pm watershed – gives our competitors an unfair advantage. ITV will, therefore, be working to ensure that the regulatory framework within which we all have to operate is more equitable in the future.

The future

At a policy level, ITV believes it is very important to get the regulatory framework and revenue-generating equation right and that, post-Broadcasting Bill, much work still needs to be done. Digital television will pose additional challenges and business opportunities for our channel.

Provided we get these issues right, ITV can go on doing what it has done so successfully in the past: producing and broadcasting excellent pro-grammes, which make it 'Britain's Most Popular Button'.

62

British Sky Broadcasting

Ray Gallagher
*Director of Public Affairs, British Sky
Broadcasting*

In 1989, Sky Television became the first broadcaster to offer UK viewers multi-channel choice. British Sky Broadcasting was created in November 1990 from the merger between Sky Television and British Satellite Broadcasting.

The business has been transformed since those early days in 1989, from a four-channel network with accumulated losses of over £1.5 billion to its present position as the biggest satellite broadcast network in the world, offering 40 channels to more than 5.65 million homes throughout the UK and Eire.

BSkyB continues to lead the television revolution in the UK and now offers alongside its own services a wide range of independent channels, delivering even more choice for the nation's growing multi-channel market. This increased variety is particularly popular with young people and families. More than one in three children now live in a Sky home.

The breadth and depth of the programming, from live televised sports to non-stop news to first-run movies to popular series, provides both new opportunities for sponsors and advertisers, as well as more choice for viewers. BSkyB has also been a catalyst for employment – in television and other related industries, generating millions of pounds of economic activity. Through this drive and vision, BSkyB will continue to lead the whole television revolution, creating new offers from which the entire television industry can benefit.

The business

BSkyB's business comprises three core activities; programming, distribution and advertising. In all three, BSkyB has been the main force for change delivering a dramatic increase in choice for UK viewers and a host of new quality programmes previously unavailable on British television.

New technology has been developed to deliver a wide selection of channels to subscribers who receive them through a satellite dish or by cable. Advertisers have been offered fresh strategies allowing them to use a variety of media to target their chosen audiences.

It is this innovative approach that has enabled BSkyB to provide an alternative to the terrestrial channels which for so long have been the dominant force in the market.

Programming

BSkyB's multi-channel service provides viewers with the widest possible choice of quality programmes, from television movie premieres, to 24-hour news as it happens, to the best in live sport, new series and dramas. This service is constantly being developed and extended. Sky screens an average of 30 new movies a month, and covers 100 different sports every year.

Distribution

BSkyB has invested heavily in subscriber management, and customer relations through state-of-the-art technology and quality staff training. The use of two methods of distribution, DTH (direct to-home via satellite dish) and cable, maximises the number of viewers able to receive multi-channel TV. In addition to individual homes, the Sky service is received in pubs and clubs, while shared dishes carry it into blocks of flats, hotels, and Her Majesty's forces in the UK.

At 30 September 1996, BSkyB's multi-channel package was received by more than 5.65 million subscribers in the UK and Eire. Of these, 3.3 million received the programmes through DTH and 2.35 million via their cable operator.

BSkyB is determined to remain at the cutting edge of change in television. It has committed itself to the future of multi-channel broadcasting by leasing capacity on a range of Astra's digital satellites, due to launch in autumn 1997.

The satellite dish market

BSkyB's DTH customers own or rent the equipment necessary to receive the signals. Demand has been such that the market for satellite dishes alone is worth more than £100 million a year. Competition from the major retailing multiples has seen prices for satellite dishes fall as low as £79, making the entry cost for satellite TV viewers ever more affordable.

BSkyB and cable television

BSkyB is the largest supplier of programming to cable operators. All broadband cable systems carry Sky channels. BSkyB's policy has been to make its programming as widely available as possible, and most cable subscribers can enjoy the same programme choice as BSkyB's DTH subscribers.

Advertising

BSkyB's multi-channel service is increasingly attractive to advertisers. Whatever the target market, there is scope for integrated campaigns. Advertisers can buy spots on the wide variety of Sky channels and sponsor airtime. They can use Sky Text services and the Sky TV guide, and there are opportunities for joint promotions and merchandising.

It has created real competition for the terrestrial broadcasters, in terms of both price and flexibility. In March 1996, during the week of the Bruno–Tyson fight, cable and satellite viewing took more than 10 per cent of the overall television audience for the first time. It also surpassed the share of a terrestrial broadcaster for the first time. In August it set a new record of 11.7 per cent of total UK viewing.

Recent surveys have shown that in multi-channel homes more than a third of all viewing is taken by the satellite channels. Sky's 12 channels take around 18 per cent of total viewership in satellite homes.

In the financial year 1995–96, Sky's advertising revenue increased by 20 per cent to £110 million. This compared with an average increase of just over 5 per cent for the terrestrial channels.

Targeting

The complexity of today's markets, with increasingly segmented consumer groups being served by more and more niche products, requires much more from an advertising medium than the ability to reach a mass market. Sky can offer a variety of media opportunities, spot advertising on a wide range of channels, sponsorship, text services and publications, opportunities for joint promotions and merchandising. This offers advertisers unique targeting opportunities, making television advertising much more effective than on traditional terrestrial broadcasts.

The Sky audience

All forecasts about the extent of satellite and cable penetration between now and the end of the decade predict steady, positive growth. Opinions vary as to the relative proportions of dish and cable homes, but projections suggest that the total number of homes with Sky will be over nine million by the year 2000. This represents a 40 per cent penetration of UK homes. In a fiercely competitive global market, BSkyB is a British success story.

63

Commercial Radio

Steve Cox
Radio Advertising Bureau

Commercial radio has existed in the UK for nearly a quarter of a century, and yet it is only in the last five years that it has truly come of age. It may seem strange now but during the Eighties and early Nineties, the industry had struggled to escape the tag of 'the 2 per cent medium' – a figure referring to the percentage of all advertising revenue spent on radio.

Despite massive advances in terms of listenership and number of stations, advertisers still appeared unconvinced that radio had any value in marketing their brands other than for traditional 'tactical' support. As we shall see, this view has now changed, but in a benchmark survey carried out by the RAB in 1992, the medium's principal unique selling propositions (USPs) as listed by over 200 advertisers were:

- *low cost* – radio was regarded as being relatively cheap, both in terms of commercial production and buying airtime;
- *speed* – radio offered advertisers the flexibility to decide to make a commercial, create it the same day, and transmit it on air the following day;
- *local flexibility* – the proliferation of local stations provided advertisers with the option of supporting a network of retail outlets with minimal wastage.

All of this encouraged retailers and publishers to use radio for tactical reasons (promoting sales, or Sunday's newspaper), but, at that time, few advertisers believed that radio could play a role in strategic brand support.

This position is now changing as users increasingly learn to appreciate the power of the medium and its ability to access enormous numbers of potential customers, attracted in growing numbers from the BBC.

At the same time, a number of significant events have occurred that together have resulted in a marked change in advertisers' perceptions of radio and a corresponding increase in advertising revenue for the medium.

Recent growth

Classic FM launched in 1992 and was the first fully national commercial radio station. It was followed shortly afterwards by Virgin and there are now four national or near-national commercial stations broadcasting. It is clear that, for some advertisers, the existence of national stations has led them to revise their views about radio's potential role in their marketing mix. Radio may still be most regularly used as support to another medium, but it is now sometimes strategic rather than tactical support.

This has been backed up by an intensive generic marketing campaign mounted by the Radio Advertising Bureau. Also founded in 1992, the RAB is funded by all commercial stations and has carried out extensive research into how radio advertising works and how best advertisers can take advantage of this. Operating as a free consultancy service for advertisers and their advertising agencies, the RAB has received considerable acclaim for its role in changing advertisers' perceptions and enabling them to appreciate that the medium is far more than simply TV without pictures, but has its own unique benefits which can be used solus, or in conjunction with other media, to promote brand sales.

Linking into this, in 1992 commercial radio also revised its method of measuring audiences and introduced RAJAR, one of the largest media research studies in the world, to enable advertisers to plan their campaigns more effectively. Now advertisers can target their radio advertising with startling accuracy – even down to reaching the listeners of individual BBC programmes, like Radio 4's *Today*, when they switch to a commercial station.

The combination of these factors, together with continued growth in listening to commercial radio, has led to an explosion in advertising revenue spent in the medium. After enduring 21 years as the '2 per cent medium', commercial radio now has grown rapidly to a point where it is currently taking close to a 5 per cent share of all display advertising expenditure.

Recent trends

The commercial radio industry is regulated by the Radio Authority which is responsible for awarding all new commercial licences and monitoring existing licence holders to check they are fulfilling the conditions under which they hold their licences. They are committed to a programme of expanding the number of commercial stations broadcasting.

Currently around 180 are on air, and this looks set to increase to around 250 by the end of the decade. The Radio Authority's remit is to only award new licences to stations offering a different style of programming from those already broadcasting in the area concerned, so that each new station broadens choice for that area's listeners.

This has also had significant benefits for radio advertisers. If each station in any given area has a different programme format, it tends to attract a different type of audience; as a result, the existence of more stations offers the opportunity to reach discrete target groups, with minimal levels of wastage, in a suitable programme environment.

Much of this development has occurred in urban areas. Radio listeners in London (the most developed UK radio market) can choose from over 20 commercial stations, and in Manchester there are 9 commercial options. It seems likely that many of the planned new stations will also be allocated to large centres of population.

This expansion will revolve around local stations, since the BBC is highly unlikely to surrender any more frequencies to the commercial sector (it currently holds around 60 per cent – in general the best 60 per cent). It is, therefore, certain that there will be no more national commercial stations in the next five years broadcasting within the current frequency spectrum.

However, there may be opportunities for more national stations in the future should Digital Audio Broadcasting really take off. DAB is already technically possible, and the radio industry is currently conducting experiments in digital transmission. At present, much of the investment is coming from the BBC, as development is expensive and there is as yet little incentive for commercial stations to invest in something that, if successful, will open up the airwaves for competitors.

For the listener, DAB transmission means that signals may be received and reproduced with CD quality both on FM and AM. Six stations can transmit using DAB in the frequency space occupied by one 'traditional' station, opening up tremendous opportunities for station proliferation. However, it requires both new transmission equipment and new receiving sets, and herein lies a problem.

Currently, receivers are very expensive, and few listeners are likely to invest in them. In fact it is possible that this may not happen until the major car manufacturers begin to include them as standard in new models. Eventually (if the VCR 'model' is followed) consumers will begin to purchase the new DAB radios as 'standard', but this is likely to take some time.

Summary

So then, to summarise the developments of the last few years. Proliferation of stations, including new national options, combined with a period of intensive research and marketing has changed advertisers' perceptions of radio as a viable advertising medium.

When the RAB recently repeated the same survey mentioned earlier amongst around 200 advertisers, their views on radio's USPs had changed significantly from those held in 1992. The three most popular were:-

- *low cost* radio is still regarded as being relatively cheap, despite increases in airtime costs brought about by increased demand;
- *audience* radio is now perceived as offering mass coverage with the option of targeting discrete target groups with low levels of wastage;
- *listener relationship* due largely to the work of the RAB, radio is perceived as benefiting from a unique relationship with its listeners that offers advertisers new ways to convey strategic brand messages above and beyond radio's 'traditional' tactical strengths.

Clearly the last five years have been very successful for commercial radio. The encouraging news is that independent forecasters see this growth continuing, as Figure 63.1 from the Advertising Association shows.

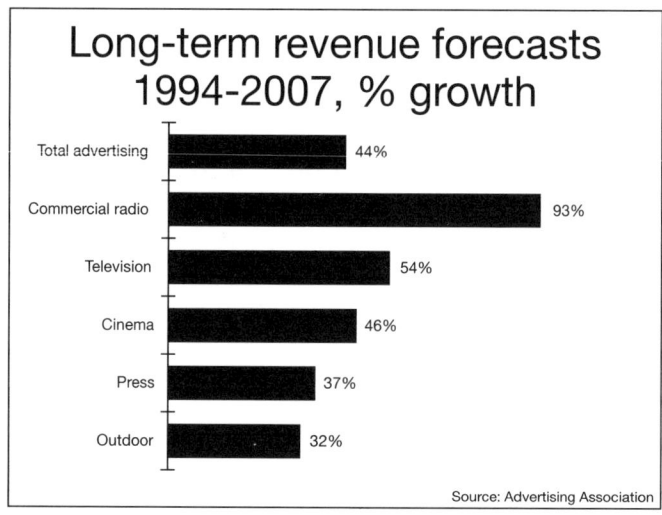

Figure 63.1 Long-term revenue forecasts 1994–2007, % growth

Commercial radio thus seems set to be one of the UK's fastest-growing media for some considerable time to come yet.

64

National Newspapers

David Pollock
*Director, The Newspaper Publishers
Association*

Changes in the industry

National newspapers today face unprecedented changes in the media industry, with increasing competition from developments in electronic media, as well as the changing nature of the society in which we live. The growth of entertainment from screen-based sources takes up more of the leisure time of potential readers, while longer working days and decreased leisure hours present further challenges. Newspapers are meeting these developments with unprecedented investment in promotion and marketing.

While the general explosion of media choice has had an effect on newspaper circulation levels, the figures show that Britain's national press is remarkably resilient. In 1994 (the latest year for which full European data are available) 8 of the top 20 European titles by circulation were British – yet their sales totalled 51 per cent of the total of those top 20. In the first six months of 1996, national dailies sold more than 14 million copies a day, a rise of more than 150,000 a day for the same titles over the same period in 1995.

Over the last decade the circulation of the broadsheet newspapers has increased by 7 per cent, further enhancing their value as an advertising medium. As noted below, the role of the popular press, as an advertising medium, has also stood up well. The price and promotional initiatives of recent years have brought a 12 per cent growth since 1993 in the broadsheet daily sector by attracting new readers as well as increasing the frequency of purchase of the individual titles. While some readers may move between titles depending on the best price or promotional offer, they nevertheless remain loyal to national newspapers.

Advertising

Advertising is a very substantial component of national newspaper publishers' revenue (£1.45 billion or over 52 per cent in 1995, against a total annual turnover of £2.75 billion) and this is showing consistently high growth.

Over the past decade display advertising revenue (currently 67 per cent of the total for the broadsheets and 89 per cent for popular newspapers) has grown steadily at an annual rate of over 7 per cent in both the broadsheets and populars, as might be expected with the growth of corporate profitability and consumer expenditure, in addition to increased competitiveness amongst advertisers.

In the future, advertisers will find new options for reaching their customers as media continue to fragment, with multichannel television, more cable and new satellite networks. However, increasing fragmentation of other media will confirm the attractiveness of national newspapers as a most effective and economic way to reach customers – nationwide or regionally.

Classified advertising is an established marketplace, which has grown by over 7 per cent in broadsheets and by as much as 12 per cent in populars during the last decade.

A market is beginning to develop, especially for classified advertising placed in electronic newspapers. However, their readership is different from the traditional newspaper and at the moment it is the printed newspaper which provides most of the advertisements to establish this electronic marketplace. Electronic newspapers will become an established medium in the future and will develop niche markets, but there is likely to be no significant erosion of advertising in the printed medium over the next decade.

Developing the industry

While newspaper publishers' revenues are supported by current buoyant advertising levels, they have had to withstand some hefty increases in the price of their main raw material – newsprint – which represents some 30 per cent of national newspaper costs. Not only has newsprint increased in price; but so too has the paper used to produce colour supplements.

Against this background, many newspapers have been reviewing their businesses. The health of many individual titles is good, and publishers continuously monitor the requirements of their core readers, delivering products to a standard, and meeting a diversity of interest, which have never been greater.

All national newspaper publishers have interests in other media, whether by diversification into electronic newspapers or by means of strategic stakes in television, radio, satellite broadcasting or regional papers. They have become multimedia players to enable them to compete in the global media marketplace and are well placed to adapt to changes in the media industry.

The future – the reading habit in an electronic age

Changes in reading habits will inevitably affect readership, with older readers not being replaced by younger ones at the same rate. Although the habit of reading newspapers has shown some decline over the past decade, national newspapers are following long-term strategies to encourage young readers to develop their newspaper-reading experience. Several newspapers have produced targeted sections designed to appeal to a younger readership; still others are following other strategies, targeting the student market or developing promotions aimed at young people.

Electronic versions of national newspapers on the Internet are already established (see Table 64.1). They are here to stay and have the potential to become a powerful medium. While a growing number of national newspaper titles are now on-line, however, this development is currently more about promotion than directly building revenue. Electronic publishing can extend the brand of an established newspaper. Experience is showing that, of the new readers brought into an electronic newspaper, some become readers of the 'parent' title. In effect, electronic publishing can increase newspaper readership, rather than the reverse. This trend of dual readership is likely to continue at least in the medium term.

Table 64.1 UK National Newspapers on the World Wide Web

Daily/Sunday Telegraph	http://www.telegraph.co.uk
Express	http://www.research.expressnewspapers.co.uk
Financial Times	http://www.ft.com
Guardian	http://www.guardian.co.uk
Times/Sunday Times	http://www.the-times.co.uk

Looking further ahead, the question is whether electronic newspapers will ever become replacements for the printed medium. At the moment they are alternative delivery systems for the newspapers and are likely to remain so. Although they have the potential to become replacement vehicles for the printed newspaper for some readers, huge investment would be required before they could deliver significant returns; and the printed word is likely to remain the most convenient format for many readers.

Meanwhile, the continuing investment by publishers in the national press will ensure that newspapers are strong and sufficiently robust to face the competition and changes in the marketplace.

Continuing adaptation

National newspapers have always adapted to change and will continue to do so. Publishers have responded to the changing marketplace by increasing the value of their weekend titles with extra sections and supplements, especially for finance, sport, IT, travel and women's interests.

In particular, they are developing the Saturday package, resulting, for the broadsheet market, in Saturday circulations typically increased by some 20 per cent over weekdays. Against a background when the price of newsprint has risen sharply, this growth in sections demonstrates continuing editorial innovation.

More effort is going into promotion, building up databases on potential readers and offering discounted long-term subscription deals.

Production costs have been reduced due to the development of advanced computer systems for both editing and production processes. There is a growing tendency to share contracted printing facilities away from London and, in order to improve distribution and sales overseas, many titles already print editions outside the UK.

The continued steady growth of advertising revenue and the well-established feedback mechanisms of newspapers give just cause for optimism for the future.

National newspapers will remain a buoyant, strong and influential mass-market medium over the next decade and thereafter, giving publishers the incentive to continue to invest in their titles, optimising the benefits of new technology.

National newspapers have adapted well in the past to structural changes in the media and to changing consumer behaviour over the years. They will continue to do so and will remain a powerful medium.

65

Regional Newspapers

Dugal Nisbet-Smith, CBE
Director, The Newspaper Society

Rationalisation before regeneration

Britain's regional newspapers have come under the spotlight in the past year, as a sweeping series of management buy-outs, mergers and acquisitions wrought a swift and radical shake-up in the ownership structure of the industry.

In just 10 months, from October 1995 to August 1996, some £1.3 billion was spent on 20 major acquisitions – more deals than in almost any other media sector. This has had the positive effect of placing most of the major newspaper groups, previously owned by large conglomerates such as Thomson, Reed Elsevier, EMAP and Pearson, in the hands of entrepreneurial and specialist managements with a personal investment in their business success.

Others queued up to buy regional groups; both broadcasters and national newspaper publishers have been among the contenders, including David Montgomery of the Mirror Group, Lord Hollick of MAI/United, Carlton Communications and Scottish Television, which bought Caledonian Publishing, publishers of *The Herald* (Glasgow) for £120 million.

The result is that United News & Media, owners of the fourth-largest regional press publisher United Provincial Newspapers, and the Daily Mail & General Trust, owners of Northcliffe Newspapers Group, ranked at number two, are the only major diversified media groups left with significant interests in regional newspapers. In 1995, the top five regional press groups were all owned by multinationals.

The new breed of publisher

Trinity International Holdings, now the largest regional press publisher, after investing £327 million in buying most of the Thomson Regional Newspaper group, is an example of this new breed: the regional press specialist who understands the local market will exploit his local brands by diversification into new media and will not be subject to the other priorities of a multinational media portfolio.

Johnston Press is another group which has nearly doubled the number of newspaper titles it publishes, following its acquisition of EMAP Regional Newspapers for £211 million. Newsquest, set up with the backing of US venture capitalists Kohlberg Kravis Roberts, after a £205 million management buy-out of Reed Regional Newspapers, bought Westminster Press from Pearson for £305 million.

These mergers and acquisitions are set to continue, aided by changes in the Broadcasting Act which, within limits, frees print and broadcasting media to buy each other. We will see the increasing polarisation of the regional newspaper market. The top 20 regional press publishers currently dominate 80 per cent of circulation. The big will get bigger; the small will stay small, and the middle will disappear – either joining the super league by their own expansion or becoming the next course on someone else's table.

Future trends

Costs will continue to be driven down; the numbers of managers, full-time journalists, production and administration staff are expected to fall, but systems and marketing staff will grow.

Regional newspaper publishers are actively investing in new technology and electronic systems to enable them to tap into additional revenue sources. There will be new and growing revenue from related media and marketing activities. But the core business of the industry will remain newspaper-based for at least the next decade.

Media are moving from mass marketing to one-to-one marketing. Major mass-communication channels are fragmenting and audiences are becoming increasingly difficult and costly to reach. This trend favours regional and local newspapers which can deliver target audiences in a cost-effective way.

The local franchise

So why are so many people clamouring to get a slice of the regional press?

Largely because they can foresee the 'retreat to localness' and want to ensure they are in a position to control the unique local information franchises – the most valuable asset held by local newspapers.

Many feel that the future lies in developing comprehensive databases on millions of homes, businesses, advertisers and readers. The key is in controlling access to local markets via a whole range of different media. Local newspapers, concentrating on their very 'localness', will remain at the heart of the industry.

There is growing investment and diversification into electronic publishing, with many groups developing Internet sites, audiotex and other electronic services for their readers. There are also tie-ups with local radio and cable television stations. Some groups have set up their own broadcasting operations. One example is Midland Independent Newspapers which launched Birmingham Live in 1996, as part of the Mirror Group's Live TV.

We are also seeing a growth in strategic alliances between newspaper groups, particularly in non-competitive areas but also in the lucrative area of letterbox marketing, as well as advertising. Eight groups have already joined forces to create Adhunter, a national classified advertising database on the Internet.

Pressures on newspapers

The explosion in media choice has inevitably had an effect on circulation levels. This is not peculiar to newspapers nor indeed to Britain's print media. The rapid growth in sources of news and information, coupled with longer working hours, has impacted on print globally.

Many publishers feel that, in the long term, the growth of up to 200 television channels, numerous radio stations and electronic media services – leading to smaller, fragmented audiences – will only serve to strengthen regional and local newspapers. Local audiences will turn to them as relevant content providers and advertisers will turn to them for their ability to deliver local, niche audiences.

Newspaper publishers were hit by price rises in their main raw material – newsprint – of up to 50 per cent during 1995. This factor, coupled with the nationals' cover price war, led to an uncomfortable year for most regional publishers and resulted in sweeping cost-cutting measures. Although there was a brief respite from the price war in late 1995, the pressure only really lifted half-way through 1996 as newsprint prices began to fall.

Strengths of the regional press

The regional press is still the second-largest advertising medium in Britain, taking nearly £2 billion (£1,963 million or 21.1 per cent of the total adspend) in 1995, substantially more than all other media except television.

Despite the slow decline in sale, the regional press is read by nine out of ten adults (40 million people) every week and is considered the most trusted, responsible medium in the country.

Analysts remain optimistic about the future for the print media in general, predicting that it will remain a core component of Britain's media sector for many years to come. The regional press in particular, dismissed by some as 'mature', is largely under new management, remains highly profitable, and is gearing up for a robust role in the multimedia future.

66

Magazines

Peter Dear
*Deputy Chief Executive, Periodical
Publishers Association*

Market diversity

Estimates of the total number of magazine titles published today in the UK vary and depend upon the definition employed. British Rate and Data (BRAD) lists more than 6,500 separate titles which take advertising.

In general, magazines are defined as either 'consumer' titles, providing people with leisure-time information and entertainment, or 'business and professional' titles, providing people with information relevant to their working lives. A distinction is often made between 'general consumer' and 'consumer specialist' titles. The former have wide appeal, while the latter are specifically aimed at groups of people with particular interests, such as rock music or sailing. Another growing area is the customer magazine market, whose titles are sent out by companies to their customers and prospects, and usually include articles about the companies, their products and services.

There are many other sorts of magazines – newsletters and comics, for example. Increasingly, magazines are publishing material by electronic means, most recently and most notably by the Internet and other on-line services (see Chapter 67).

The magazine industry has experienced a decade of rapid growth, with publishers catering for an ever-increasing range of new and more specialised markets. Over the last ten years the total number of magazines has increased by 33 per cent. The industry is characterised by a regenerative process, with new titles launched as others are closed. The diversity of the market is a product of the number of titles in the various sectors. The growing number of titles being launched for tightly defined target audiences reflects the increasing variety of lifestyle patterns and the trend towards business specialisation.

The leading magazine titles are owned by a handful of major publishing companies. Reed Elsevier is the largest publisher in the UK, owning, on the consumer side, IPC Magazines and, on the business and professional side, Reed Business Publishing. Other leading consumer publishers include BBC Magazines, Condé Nast, D C Thomson, EMAP Consumer Magazines, G&J of the UK, H Bauer, The National Magazine Company and Reader's Digest.

Among other important business and professional publishing groups are EMAP Business Communications, Haymarket Business Publications, Miller Freeman and VNU Business Publications. Several publishing houses have portfolios which include both consumer and business titles. At the other end of the scale, the industry is characterised by a large number of small, independently published titles which tend to cater for very specialised markets.

Most magazines derive income from both the sale of copies and the sale of advertisement space. Industry statistics show that magazine revenue is approximately £3 billion, with revenue to the publishers, after taking out costs for distribution and newstrade, about £2.3 billion.

A characteristic of the industry is the use of magazines to develop other revenue streams such as exhibitions, directories, database marketing, direct mail – and increasingly electronic publishing. According to the latest figures from the Department of Trade and Industry, these other activities take total revenue for the sector to around £3.5 billion. Periodical Publishers Association (PPA) members account for about 80 per cent of the magazine industry's revenue.

The consumer press derives the majority of its revenue from copy sales. This proportion has been on the increase. In contrast, advertising accounts for more than 70 per cent of total revenue in the case of the business and professional press.

In a major study called Media Futures, the Henley Centre forecasts that the number and diversity of magazines will continue to grow due to:

- continued expansion and fragmentation of leisure interests across society as a whole;
- demand for specialist titles from the baby boomers as they move into retirement;
- polarisation between income groups and a consequent increase in the

diversity of lifestyles, needs and aspirations;
- young people's need to assert their individuality – the continuing fragmentation of social identities;
- growth in the 'knowledge society' and the accompanying increase in demand for informational content.

The Henley Centre believes the traditional distinction between business and consumer magazines will become increasingly blurred as a result of the increase in part-time working, the adoption of more flexible working patterns and the growth of the small office, home office (SOHO). New media offer magazine publishers an opportunity to exploit their content through alternative distribution channels.

Circulation

Over the past five years, circulation of consumer magazines has continued to rise, reaching 12 per cent overall since 1991. Consumer spending on magazines has risen at an even faster rate (43 per cent) due to robust increases in cover prices. In the case of business and professional magazines, overall figures are much increased over the past decade, with the major growth being in controlled circulation (free) titles.

The establishment of the new basic ABC (Audit Bureau of Circulation) certificate and the introduction of the more detailed ABC Profile in 1991 for business and professional magazines, now provide the publisher and media buyer with certified demographic and related data.

Circulation growth has taken place against a background of increases in cover price. Over the past decade, they have gone up by more than the rate of inflation: in 1994, for instance, when inflation was 2.5 per cent, average cover prices rose by 7.5 per cent. The average cover price of weekly consumer magazines is 63p while for monthly consumer magazines it is £1.83 (Advertising Association, 1995). Ten years ago these figures were 27p and 85p respectively. These increases have been greater than those in other areas of the press. But despite these increases UK consumer magazines still remain among the least expensive in Europe.

The expenditure on consumer magazine sales in the UK is over £1.5 billion (Wessenden Marketing/PPA). Consumer magazine publishers receive about £750 million net from cover price revenue.

The vast majority of magazines are sold through retail outlets, the subscription market for consumer magazines remaining very small in the UK and Eire, with trade estimates at around 5 per cent of annual volume. Various subscription initiatives being undertaken by publishers are likely to enhance future levels. In the US more than three quarters of magazine copies are sold by subscription, while in Germany 43 per cent of copies are sold in this way. Approximately 24 per cent of business and professional magazines are sold through subscriptions. The hand delivery of subscription copies by independent distributors is still in its infancy. The total magazine postal business of some 500 million magazines a year, handled by Royal Mail and other carriers, represents about 30 per cent of total circulations.

According to a recent study by Wessenden Marketing (Magazine Retailing Towards 2000) significant changes are expected in the newstrade. The greatest change is forecast in the growth in the volume of magazine sales through supermarkets and hypermarkets.

There are relatively more monthly titles in the business and professional press than in the consumer press. Nevertheless, weeklies account for more than half the circulation in the sector. Controlled circulation (free) titles represent the majority of the business and professional magazine market.

Advertising

Approximately £1.4 billion per annum is spent on advertising in magazines. Following the general economic recession in the early 1990s, magazine advertisement revenue is once again growing.

Overall, magazines took 17.8 per cent of advertising expenditure in 1995; consumer magazines' share is 6.5 per cent, while that for business and professional titles is 11.3 per cent. Advertising accounts for about 38 per cent of consumer magazines' revenue. In the case of business and professional publications, the proportion of revenue derived from advertising is 72 per cent.

In contrast to newspapers, a very high proportion (78 per cent) of consumer magazine advertisement revenue is derived from display advertising, with only a relatively small amount (21 per cent) coming from classified/recruitment. The proportion of classified advertising has, however, increased in recent years. In the case of business publications, 71 per cent of advertisement revenue derives from display, with classified accounting for 29 per cent, and this proportion of business press advertising revenue coming from classified is on the increase. According to the Advertising Association's (AA) latest forecast, business magazines will be the second fastest-growing medium in 1996, with a predicted growth of 6 per cent in real terms.

Recent years have seen a substantial growth in demand from advertisers for special advertisement features, more commonly dubbed 'advertorials', and sponsored editorial. The personal one-to-one relationship which magazines enjoy with their readers has been a key factor in attracting advertising revenue of this kind. While advertisers make use of special advertising opportunities in most kinds of consumer and business and professional magazines, they are a particular feature of women's, fashion and home-interest titles.

Between 1994 and 1995, the number of pages in consumer magazines carrying advertising of this nature grew by 17.2 per cent. There has been a 170 per cent increase since 1991.

To assist advertisers and publishers in this developing area, PPA has published a set of guidelines in conjunction with the British Society of Magazine Editors.

Readership

More than 80 per cent of adults – and 84 per cent of women – read a consumer magazine.[1]

Reading of business magazines among business decision-makers is even higher, with 95 per cent regularly reading a magazine relevant to their market. The targeted nature of magazines means that readership in relevant groups tends to be particularly high.

Overall, the number of readers-per-copy is higher for magazines than newspapers. Reported readers-per-copy figures vary quite considerably from magazine to magazine.

Only a few general interest magazines, such as the TV listings titles, have reader profiles that closely mirror the population profile. Most titles are weighted to a demographic group or groups – reflecting the strongly targeted nature of the medium.

Over the past few years gross readership of magazines has been on the increase according to the National Readership Survey, while readership of newspapers has been in decline. While readership figures give an indication of the number of people who see a publication, other measures, such as time spent reading and amount read, can give additional information on the quality of that readership.

Over a quarter of British adults – 12 million people – are average-issue readers of at least one specialist magazine. Significantly, these people are above-average wage earners; nearly half are light viewers of commercial television; and 90 per cent of them read the advertising in these magazines. The largest specialist sector is music magazines, which attracts 18.3 per cent of the population.

Business and professional magazines enjoy high coverage in the specialist markets they serve. Individual titles – in particular the market leaders –

---

[1] These figures relate to the 200 magazines on the NRS (out of over 2,000 consumer magazines)

can achieve high readership levels, particularly if they are regarded as 'required reading': 95 per cent of business and professional people regularly read the publications relevant to their sector. On average, four different publications are read.

Advertising effectiveness

Several studies provide information about the communication effectiveness of magazines. A compilation of research studies, *How Magazine Advertising Works* (1995), presents a synthesis of more than 50 key studies of the consumer magazine sector over the past ten years and acts as a comprehensive one-stop reference source about magazine advertising. Some important recent studies include:

- *Ad Track*   In 1994, IPC Magazines commissioned Millward Brown to produce a continuous tracking study over 48 weeks, interviewing nearly 10,000 women who had read a magazine in the past year (about 90 per cent of all women). Twenty-four brands advertising in magazines were tracked, with half of these also using TV. The two main questions asked concerned awareness of the advertising and purchase consideration. The research showed that, averaging all campaigns, magazines delivered an awareness rating of 13 per cent – exactly the same as TV but at half the cost. In the case of purchase consideration, the study conclusively proved that magazine campaigns can increase people's willingness to consider buying a product.
- *Media values*   In 1992, Research Services Ltd set out to establish how magazine reading compares with other media consumption, and how magazines meet the needs and interests of their readers. Comparisons with the Media Involvement Study of 1983 show that the media explosion of the past decade has not eroded readers' close relationship with their magazines. The study provides qualitative information detailing consumers' attitudes to various media and various types of magazines.
- *The Media Multiplier*   In 1991, the International Federation of the Periodical Press (FIPP) published the findings of research covering 100 advertising campaigns, which demonstrated that the combination of print and television has a multiplying effect on communication effectiveness. The study also confirmed that a mixed schedule using both print and television delivers better coverage and frequency against a target audience than does a schedule using television alone.
- *Magazines into 2000*   During 1995, the Henley Centre produced a magazine-industry forecast which also examined the effectiveness of advertising and editorial within different media. The report concluded that

consumers are more likely to act as a result of seeing advertising in magazines than as a result of seeing advertising in other media – and this is particularly true of ABC1 consumers.

Magazines are an effective medium not only when used in isolation but also when used in conjunction with television. Television, although a very powerful advertising medium, has its limitations, and these are precisely where magazines have their strengths. Television cannot provide evenly balanced coverage across all sectors of the population as many people are simply light viewers of commercial television. These light viewers, however, do read magazines and an appropriate selection can improve targeting. Magazine advertisements are permanent and portable: the reader can hold and study an ad for as long as desired. The reader is in control of his or her own exposure. Thus, magazines and TV complement one another and a mixed schedule of TV and magazines is even more effective than TV on its own. Research demonstrating this point is detailed in the Media Multiplier study.

Business and professional magazines are an integral part of most people's working lives – and are read intensively and used extensively. New research from NOP provides evidence about the way such magazines are regarded and valued. The findings indicate business and professional titles are read avidly, relied on as a primary information source and are actively used in every arena of business life.

67

Customer Magazines

Julian Treasure
*Chairman, Association of Publishing
Agencies and TPD Publishing Ltd*

Contract publishing is no longer a niche activity: it is now a £200 million industry and one of the few marketing sectors which has grown rapidly and continuously over the last five years. And we are still just scratching the surface. In a recent survey of UK marketing directors conducted by RSGB, only one in ten major organisations were producing a customer magazine.

Since 1989 the contract publishing industry has grown by over 200 per cent compared with expenditure in customer magazines, which actually went down over the same period. As with any form of marketing, few companies have the desire or time to handle the complex activity in-house, so the last few years have seen the rise of the specialist contract publishing agency.

Already the customer magazine market is bigger than the cinema advertising medium and it is catching up on radio and outdoor advertising. Customer magazines now account for five of the top 20 magazine titles by circulation.

Value-added marketing

A customer magazine is value-added marketing; the medium itself enhances the message. With thousands of words and dozens of pictures, magazines can easily handle complex messages. The best magazines will be useful and entertaining, and generate attention levels of which other forms of marketing can only dream.

High-quality customer magazines can create new clients and increase loyalty among your existing customers, helping them to get more out of their relationship with you. As a result, the lifetime value of your customers can increase dramatically, with a direct effect on profits and revenues alike.

Unlike advertising, which, to be effective, has to concentrate on a single proposition, magazines have the unique ability to convey a number of complex messages that would be impossible to get across using traditional media. They offer customers who are buying an intangible service, such as insurance or mobile-phone airtime, something tangible, something they can see and feel, thus imbuing the service with a whole range of values and reinforcing the brand's identity.

Why use a specialist publishing agency?

As the market for customer magazines has grown, so too has the number of specialist contract publishing agencies. As with any form of marketing, few companies have the desire or time to handle this complex activity in-house. Clients have quickly seen the benefits of using publishing agencies – better quality, more flexibility, far less internal resource commitment, less risk of error and better value for money – as professional publishing expertise is brought to bear.

As a result of this, customer magazines have become more sophisticated machines. Editorial quality and credibility are all important in the make-up of any customer magazine. Publishing companies have a more sophisticated and long-term view on what is expected and needed than ever before.

The other significant growth area is that of third-party advertising. Until quite recently, most customer magazines took few outside advertisements. But now thanks to increased circulations, improved content and more communication with media buyers, ad revenue is on the increase. In the case of *O* magazine, for example, which TPD Publishing produces on behalf of Orange plc, the magazine has a strong balance of editorial and advertising, including very specific lifestyle and top-brand advertisers. To put this figure in perspective, 59 per cent of customer magazines now carry third-party advertising, generating £54 million in ad revenue in the year.

What some clients do tend to forget is that customer magazines, like any other marketing communication, need to be of a high quality to succeed. This is especially true where the issue of advertising is concerned. Relevant and appropriate advertising has a key role to play in the development of quality publications, but clients are deceiving themselves if they assume that customer magazines can be produced for free.

Market leaders

The UK is really leading the field in contract publishing and there are significant opportunities for companies to expand abroad. TPD Publishing, for example, now publishes many of its titles in several languages and to audiences across the world.

Other opportunities include the vast potential of media convergence, where traditional publishing methods meet with the relatively new multimedia marketplace. Equally important is the tailoring of magazines to tap detailed customer bases, allowing the production of many different versions of a publication, but specifically adapted to meet individual readers' needs.

The market growth and potential are phenomenal. Two years ago, Microsoft's UK arm set aside more than £500,000 to launch a combined customer magazine and loyalty programme. The launch of *Microsoft Advantage* was designed to help Microsoft give its customers added value. The results have been outstanding. According to John Leftwich, Microsoft's General Manager for End User Customer Unit, Europe: 'Microsoft's goal is total customer satisfaction. Research has shown that our most satisfied customers are those who receive *Microsoft Advantage* magazine. We consider the magazine to be making a significant contribution towards achieving our objectives.'

Appendix I
Contact Addresses

2Cs Communications
33–34 Alfred Place
London WC1E 7DP
United Kingdom
Contact: Richard Birtchnell, Director, Special Projects
Tel: (44) 171 631 0332
Fax: (44) 171 631 0262
E-mail: 2CsComms@gpo.sonnet.co.uk
Website: http://www.2Cs.co.uk

ABB Corporate Communications
PO Box 8131
CH 8050 Zurich
Switzerland
Contact: Michael Robertson, Assistant Vice President
Tel: (41) 1 317 7304
Fax: (41) 1 312 1543
E-mail: michael.robertson@chmar.mail.abb.com
Website: http://www.abb.com

Account Planning Group
16 Creighton Avenue
London N10 1NU
United Kingdom
Contact: Alan Cooper, Chairman
Tel: (44) 181 444 3692
Fax: (44) 181 883 9993
E-mail: apg.mail@easynet.co.uk
Website: http://www.easynet.co.uk/apg

Advertising Standards Authority
2 Torrington Place
London WC1E 7HW
United Kingdom
Tel: (44) 171 580 5555
Fax: (44) 171 631 3051
Website: http://www.asa.org.uk

Andersen Consulting
2 Arundel Street
London WC2R 3LT
United Kingdom
Contact: Cheryl Freeman, Maritime Region Marketing Director
Tel: (44) 171 438 5430
Fax:: (44) 171 304 8239
E-mail: cheryl.freeman@ac.com
Website: http://www.ac.com

BNFL Corporate Communications Unit
The Management School
University of Salford
Salford M5 4WT
United Kingdom
Contact: Dr Richard J Varey, Director
Tel: (44) 161 745 5884
Fax: (44) 161 745 5442
E-mail: r.j.varey@bms.salford.ac.uk
Contact: Mohammed Mirza, Academic/Communications Consultant
Tel: (44) 161 745 5491
Fax: (44) 161 745 5442
E-mail: m.t.mirza@bms.salford.ac.uk

British Broadcasting Corporation
Broadcasting House
Portland Place
London W1A 1AA
United Kingdom
Contact: Colin Browne, Director of Corporate Affairs
Tel: (44) 171 765 5531
Fax: (44) 171 765 3243
E-mail: colin.browne@bbc.co.uk
Website: http://www.bbc.co.uk

British Direct Marketing Association
Haymarket House
1 Oxendon Street SW1Y 4EE
United Kingdom
Contact: David Robottom, Director of Development
Tel: (44) 171 321 2525
Fax: (44) 171 321 0191
E-mail: dma@easynet.co.uk
Website: http://www.dma.org.uk

British Gas Energy
Room 12, 45 The Adelphi
1–11 John Adam Street
London WC2N 6HT
United Kingdom
Contact: Simon Lewis, Director, Corporate Affairs
Tel: (44) 171 269 4938
Fax: (44) 171 269 4849
E-mail: LEWISSD@BGEP.CO.UK

British Nuclear Industry Forum
22 Buckingham Gate
London SW1E 6LB
United Kingdom
Contact: Roger Hayes, Director General
Tel: (44) 171 828 0116
Fax: (44) 171 834 5929
E-mail: bnif@easynet.co.uk

British Sky Broadcasting Ltd
Grant Way
Isleworth
Middx TW7 5QD
United Kingdom
Contact: Ray Gallagher, Director of Public Affairs
Tel: (44) 171 705 3712
Fax: (44) 171 705 3113
E-mail: gallagher@sky.bskyb.com
Website: http://www.sky.co.uk

BT Laboratories
Martlesham Heath
Ipswich IP5 7RE
United Kingdom
Contact: Professor Peter Cochrane, Head of Advanced Applications
    Technologies
Tel: (44) 1473 644712
Fax: (44) 1473 647431
Contact: Mike Lyons, Head of Business Modelling Group
Tel: (44) 1473 646852
Fax: (44) 1473 647410
Website: http://www.labs.bt.com/people/cochrap

Burson-Marsteller
24–28 Bloomsbury Way
London WC1A 2PX
United Kingdom
Tel: (44) 171 831 6262
Fax: (44) 171 430 1033
Website: http://www.bm.com
Contact: Michael Seymour, Managing Director, Issues and Crisis
    Management
E-mail: mike_seymour@bm.com
Contact: Professor Alan Watson CBE, Chairman, Europe
E-mail: alan_watson@yr.com

Cable Communications Association
Artillery House
Artillery Row
London SW1P 1RT
United Kingdom
Contact: Michael Hayes, Former Director of Marketing
Tel: (44) 171 222 2900
Fax: (44) 171 799 1471
Website: http://www.cable.co.uk

Campaign Magazine
174 Hammersmith Road
London W6 7JP
United Kingdom
Contact: Claire Beale, Associate Editor
Tel: (44) 171 413 4294
Fax: (44) 171 413 4507
E-mail: 100560.1626@compuserve.com

Caroline Bainbridge Communications Planning
14 Chesney Court
Shirland Road
London W9 2EG
United Kingdom
Contact: Caroline Bainbridge, Principal
Tel: (44) 171 286 1584
Fax: (44) 171 289 1194

Charles Barker plc
56 Dean Street
London W1V 6HX
United Kingdom
Contact: Tim Sutton, Chief Executive
Tel: (44) 171 494 1331
Fax: (44) 171 439 1071
E-mail: tims@cbarker.co.uk
Website: http://www.cbarker.co.uk

Chartered Institute of Marketing
Moor Hall
Cookham
Maidenhead, Berks SL6 9QH
United Kingdom
Contact: Steve Cuthbert, Director General
Tel: (44) 1628 427001
Fax: (44) 1628 427009
E-mail: marketing@cim.co.uk
Website: http://www.cim.co.uk

Confederation of British Industry
Centre Point
103 New Oxford Street
London WC1A 1DU
United Kingdom
Contact: Sir Colin Marshall, President
Tel: (44) 171 379 7400
Fax:(44) 171 240 8289
E-mail: cbi-information@geo2,poptel.org.uk
Website: http://www.cbi.org.uk

Countrywide Porter Novelli
39 High Street
Banbury
Oxon OX16 8ET
United Kingdom
Contact: Peter Hehir, Chairman
Tel: (44) 1295 272288
Fax: (44) 1295 271757
E-mail: peter.hehir@countrywide.e mail.com
Website: http://www.countrywidepn.co.uk

Stuart Crainer, Author
22 Ruscombe Road
Twyford
Berks RG10 9JL
United Kingdom
Tel: (44) 1734 340035
Fax: (44) 1734 340035
E-mail: stuartc@firenet.net

Duckworth Finn Grubb Waters
41 Great Pulteney Street
London W1R 3DE
United Kingdom
Contact: Chris Forrest, Planning Director
    Rachel Walker, Account Planner
Tel: (44) 171 734 5888
Fax: (44) 171 734 3716
E-mail: dfgw@easynet.co.uk
Website: http://www.dfgw.co

Easy i Ltd
42 The Square
Kenilworth CV8 1EB
United Kingdom
Contact: Iain McLeod, Managing Director
Tel: (44) 1926 854111
Fax: (44) 1926 854222
E-mail: easyi@easynet.co.uk
Website: http://www.thebiz.co.uk

Electronic Commerce Association
Ramillies House
1–9 Hills Place
London W1R 1AJ
United Kingdom
Contact: Roger Till, Chief Executive
Tel: (44) 171 432 2500
Fax: (44) 171 432 2501
E-mail: roger.till@eca.org.uk
Website: http://www.eca.org.uk

Energy from Waste Association
26 Spring Street
London W2 1JA
United Kingdom
Contact: Ray Palin, Director
Tel: (44) 171 402 7110
Fax: (44) 171 402 7115

FireCrystal Communications
699 River Road
Yardley, PA 19067
USA
Contact: Alfred Glossbrenner
Tel: (1) 215 736 1213
Fax: (1) 215 736 1031
E-mail: gloss@gloss.com

GPC Market Access
Rue D'Arlon 50
B1000 Brussels
Belgium
Contact: John Duhig, Consultant
Tel: (32) 2 280 1700
Fax: (32) 2 230 5706
E-mail: 100670.752@compuserve.com

Hallmark Marketing Services Ltd
Canister House
27 Jewry Street
Winchester
Hants SO23 8RY
United Kingdom
Contact: Tom Watson, Managing Director
Tel: (44) 1962 863850
Fax: (44) 1962 841820
E-mail: 100540.101@compuserve.com

Hill & Knowlton
5 Theobalds Road
London WC1X 8SH
United Kingdom
Contact: Edward Bickham, Managing Director, Public Affairs and
    Corporate Policy
Tel: (44) 171 413 3050
Fax: (44) 171 413 3113
E-mail: vjethwa@hillandknowlton.com
Website: http://www.hillandknowlton.com

Incorporated Society of British Advertisers Ltd, The
44 Hertford Street
London W1Y 8AE
United Kingdom
Contact: Bob Wootton, Director of Media Services
Tel: (44) 171 499 7502
Fax: (44) 171 629 5355
Website: http://www.isba.org.uk

Independent Television Association
200 Gray's Inn Road
London WC1X 8HF
United Kingdom
Contact: Barry Cox, Director
Tel: (44) 171 843 8122
Fax: (44) 171 843 8159

Information Society Initiative
Heather Court
Maidstone Road
Sidcup, Kent DA14 5HH
United Kingdom
Infoline (UK): 0345 152000
E-mail: info@isi.gov.uk
Website: http://www.isi.gov.uk

Institute of Practitioners in Advertising
44 Belgrave Square
London SW1X 8QS
United Kingdom
Contact: Janet Hull, Director of Advertising Effectiveness
   Nicolas Phillips, Director General
Tel: (44) 171 235 7020
Fax: (44) 171 245 6079
E-mail: mark@ipa.co.uk
Website: http://www.ipa.com

Institute of Public Relations
The Old Trading House
155 Northburgh Street
London EC1V 0PR
United Kingdom
Contact: Simon Lewis, President
    Jeremy Weinberg, Press and Marketing Officer
Tel: (44) 171 253 5151
Fax: (44) 171 490 0588
E-mail: info@ipr1.demon.co.uk
Website: http://www.ipr.press.net

Interactive PR News
12021 Wilshire Boulevard, Suite 861
Los Angeles CA 90025
USA
Contact: Alan Coon, Editor
Tel: (1) 310 442 9149
Fax: (1) 310 826 9591
E-mail: editor@interactivepr.com
Website: http://www.ijumpstart.com

International Association of Business Communicators
c/o Tara Purnell
Watson Wyatt Worldwide
Watson House, London Road
Reigate, Surrey RH2 9PQ
United Kingdom
Contact: Gloria Walker, President, UK Chapter
Tel: (44) 171 493 6793
Fax: (44) 171 409 0551
Contact: Kevin Thomson, Vice President, Professional Development
Tel: (44) 1628 473217
Fax: (44) 1628 474011
Contact: Tara Purnell, Administrator
Tel: (44) 1737 241144
Fax: (44) 1737 241496
E-mail: tara_purnell@watsonwyatt.co.uk
Website: http://www.iabc.com/chapters/euroafrica/uklondon

International Consultants Organisation
c/o PRCA
Willow House, Willow Place
London SW1P 1JH
United Kingdom
Contact: Peter Hehir, President
Tel: (44) 1295 272288
Fax: (44) 1295 271757
E-mail: peter.hehir@countrywide.e-mail.com
Website: http://www.martex.co.uk

International PR Association
Case Postale 2100
CH 1211 Geneva 2
Switzerland
Contact: Roger Hayes, President

Jameson Investor Relations Inc
900 North Lake Shore Drive
Chicago IL 60611
USA
Contact: Pamela A. Jameson CFA, Principal
Tel: (1) 312 751 8742
Fax: (1) 312 751 9924
E-mail: PAJCHI@aol.com

Leo Burnett Ltd
35 West Wacker Drive
Chicago IL 60601
USA
Contact: Kate Lynch, Media Director, Europe
Tel: (1) 312 220 5959
Fax: (1) 312 220 3299
E-mail: Kate_Lynch@chi.leoburnett.com
Website: http://www.leoburnett.com

Lion's Den Communications Management Ltd
Devonshire House
12 Barley Mow Passage
London W4 4PH
United Kingdom
Contact: John Clare, Managing Director
Tel: (44) 181 742 0392
Fax: (44) 181 742 0393
E-mail: john@lionsden.co.uk

Lloyds of London
1 Lime Street
London EC3M 7HA
United Kingdom
Contact: Peter Hill, Head of Corporate Communications
Tel: (44) 171 327 5110
Fax: (44) 171 327 5232
E-mail: peter.j.hill@lloydsoflondon.co.uk
Website: http://www.lloydsoflondon.co.uk

Lucas Industries
46 Park Street
London W1Y 4DJ
United Kingdom
Contact: Gloria Walker, Manager, Public Affairs
Tel: (44) 171 493 6793
Fax: (44) 171 409 0551
E-mail: 101743.210@compuserve.com

Manning, Selvage & Lee
123 Buckingham Palace Road
London SW1W 9SH
United Kingdom
Contact: Jackie Elliot, Chief Executive
Tel: (44) 171 878 3000
Fax: (44) 171 878 3030
E-mail: jackie_elliot@mslpr.com
Website: http://www.mslpr.com

Marketing & Communication Agency Ltd, The
Court Garden House
Marlow, Bucks SL7 2AE
United Kingdom
Contact: Kevin Thomson, Chairman
Tel: (44) 1628 473217
Fax: (44) 1628 474011
E-mail: info@source.mca.co.uk

McCann-Erickson
36 Howland Street
London W1A 1AT
United Kingdom
Contact: Amy Smith, Marketing Director
Tel: (44) 171 580 6690
Fax: (44) 171 915 2006
E-mail: Amy_Smith@McCann.com
Website: http://www.mccann.com
Contact: Gerard O'Neill, Member, McCann Strategy Group
Tel: (353) 1 661 9147
Fax: (353) 1 661 0312
E-mail: henleyci@iol.ie

Medialink Worldwide Inc
14 Soho Square
London W1V 5FB
United Kingdom
Contact: David Davis, Senior Vice President, International
Tel: (44) 171 439 1774
Fax: (44) 171 439 1378
E-mail: ddavis@medialink.com
Website: http://www.medialinkworldwide.com

Microsoft Ltd
Microsoft Place
Winnersh Triangle
Wokingham
Berks RG41 5TP
United Kingdom
Contact: Shaun Orpen, Director of Marketing Services
Tel: (44) 1734 270001
Fax: (44) 1734 270002
Website: http://www.microsoft.com

Mike Monkman Media
41 Owl Way
Hartford, Huntingdon
Cambs PE18 7YZ
United Kingdom
Contact: Mike Monkman, Principal
Tel: (44) 1480 450833
Fax: (44) 1480 459933

Neomedion Ltd
The Mount
Lower Dicker
East Sussex BN27 4BE
United Kingdom
Contact: Charles Dawson, Managing Director
Tel: (44) 1323 442742
Fax: (44) 1323 442741
E-mail: cdawson@ibm.net

Newspaper Publishers Association Ltd, The
34 Southwark Bridge Road
London SE1 9EU
United Kingdom
Contact: David Pollock, Director
Tel: (44) 171 928 6928
Fax: (44) 171 928 2067
E-mail: 106124.1730@compuserve.com

Newspaper Society, The
Bloomsbury House
74–77 Great Russell Street
London WC1B 3DA
United Kingdom
Contact: Dugal Nisbet Smith CBE, Director
Tel: (44) 171 636 7014
Fax: (44) 171 631 5119
E-mail: ns@newspapersoc.org.uk
Website: http://www.newspapersoc.org.uk

Origination (AMC Associates)
36 West Hill Road
London SW18 1LN
United Kingdom
Contact: Burce P Abrahams
Tel: (44) 181 870 3239
Fax: (44) 181 870 3239

Periodical Publishers Association
Queen's House
28 Kingsway
London WC2B 6JR
United Kingdom
Contact: Peter Dear, Deputy Chief Executive
Tel: (44) 171 404 4166
Fax: (44) 171 404 4167
E-mail: info1@ppa.co.uk
Website: http://www.ppa.co.uk

Politics International
92 Horseferry Road
London SW1P 2EE
United Kingdom
Contact: Nicholas Comfort, Political and Media Consultant
Tel: (44) 171 976 0020
Fax: (44) 171 976 0021
E-mail: pi@politicsint.co.uk

Public Policy Unit
50 Rochester Row
London SW1P 1JU
United Kingdom
Contact: Arthur Pryor, Head of Competition and Regulation Group
Tel: (44) 171 828 6088
Fax: (44) 171 828 7217

Public Relations Consultants Association
Willow House
Willow Place
London SW1P 1JH
United Kingdom
Contact: Chris McDowell, Director
Tel: (44) 171 233 6026
Fax: (44) 171 828 4797
E-mail: prca@martex.co.uk
Website: http://www.martex.co.uk/prca/index.htm
Contact: Jackie Elliot, Chairman
Tel: (44) 171 878 3000
Fax: (44) 171 878 3030
E-mail: jackie_elliot@mslpr.com

Radio Advertising Bureau
77 Shaftesbury Avenue
London W1V 7AD
United Kingdom
Contact: Steve Cox, Advertising Consultant
Tel: (44) 171 306 2500
Fax: (44) 171 306 2505
E-mail: steve@rab.co.uk
Website: http://www.rab.co.uk

Sampson Tyrrell Enterprises
6 Mercer Street
London WC2H 9QA
United Kingdom
Contact: Johnnie Seidler, Account Director
Tel: (44) 171 574 4000
Fax: (44) 171 574 4100
E-mail: johnnie@stenter.com

Shandwick International plc
18 Dering Street
London W1R 9AF
United Kingdom
Contact: Lord Chadlington, Chairman
    Daphne Luchtenburg, European Marketing Manager
Tel: (44) 171 355 1908
Fax: (44) 171 499 1752
E-mail: dluchtenburg@shandwick.com
Website: http://www.shandwick.com

Simons Palmer Denton Clemmow Johnson Ltd
19–20 Noel Street
London W1V 3PD
United Kingdom
Contact: Alan Cooper, Director
Tel: (44) 171 287 4455
Fax: (44) 171 734 2658
E-mail: planning @simonspalmer.netkonect.co.uk

Slogo Register, The
140 Salmons Lane
Whyteleafe
Surrey CR3 0HA
United Kingdom
Contact: Timothy R V Foster, Principal, Consultant Editor
Tel: (44) 181 736 2225
Fax: (44) 181 736 2011
E-mail: fostair@atlas.co.uk
Website: http://www.thebiz.co.uk/slogos

SMI Group Ltd
1 Down Place
London W6 9JH
United Kingdom
Contact: Alex Letts, Chairman
Tel: (44) 181 563 2222
Fax: (44) 181 741 2294
E-mail: alex@smigroup.com
Website: http://www.smigroup.com

Smythe Dorward Lambert Ltd
55 Drury Lane
London WC2B 5SQ
United Kingdom
Contact: Colette Dorward, Managing Director
Tel: (44) 171 379 9099
Fax: (44) 171 379 7156
E-mail: info@smythe.demon.co.uk
Website: http://www.smythe.co.uk

Solutions Organisation, The
Southview
8 Stonehill Close
London SW14 8RP
United Kingdom
Contact: Clive Bonny, Director
Tel: (44) 181 876 1454
Fax: (44) 181 878 6970

Synopsis Communication Consulting
62–68 Rosebery Avenue
London EC1R 4RR
United Kingdom
Contact: Bill Quirke, Principal
Tel: (44) 171 713 7477
Fax: (44) 171 833 8040
E-mail: info@synopsis-communication.co.uk

TPD Publishing Ltd
Long Island House
1–4 Warple Way
London W3 0RG
United Kingdom
Contact: Julian Treasure, Chairman
Tel: (44) 181 740 1740
Fax: (44) 181 740 1741
E-mail: julian.treasure@tpdgroup.co.uk

UXL Ltd
62–63 Webber Street
London SE1 0QW
United Kingdom
Contact: Jeremy Keohane, Client Director
Tel: (44) 171 633 0300
Fax: (44) 171 928 7989
E-mail: jem@uxl.co.uk
Website: http://www.uxl.co.uk

Dr Jon White, Consultant
78 Claremont Road
London N6 5BY
United Kingdom
Tel: (44) 181 340 4422
Fax: (44) 181 340 4488
E-mail: 100541.3027@compuserve.com

William M Mercer Ltd
Mercer House
Thames Side
Windsor
Berks SL4 1QN
United Kingdom
Contact: Neville Hobson, Senior Consultant
Tel: (44) 1753 842188
Fax: (44) 1753 830186
E-mail: neville@netcomuk.co.uk
Website:: http://www.mercer.com

Words Into Action
98 Chestnut Lane
Amersham
Bucks HP6 6EE
United Kingdom
Contact: Annette Allen, Director
Tel: (44) 1494 724695
Fax: (44) 1494 721816
E-mail: a.allen@netcom.co.uk

Index

Index of Advertisers